D0465969

The Case
for Gold

The Case
for Gold

**A MINORITY REPORT
OF THE U.S. GOLD
COMMISSION**

Second Edition

REP. RON PAUL

MISES INSTITUTE

Copyright © 1983 by the Cato Institute
Copyright © 2011 Foreword to the Second Edition by the Ludwig von Mises
Institute and published under the Creative Commons Attribution License 3.0
http://creativecommons.org/licenses/by/3.0/

Co-Publishers:
Ludwig von Mises Institute
518 West Magnolia Avenue
Auburn, Alabama 36832
Mises.org

Laissez Faire Books
808 St. Paul Street
Baltimore, Maryland 21202
LaissezFaireBooks.com
lfb.org

ISBN: 978-1-61016-199-2

CONTENTS

Acknowledgements

The authors would like to thank Christopher Weber, Murray Rothbard, and John Robbins for their assistance in researching, drafting, and editing this report.

FOREWORD TO THE SECOND EDITION

This country had the chance to avoid the disastrous meltdown of 2008 and following, the one that has led to nationalization of industries, the creation of oceans of paper money, and the destruction of so many American dreams. The answer that might have been is the one you hold in your hands: the minority report of the U.S. Gold Commission of 1982, written by Ron Paul and signed by Lewis E. Lehrman. It provides an outstanding history, wonderful theoretical analytics, and a proposal for the return of sound money, which is gold.

Alas, it was the minority report and therefore killed by political forces. Of course, the fix was in from the beginning. The Commission only came to exist in the first place as payoff to certain "goldbugs" in the Republican Party in those years. Ronald Reagan was one of them. So his influence was part of the reason the Commission was created. But it wasn't created to institute a gold standard. It was created to bury the idea once and for all.

Ron Paul wouldn't let it happen. The result was this book, which remains a mighty case for sound money and the blessings that change would bring to this country. A gold currency would restore economic stability and growth. It would eliminate unemployment. It would force government to spend only what it can collect in taxes. It would rein in the welfare state and the warfare state. It would give the people control of money again. It would restore what we used to call freedom, which is a core of social and civic life that is impenetrable and inaccessible to government planners.

With a gold standard, the Fed could disappear. The banking industry would become an industry like any other, subject to the profit-and-loss test and given no guaranteed bailouts at taxpayer expense. The financial industry would be forced to surrender its love of socialism (for losses, not gains) and become honest again. We would all start living within our means and thriving off private wealth rather than depending on the public sector to save us.

Trade with other nations would benefit. Protectionist wars rooted in currency manipulation would cease. Policy options in Washington would be mercifully restricted to only what Washington could afford to do and afford to enforce. Vast swaths of the public sector as we know it would have to just pack up and go home. This would be the greatest blessing visited on this country in a century. But can you see why Washington isn't interested? It has nothing to do with disagreements over economic theory. It is all about who has power in society. Paper money gives power to tyrants. Sound money, that is gold, gives power to the people and the free markets they control.

So, yes, we should have listened to Ron in 1982. The thing is that he—wisely and bravely—never stopped talking about this issue. It turns out that this book, this minority report, is the work of a prophet. It tells the truth and shows the way. It should be our manifesto again. This timeless statement on behalf of economic truth can be our guide.

They didn't listen then. But maybe they'll listen now. We need monetary freedom more than anything else. The way digital markets are advancing, it might come about with or without Washington's permission. As Ron has always known, paper money cannot last. Either it has to go, or the American dream has to go. They cannot forever live side by side.

Llewellyn H. Rockwell, Jr.
December 2010

FOREWORD

More and more people are asking if a gold standard will end the financial crisis in which we find ourselves. The question is not so much *if* it will help or *if* we will resort to gold, but *when*. All great inflations end with the acceptance of real money—gold—and the rejection of political money—paper. The stage is now set; monetary order is of the utmost importance. Conditions are deteriorating, and the solutions proposed to date have only made things worse. Although the solution is readily available to us, powerful forces whose interests are served by continuation of the present system cling tenaciously to a monetary system that no longer has any foundation. The time at which there will be no other choice but to reject the current system entirely is fast approaching. Although that moment is unknown to us, the course that we continue to pursue will undoubtedly hurtle us into a monetary abyss that will mandate a major reform.

That moment may come very soon—it nearly arrived in the 1979 dollar crisis—but I hope it will not arrive for several years. That way a greater understanding among more people will prompt a wiser choice in establishing the new order. The minority views of the Gold Commission deal precisely with this task. In planning for a constructive monetary reform the errors of the past and the myths that have evolved around money must be fully understood and explained. In this report we have made an effort to analyze the American experience with gold and to refute the clichés used to condemn the use of gold as money. No one program is indispensable in outlining the transition from paper to gold. Every day conditions are different. Today we need a program different from the one necessary three years ago, and in three years the conditions again will change. We certainly do not have the same problem faced by the Germans in 1923, but in 1986 we may. Nevertheless, outlines of different methods of achieving a convertible currency can be made; we have done so in these views.

Briefly, we offer two methods, one through the legalization of competing currencies, the other a government-directed gold standard of the classical variety. Only future events and attitudes will determine the best method. We do know that current monetary policy cannot continue indefinitely, and we are obligated to prepare for better times.

This report establishes the foundation on which a sound monetary system can be built.

The date the Gold Commission officially voted and rejected the gold standard—a foregone conclusion from the very beginning—the *Wasnington Post* headline read, "Commission Votes Against Revival of Gold Standard." A reporter called to ask my reaction, assuming I would be greatly disappointed. But my response was the opposite. "I'm delighted," I said, "the news is that the gold standard was considered and the (temporary) rejection deserves a top front page headline by the *Washington Post*." The fact that for the first time in over 100 years a government body was seriously discussing the issue of gold as money is a major achievement. It may even be argued that this was the most significant discussion since the Constitutional Convention when the Founding Fathers condemned the Continental and tried to protect us from the ravages of another political currency. Even the 25 volumes published by the National Monetary Commission in 1912 largely avoided the issue of money and concentrated only on banking procedures. Yes, the news on the gold standard was noteworthy, but not quite for the reason suspected by the *Washington Post*.

Making a significant change in policy takes time and effort. Rejecting the paper standard will not occur overnight. The destruction of the dollar, once "as good as gold," literally took 58 years (1913–1971). Paper did not defeat gold in one battle. Gold will achieve success in a shorter period. Already the initial steps have been taken. Legalization of gold ownership in 1974 (thanks to Philip Crane, Jesse Helms, and others) and of gold clause contracts in 1977 have certainly been positive developments. The gold coin as recommended by the Gold Commission is another major step in creating a climate for general acceptance of a gold standard. A U.S. gold coin minted by the U.S. Treasury for the first time in 50 years is a significant event and heralds a new era in U.S. monetary history.

The debate in the news media that accompanied the establishment of the Gold Commission made millions of Americans aware of the issue. This public attention will, in the long run, be quite beneficial and is absolutely necessary before gold is generally accepted as money once again.

This report makes the point that we need not *return* to a gold standard—which had many shortcomings—but we can learn from the mistakes of the past, improve upon past systems, and go *forward* to a modern gold standard. By contrast, all the effort and planning imaginable cannot make paper money work. There is no way paper can be "improved" as money. Whenever governments are granted power to purchase their own debt, they never fail to do so, eventually destroying the value of the currency. Political money always fails because free people eventually reject it. For short periods individual countries can tell their citizens to use paper, but only at the sacrifice of personal and economic liberty.

Governments can fool people for a while with paper money, but it's inevitable that trust in the money—something absolutely required for it to serve as a medium of exchange and to allow economic calculation—will be lost. Governments have power to declare paper to be legal tender, but they do not have power to make that money trustworthy. As governments more and more insist on paper alone serving as money, less and less trust is placed in it. It's hardly a surprise that the decade of the 1970s, a decade of paper money, has brought us the decade of the 1980s—a destroyed bond and mortgage market, persistent and devastatingly high interest rates, and a faltering economy.

If the nature of money is understood and one observes how the destruction of money occurred during the past 50 years, and especially during the past 10, it's easy to see why interest rates are high. Most people today see the economic problems we face as the result of high interest rates and a "shortage of money," yet the high interest rates are merely symptoms of an untrustworthy currency. When one deals with currency that has no predictable value and in the long run is steadily depreciating, a "shortage" will always occur. The shortage, however, is in purchasing power and trust, and not in nominal dollars. Ironically, the more dollars created to satisfy this "shortage," the greater is the loss of purchasing power and trust.

This report was written to demonstrate as clearly as possible the choices available to us: political (paper) money or commodity (real) money. It is imperative that we make it clear to the American people the alternatives they have, and that they make the correct choice. Making the wrong choice will jeopardize our political freedom and destroy the possibility of restoring a truly productive economy. Making the correct choice—limited government, free market, private property, and sound money—ensures liberty and prosperity.

I'm firmly convinced that major economic and political decisions will be forced upon us in the 1980s. The current system is "running out of steam" and is slowing to a stop. New ideas as well as a "new" money are required to keep society's train from rushing downward from our magnificent peak of economic prosperity and political freedom.

I hope this report will help prevent needless suffering and show the way to an honest money system in which the people are in charge, not politicians and the bankers.

Washington, D.C.   Ron Paul
July 1, 1982   Member of Congress

We live in an age of inflation. Punctuated by brief moments of austerity and declining prices, the world of work hurtles without compass toward a rendezvous with catastrophe.

Usually defined as too much money chasing too few goods, inflation is really the depreciation of money, a process of monetary destruction. But a stable monetary standard is essential in a market economy—it is the indispensable standard of commercial value. Stable money is, in fact, bound up with civilization itself. The depreciation of the commercial standard of civilization—money, as with the depreciation of moral and legal standards of value, brings chaos and disorder. For a generation we have seen the debasement of these standards not only in commerce, but also in our public life, our schools, our families, our art, and our science. It is no exaggeration to say that the survival of Western civilization in general, and America in particular, is at stake in the struggle over standards of value.

Monetary Revolution

When stable political institutions are overturned, the result is revolution. Inflation and deflation are revolutions in the world of commercial affairs. And history shows that a price revolution often precedes a political revolution. Lenin in Russia, Hitler in Germany, and Mao in China—to name just three examples—came to power after great inflations.

Today, we have a permanent financial crisis at home and throughout the world because men and women no longer trust the American dollar. No longer a just and honest measure of the value of work, the dollar has ceased to be the stable standard of economic worth the world over. Since 1971, when President Nixon cut the dollar's final link to the gold standard, our currency has been nothing but a printed piece of green paper, or an impulse on a computer tape, manipulated by a government-created monopoly bank called the Federal Reserve System. What the Post Office has done to the currency of communications—the mail—the Fed monopoly has done to the currency of commerce—the dollar.

Working people understandably refuse to hold the depreciating dollar for long periods. They spend it quickly for a house, a car, an antique, a rare coin—anything real. At best they lend their dollars for short periods to the highest bidder, usually the U.S. government or money market funds, which do not build factories or hire unemployed workers.

Why have producers and consumers alike lost faith in our commercial standard of value? It is because the U.S. government, the Federal Reserve, and the dependent private banks have created more dollars than Americans want to hold. These paper and credit dollars were often printed to pay for the colossal budget deficits, created by special-interest government in Washington. And often the manipulation of credit by the Fed was an indirect effort to manipulate voters by manipulating the banking system and the economy. Even during short periods of dollar scarcity, such as 1981–1982, the Fed has denied credit to the economy in order to correct for previous periods of excess. Fed manipulation causes inflation *and* deflation.

What the Fed and the politicians have forgotten is the sacred link between the value of the dollar and the value of work. The manipulation of the quantity of money does not create prosperity.

Money does not make wealth. Only hard work creates wealth.

Real Money for Real Work

A craftsman labors many hours to create a product. If he exchanges the product for Federal Reserve notes, he receives for his work a paper dollar that costs almost nothing to produce. But if he exchanges the valuable product of his hands for gold coins, he takes for his work the real product of labor offered by miners and coin makers. All producers desire to trade proportional product values of honest work—both in quality and quantity. Producers and consumers use money to make the exchange—and to save.

But the paper dollar, with which Americans are paid today, is not real money. Almost no real work is required of the government to produce the mass-printed paper dollar bill. So with its marginal cost of production almost zero, our paper money has no real underlying value. Nor is the paper dollar *linked* to anything of real value. Yet it is legal tender. That is, the U.S. government requires Americans to accept paper money without intrinsic value in payment of all debts, public and private. In exchange for real work and real values, Americans by law must accept paper money—unless the contract specifies otherwise.

Today, we live in a crisis of inflation and deflation caused by government manipulation of paper money and bank credit. The unhinged federal government deficits are the visible manifestations of government finance run amok.

The Dangers Confronting President Reagan

Four financial forces now conspire to destroy the President's economic program: rising federal spending; the permanent federal deficit; the Treasury demand for credit to finance the deficit; and the unpredictable creation and destruction of excess money and credit by the U.S. central bank, the Federal Reserve System. Together, these forces cause extreme price volatility, high interest rates, and economic stagnation.

Total government credit demand is running at $150–200 billion a year, and rising. But personal savings are only about $100 billion. Net national savings equal approximately $200 billion. The impact of the government demand for credit has dazed the Fed and the market. The government absorbs almost all the savings, and business languishes. The Federal Reserve wanders around Wall Street amidst the chaos of the capital markets, which are virtually shut down for all but the U.S. Treasury and the highest quality utility and telephone credits, themselves government wards. Moreover, with the defense buildup, even the rate of growth of federal spending may not slow down. And it is government borrowing at present levels, joined to Fed manipulation, which has immobilized the money and capital markets.

Previous administrations sowed chaos. President Reagan may reap the whirlwind.

Indifference to Deficits

The present crisis is not unique.

Financial disorder greeted Margaret Thatcher in 1979 when she was elected Prime Minister of England. In 1958, economic chaos and war destroyed the Fourth Republic in France. But President Charles DeGaulle and his financial advisor, Jacques Rueff, understood the causes of the French financial collapse. The causes were budget deficits (financed indirectly by the Bank of France), a manipulated currency, and an overregulated economy. In creating the Fifth Republic, Rueff and de Gaulle reformed the currency, balanced the budget, and began the deregulation of the economy. The result for France was a decade of economic growth and political stability.

Here in the United States, two past decades of Keynesian policies have failed under Lyndon Johnson, Richard Nixon, and Jimmy Carter, while Thatcher's current monetarist policies are coming to naught in England because they depend too much on central bank manipulation of the money supply. Well-intentioned monetarist policies, officially adopted by the Reagan administration and the Federal Reserve, are doing no better in the United States.

Neither monetarists nor Keynesians understand the mechanism by which inflation and deflation is transmitted—how the federal deficit and credit demands influence interest rates and tend to cause inflationary and deflationary Fed monetary policy. Both supply-siders and monetarists are unsure of the links between federal spending, budget deficits, rising interest rates, growth in the money supply, inflation and economic stagnation. But as the monetarists, Keynesians, and supply-siders war among themselves, they now agree, ironically, on one thing: *Budget deficits don't matter*. And they are all *tragically* wrong. The indifference of academic economists to budget deficits is an economic heresy which ravages the world. And the wages of sin are upon us—the highest real rates of interest in the last 20 centuries.

Meanwhile, because of the Reagan administration's uncertain policy towards deficits and the Fed, and the effect of deficits on capital formation and economic growth, we now endure the major financial crisis of postwar American history.

Rising Treasury credit demands, on and off budget; historically high interest rates; and a political decision by the Fed to create excess credit again could cause a complete collapse of the U.S. capital markets.

Once the wonder of the Western world, American long-term capital markets have already ceased to exist as our forefathers knew them.

There Are Solutions

But we need not accept the destruction of our money and our economy. The remedies are available and they are historic American remedies. We could establish the gold standard, balance the budget without raising taxes, and reform the procedures of the Federal Reserve. That is what this report is about.

It is about financial disorder in America. We try to show, in outline form, where we have been, where we are now, and where we must head. We lay out a financial policy for the rebirth of the American economy, a lasting policy which we deeply believe will lead to full employment and growth in a free economic order.

Even without such a sound financial policy, we are repeatedly told by critics that we shall still survive as a country. True, it is the lot of working people and businessmen to survive, especially in America. But to what end? Permanently high unemployment, inflation, and interest rates? Increasing bankruptcies? Wage and price controls? Is this the stuff of the American dream?

We can achieve financial order, but only with real leadership and real money.

New York, New York   Lewis E. Lehrman
July 1, 1982

INTRODUCTION

The United States is now in the most serious recession since the 1930s. The most staid and sober magazines and newspapers are writing openly about the possibility of depression. Sectors of the economy have already entered the depression stage; more are threatening to follow. The number of personal and business failures more than doubled from 1971 to 1981, and the early figures for 1982 indicate that failures are up 50 percent over 1981. Interest rates remain near record highs; unemployment has reached nine percent and is moving upward. The only sign of improvement is a slower rate of increase—but still an increase—in the cost-of-living. Annualized increases in the Consumer Price Index are now down near the levels that prompted President Nixon to impose price and wage controls in 1971.

How did the economy get into such a poor condition? Can it be blamed on the Reagan administration's new policies, as some would like to do? Or is there a more fundamental reason for our present crisis?

It is the conclusion of the signers of this report that there is a more fundamental reason. Our present crisis has not developed in the past year; it has been growing for at least a decade. When President Nixon imposed price and wage controls on August 15, 1971, he also, ironically enough, severed the last link between the dollar and gold. The process begun in 1913 with the formation of the Federal Reserve System, accelerated by President Franklin Roosevelt through a confiscation of privately owned gold and a devaluation of the dollar, nearly completed in the 1960s by the withdrawing of silver certificates from circulation and the end of silver coinage, was finally completed when the international convertibility of the dollar into gold was ended in 1971.

The entire process is a catalogue of broken promises and outright theft on the part of the federal government as it sought to substitute a managed, irredeemable paper money system for a gold standard. For the past 10 years we have had a monetary system unique in our national history: no circulating silver or gold coinage, but a government monopoly of politically managed paper money. The present crisis is a result of this fundamental change in our monetary arrangements, and it will not—indeed cannot—be ended permanently unless fundamental reforms are made.

Our 10-year experiment with paper money has failed; it is time that the Congress recognize that failure. Congress has violated both the principles of sound economics and the requirements of our supreme law, the Constitution.

The Constitution forbids that anything except gold and silver coin should be made a tender in payment of debt—yet Congress has made inconvertible paper a legal tender. Economics requires a recognition that there is no such thing as a free lunch, but Congress has institutionalized the money-creating powers of the Federal Reserve in its efforts to perform the miracle of turning stones into bread.

Chapter one of this report presents an economic overview of the last 10 years, a decade of paper money. Chapters two and three detail the process by which we arrived at our present state. The fourth chapter presents the case for monetary freedom; chapter five argues the case for a gold standard, and chapter six outlines the specific reforms that will be needed to correct the blunders of the past. Finally, chapter seven will offer two views of the next 10 years, a decade with gold and a decade without.

Now Congress faces a crisis and an opportunity. We hope the arguments presented here are persuasive, and the Congress acts in a timely fashion to avert an economic calamity. For too long the federal government has been playing with Monopoly money; we must move forward to a real money system, gold.

I. The Present Monetary Crisis

In 1784 in the debate over the money issue, Thomas Jefferson said: "If we determine that a dollar shall be our unit, we must then say with precision what a dollar is." Our Founding Fathers followed that advice and in 1792 the dollar was defined as 371⁴/₁₆ grains of silver. From 1792 until August 15, 1971 the dollar was defined as a precise weight of either silver or gold. Since 1971, the dollar has had no definition (officially the definition was not legally rejected until 1976); the advice of Thomas Jefferson has been rejected entirely. For more than 10 years the dollar has been nothing more than a piece of paper with government ink on it.

More and more Americans have come to recognize this, and a loss of confidence in the currency has paralleled this recognition. The monetary authorities say it is unnecessary to have a precise definition of the dollar, claiming: "A dollar is whatever it will buy." This being the case, and the fact that the dollar buys less every day, and approximately one-third of what it bought in 1971, the dollar today is undefinable, and its value is relative. It should be obvious that this loss of definition of what the monetary unit is, is directly related to the financial and economic problems we face today.

If the dollar served as the unit of account for a single South American nation, such as Chile or Brazil, the significance of this change from a precise definition to no definition would be less. However, since World War II the dollar has been the international currency of account, used throughout the world, and held as a reserve currency by most major western nations. Even though this was done unwisely, it worked temporarily up until 1971 when the definition of the dollar was changed.

Until 1971 a dollar was ¹/₃₅ of an ounce of gold, and all nations that held the dollar as a reserve were assured that their dollars could be redeemed for ¹/₃₅ of an ounce of gold—even if American citizens were denied that same right. However, the failure of the U.S. government over many decades (Congress, the Federal Reserve, and the administration) to issue only dollars that could be redeemed led to a massive inflation of the money supply for various political reasons. This forced the United States to default on its convertibility pledge and the dollar became only something the government claimed it was. Residual trust and blind faith have allowed the dollar to serve since 1971 as money, but with ever increasing difficulty. Understanding Jefferson's advice about a precise definition of the dollar, and analyzing the problems of the last decade, during which time we have had no definition of the dollar, are crucial in our attempt to pave the way for a sound, honest, and reliable monetary system.

From 1792 to 1971 we had an imperfect money and banking system, as will be shown in chapters two and three. But during that time the dollar was always related to gold in one way or another. (It may be argued that the exception was the greenback era during the Civil War, but even then gold circulated and was used to some degree.) Even with its obvious imperfections, the gold dollar worked rather well compared with the past 10 years. Though the Depression of the 1930s was ushered in by government meddling in the economy and irresponsible money management, the gold dollar per se survived, even though debased by 41 percent. Today the dollar is troubled by a general lack of confidence. The market is anticipating that a steady depreciation will continue, thus prompting high interest rates. The purchasing power of the dollar as compared with gold has dramatically decreased over the past decade. By historic analysis, it is clear that 1971 was a significant and unique year in American monetary history.

This being the case, what in particular occurred on August 15, 1971? It was on this day President Nixon "closed the gold window," which meant that officially the American government would no longer honor its promise to foreign holders of dollars to redeem those dollars in gold. It became policy what was already known through the world, that the American government had created many more dollars—promises to pay—than it should have and no longer could live up to its monetary commitments by redeeming them in gold. A new agreement, the Smithsonian agreement, which lasted only 14 months, was claimed by President Nixon to be "the most significant monetary agreement in the history of the world," promising it would create jobs, restore financial stability, help the farmers, stimulate exports, and bring prosperity to all. "Significant" it was, but in an entirely different way, for it was this agreement that ushered in the present period of fiat paper money and monetary chaos. It has brought us the exact opposite of what was intended.

In his statement in 1971 President Nixon, as many uninformed individuals do today, blamed "speculation" for our problems and not the real culprit—government inflation. He further stated on that fateful day "that the effect of this action, in other words, will be to stabilize the dollar." How can we expect those who claimed that rejecting a gold-related dollar would "stabilize the dollar" to advise us now on solving our current financial and monetary crisis? We cannot, because they are not capable. It is necessary to look elsewhere for the solution.

Even though the declaration made in August 1971 was of great significance, overall monetary policy did not change at that particular time. This was essentially an admission of the failure of the Federal Reserve's discretionary monetary policy it had followed in various forms since 1914. Although previous deflations (particularly 1929 and 1932), and the fact we were spared from the physical destruction of World War II, prolonged the life of the dollar, the inevitable failure of discretionary policy was known by many for a long time.

When the record of the past 10 years is examined, it is clear that indicting the monetary arrangements of the past decade is justified. It is clear that discretionary monetary policy, without *any* assistance from gold, leads to serious economic instability, lack of capital formation, high interest rates, high price inflation, and intolerably high levels of unemployment. The climax of this policy came in October 1979 when the Federal Reserve was forced to change some of its management techniques. Due to international pressure, weakness of the dollar, gold at $600 an ounce, and silver over $25 an ounce, the Federal Reserve adopted a policy directed toward concentrating more on money supply than on interest rates. Monetarism was to be given a chance at solving the problems of inflation. The record from 1979 to the present offers no real hope and in many ways confirms the contention by many that the only solution will come when we have a redeemable currency.

The money supply since 1971 has been growing at unprecedented rates. Since inflation *is* an increase in the supply of money and credit, this is of critical importance. It tells us what many economic historians knew even before 1971, that when government is granted an unlimited power to create money out of thin air as the Federal Reserve has, that power is always abused. For various political reasons, excessive money is always created, bringing only trouble to the innocent citizens not receiving the "benefits" of inflation. It is tempting to pursue inflationary policies, since during all stages of inflation special interest groups benefit at the expense of others. History shows this temptation has never been resisted and the record of the money growth of the past decade confirms this to still be the case.

Money Supply	
(in billions of dollars)	
Monetary Base[1]	
December 1971	$86.6
December 1981	$169.8

M1A[2]	
December 1971	$230.4
December 1981	$364.6
M1B[3]	
December 1971	$230.6
December 1981	$442.1
M2[4]	
December 1971	$711.1
December 1981	$1842.2
M3[5]	
December 1971	$771.1
December 1981	$2187.1

All these figures indicate that the money supply in the space of 10 years has more than doubled, as measured by three of the five standard statistical series produced by the Federal Reserve. This is all the more significant, for neither the population nor American productivity increased by anything approaching that rate over the same period. Since increases in productivity and population are traditionally mentioned as reasons for increasing the money supply, neither of these factors can be used as the excuse for the massive creation of new money and credit of the Federal Reserve over the past decade. In April 1970, our population was approximately 203,000,000. By April 1980, it was 226,500,000, a 12 percent increase. Using the lowest of the money supply statistics, our money supply increased by *58 percent* over the same period. Using the largest of the money supply money figures, the money supply increased by *184 percent*. Neither figure is commensurate with a 12 percent increase in population over the decade.

As for the real growth of the Gross National Product, in 1979, GNP was $1,107.5 billion; during 1981, it was $1,509.06 billion, an increase of *36 percent*. Again that figure does not even remotely approach the growth of the money supply over the same decade.

---

[1]Bank reserves plus currency held by the public.

[2]Currency plus demand deposits at commercial banks.

[3]M1A plus checkable deposits at all depository institutions.

[4]M1B plus savings accounts and small denomination time deposits at all depository institutions and money market mutual funds.

[5]M2 plus large denomination time deposits and repurchase agreements at all depository institutions.

It is safe to say the money supply is growing three to four times faster than the real economy. Professor Milton Friedman argues that economic growth is not always related to monetary growth and that some of the best periods of economic growth in our history were associated with minimal money growth. This fact is one of the hardest to grasp by sincere economists and politicians, and yet it is most important in order to understand why commodity money is superior to paper money. Duplicating money substitutes can never replace the benefits of a *trustworthy* unit of account, one that encourages saving and prompts low interest rates. The duplication process does the opposite: It destroys trust, discourages savings, raises interest rates, slows economic growth, and does not create wealth.

Prices

The record for prices since 1971 is not very encouraging. The standard measures of price growth are the consumer price index, the producer price index, and the implicit price deflator prepared by the Departments of Labor and Commerce. Although price increases are the consequences of the government's increasing the supply of money and credit, most people still refer to these increases as inflation per se rather than the result of the inflation. Nevertheless, price increases are measurements of the harm done and are a reflection of the dollar's depreciation. Since prices are never uniform some segments of the society suffer from them more than others.

The following price statistics dramatize vividly the sharp depreciation of the currency over the past ten years.

	December 1971	December 1981
Consumer Price Index (1967 = 100)	123.1	281.5
Producer Price Index (1967 = 100)	115.4	275.3
	1971	1981
Implicit Price Deflator for GNP (1972 = 100)	96.01	193.57

Retail prices, as measured by the best statistics that the government has produced, have more than doubled during the decade of inconvertible paper money. What one Federal Reserve note purchased in 1971, it now requires approximately two and one-half Federal Reserve notes to purchase. This depreciation in the value of our inconvertible paper currency is characteristic of all such currencies throughout history. As long as the currency remains a fiat currency, one not redeemable in something of real value, we can expect the money supply to increase at unreasonable rates, depreciating the currency's value and resulting in persistent price increases of all goods and services. There is no question whatsoever that the problem of rising prices, although existing before 1971, has been made significantly worse since the closing of the gold window.

Interest Rates

Interest rates since 1971 tell the same story. They have reached heights never seen before in our history, including the greenback era of the Civil War. The prime rate soared to over 21 percent during the past decade, and higher rates are bound to occur if sound money is not restored. The supply and demand for money certainly plays a part in establishing the rate of interest, but today the inflation premium—the premium charged for the anticipation of further dollar devaluation—is the principal cause of fluctuating high interest rates. Since paper money is always depreciated by politicians, it should be expected that unless a redeemable dollar is once again established, the problem of high interest rates will not only continue but get worse. Unfortunately, high interest rates are frequently seen as a cause of inflation rather than as a result, which prompts many sincere individuals who have been victimized by these high rates to call for controls on the rates (usury laws) or for credit allocation. These policies can only make the problem worse, since they do not get to the root cause of the high interest rate: the inflation of the money supply and depreciation of the currency. Interest rates are inversely proportional to the trust the people have in the money. Until the trust is restored in the money (and in the government which has destroyed the money), high interest rates will continue. The record for interest rates for the past 10 years is a poor one and must be seen as a reflection of monetary policy.

Interest Rates Since 1971	
Conventional Home Mortgage Rate	
December 1971	7.67%
December 1981	15.98%
Low for decade	7.44% (April 1972)
High for decade	15.98% (December 1981)

Prime Lending Rate

December 1971	5.25%
December 1981	15.75%
Low for decade	4.75% (February 1972)
High for decade	21.75% (August 1981)

91-Day Treasury Bill Rate

December 1971	4.02%
December 1981	10.93%
Low for decade	3.18% (February 1972)
High for decade	16.03% (May 1981)

Bond Rates AAA Corporate Bonds

December 1971	7.25%
December 1981	14.23%
Low for decade	7.08% (December 1979)
High for decade	15.49% (September 1981)

Public Utilities

November 1971	7.96%
November 1981	15.05%
Low for decade	7.48% (December 1972)
High for decade	16.48% (September 1981)

State and Local Tax-Exempt Bonds

December 1971	5.02%
December 1981	12.91%
Low for decade	4.99% (November 1972)
High for decade	12.92% (September 1981)

U.S. Government Marketable Securities (All Maturities)

November 1971	5.37%
November 1981	12.401%
Low for decade	5.051% (March 1972)
High for decade	15.83% (October 1981)

Even with a reduction in the rate of price inflation, interest rates have remained high. This reflects the lost confidence in the currency and in the Congress's ability to deal with the problem. With deficits soaring and the Federal Reserve able to create new money at will, the lack of confidence is justified and understandable.

Bankruptcy Since 1971

Whenever a businessman complains about the economy and the difficulties he faces in maintaining a profitable business, he speaks mainly of the burden of high interest rates. Currently he sees this expense as the crippling blow to maintaining a successful business. It is practically impossible to maintain a profitable business on borrowed capital costing more than 20 percent. The interest burden has in turn led to an enormous growth in the number of personal and business bankruptcies in the past decade. Many financial institutions—in particular the savings and loans—are facing bankruptcy and are currently being absorbed by larger institutions with the assistance of tax dollars. The estimate of the number of savings and loans in danger of failing is well over 1,500. However, the proposal in Washington to "save" these institutions involves the same procedure used to "save" New York City and Chrysler—more inflation associated with a frantic effort to avoid debt liquidation by deflation.

Although bankruptcies do liquidate debt in a conventional way, large corporations, cities, states, and financial institutions are "bailed out." Financial institutions are bailed out by government-mandated and regulated takeovers by "stronger" institutions.

Those allowed to fail have been and will continue to be the smaller companies and individuals. The statistics show a rapid increase in personal and business bankruptcies since 1971—evidence of unmanageable debt service associated with high interest rates.

Business and Personal Bankruptcies and Failures Since 1971

1971	201,352
1981	519,063

These figures can be expected to increase, and they would be even worse if no firms were "bailed out" by government programs granting loans and guaranteeing loans (greater than $800 billion). These programs may keep the figures artificially low for a time, but they will obviously contribute to more inflation at a later day, a weaker economy, and the threat of even more bankruptcies later on.

Bonds and Mortgages

In the 1970s we have seen the virtual destruction of long-term financing in the United States. A key to a capitalistic economy is availability of long-term borrowing, and without its reestablishment, economic stagnation can be expected. Long-term markets cannot be restored without restoring the belief that the dollar will no longer be depreciated.

Home mortgage rates of 17 and 18 percent guarantee that a very few people will qualify for the purchase of a new home. This is destroying the housing industry and is a prime contributor to the high unemployment rate we are now experiencing.

Bonds are no longer the investment of widows and orphans, but have joined the ranks of speculative investments with investors hoping to catch minor price swings, make a profit, and then quickly sell. This is no way to build a healthy market economy. In 1945, the Standard and Poor's Index of bond prices was 121.6 for current 1945 and gold dollars. By 1981 in current dollars, it was 38, in 1945 dollars it was 9 and in gold dollars it was 2.4. It took 3.2 ounces of gold in 1945 to buy the index and .09 ounces in 1981. The bond market in Britain, which leads us by a few years in such matters, has already been destroyed.

An investment in 1971 in gold would have yielded a 17.8 percent annual return. A similar investment in a U.S. bond would have declined 5.2 percent annually in real terms.

The message of the dollar's illness came sooner in the bond market than any place else. It has moved downward since 1945, but the precipitous drop occurred in the decade since 1971. Without the reversal of long-term bond markets, true capital formation is impossible. True savings of the future will not occur under the conditions existing today, and the only credible reassurance is a precisely defined and guaranteed monetary unit.

Employment and Real Income

As one would expect when a nation's currency is depreciated by creating an excessive amount of it, the real wage of the working man is bound to go down. Even though in the early, less detectable, and more modest stages of inflation, increases in productivity can stay ahead of the depreciation and give the impression that inflation is beneficial, the results noted in the 1970s were inevitable and predict-

9

able. Real income suffered more than at any other time in American history. There was a 13 percent drop over a 10-year period.

Spendable Average Weekly Earnings	
(1967 dollars)	
December 1971	$95.04
December 1981	83.19

The recession or depression that follows periods of monetary inflation is the correction that comes as a result of malinvestment due to the false information of distorted interest rates. During a correction, as the economy tries to right itself, a period of unemployment results. If the correction is aborted and "corrected" by resumption of more inflation, each cycle will give us more unemployment. Since 1945, we can see that each cycle has gotten worse: higher interest rates, higher prices, and higher unemployment. Today, we see the unemployment levels higher than any since the Great Depression.

Unemployment	
December 1971	4.695 million (5.5%)
December 1981	9.462 million (8.9%)

Unemployment is now at a critical stage, and even if another cycle is entered and this rate is temporarily reduced, it is to be expected that without the adoption of a sound monetary system, unemployment rates will continually get worse.

Personal Savings Rate

When a currency loses its value by deliberate and steady inflation, the tendency, as more and more citizens become knowledgeable, is for a lowered savings rate. Since the exact rate of depreciation—actual price increase of goods and service—is unpredictable, it becomes impossible to anticipate and fully protect the purchasing power of savings by correctly establishing the inflationary premium on interest rates. There is a disincentive to save since price inflation is usually greater than the extra interest earned. But more importantly, it is unpredictable. Many figure it is better to buy something this year rather than next (when they will actually need it) when the price will be much higher.

1971	8.1%
1981	5.3%

Savings are discouraged even further if interest rates paid are artificially controlled by government regulations. The shift of funds from the savings and loans to the money market mutual funds is not much of a mystery. Even though savings and loans are starved for savings, they have championed the continued fixing of low interest rates on savings accounts, hoping that this special benefit will continue. Although this did help in the early stages of inflation, now when the spread is 7 percent to 12 percent between what savings and loans will pay and the market rate, we cannot expect that resumption of savings in the conventional manner will come quickly. Without true savings, capital formation is impossible. And without adequate savings, government officials are pressured to try to create "capital" by money creation, a policy that will only make the problem worse. There will be further depreciation of the currency, with more monetary inflation, thus increasing even further the disincentive to save. Only with the cessation of inflation through reinstitution of a hard currency will we see a significant increase in true savings. Economic growth depends on savings (and other things like low taxes and minimal regulations), not on the growth of the money supply as so many believe today.

Monetarism—Not the Answer

The obvious failure of the discretionary monetary system has prompted the popularization of monetarism in recent years. This is the view that the federal government should manage the nation's money system and supply, increasing the number of dollars each year by between 3 percent and 5 percent. The monetarists share our view that the Federal Reserve's discretionary policy of the last several decades has been the cause of our inflation. However, we are confident that the monetarist solution is unworkable. Since October of 1979, the Federal Reserve has directed its attention to regulating the money supply and has abandoned its traditional intense concentration on manipulation of interest rates. Yet we *now* are witnessing more erratic movement in the money supply (and interest rates) then ever before.

The excuses given are: "The monetary technicians are at fault"; "The wrong parameters are being used"; "The wrong M is being watched"; "The wrong people are in charge." The excuses are unlimited as to

11

why monetarism is failing. The explanations are always given by those monetarists who do not assume the responsibility for making monetarism work. It is certainly true that neither here in the United States nor in England has monetarist policy followed the textbook description of how monetarism should be implemented. What the monetarists will not admit nor even consider, however, is that it is not being followed because it *cannot* be followed. They prefer to believe that it is the shortcomings of the technicians rather than of the monetary system itself.

The notion that deficits do not matter so long as they are a certain percent of the gross national product, as claimed by some of the monetarists, is not acceptable. It ignores the fact that total annual borrowing of the federal government exceeds the annual deficit as the total debt is turned over more and more rapidly. A sound monetary system works hand in hand with a balanced budget, giving the citizens assurance of no possible future plans to "break the rules" and start inflating again. Many who downplay the deficit (some supply-siders, Keynesians, and monetarists) emphasize correctly that it is not inflationary if the debt is not monetized. But they fail to consider the inflationary pressures created by the real debt—the on-budget deficit, the off-budget deficit, the guaranteed loans, and the direct loans—a much larger problem than the conventionally accepted annual federal deficit. The political pressures to monetize the debt are inexorable.

Monetarism ignores man's nature and assumes that if money managers and politicians are given the power to increase the money supply at a 5 percent annual rate, they will not abuse that power. History shows that governments and the people in charge will always abuse the "right" to create money if it is granted to them.

Monetarists cannot agree on the precise definition of money. Some prefer the monetary base (bank reserves plus circulating cash); others prefer M1B (cash plus checking and transfer accounts). Since M1B is no longer satisfactory, M1A and M1B have now been dropped and M1 is presently the key M to watch, according to some. Still others believe M2 is the key M to watch. Nothing guarantees that if M1 or M2 become difficult to control, a new M will not be created. A sound monetary system cannot be this arbitrary.

The theory of monetarism advocates a deliberate and controlled monetary inflation of 3–5 percent per year to coincide with economic growth so as to produce price stability. If we don't know what the economic growth will be in the year to come—2 percent or 6 percent—we cannot know how much money to create in order to produce price stability.

We cannot wait until after the growth occurs, for it serves no purpose—the money then comes into the economy too late. The monetarists fully recognize that money growth as we have had it in the past decade is injurious to economic growth, but claim that a 5 percent growth in the money supply would not be. The truth is that any inflation—even monetarist inflation—is harmful, and that a 4 percent growth of the money supply cannot produce economic growth of 4 percent. The two are unrelated.

The central purpose of a monetary standard is trust and honesty, not stable prices. The reason gold is superior to all forms of paper is that it provides this truth and honesty, permits and encourages savings, enhances economic growth, and as a secondary benefit allows prices to adjust freely in the marketplace (yet long-term price stability is achieved more with gold than with any other standard). "Stable" prices cannot be achieved any more easily through monetary policy than they can through wage and price controls; that is, they cannot be achieved at all.

Both monetarists and gold standard advocates want to stop the present inflation. Monetarism claims that a gradual reduction in the rate of money growth can get us to where we want to be. Gradualism has not worked in England nor in the United States so far, and there is no indication that it will. Gradualism does not ensure credibility. Restoring convertibility and defining the dollar as a precise weight of gold is the only way the psychology of inflation can be broken. Although the money supply is very important, an absolute relationship of money supply to prices does not exist. Ultimately, all prices (and the value of the dollar) are set by the market, not by the monetary authorities.

Monetarism is similar to a discretionary inflationary policy in that the government remains as the monopolist fully in charge. In contrast, with a fully convertible gold standard, the people are in charge and can call the government's bluff anytime they choose by turning in their paper certificates for gold. The unit of account, as Jefferson stated, must be defined "with precision." A gold standard does this by defining the unit in a weight of gold—a paper standard provides no definition, and the unit of account is arbitrary and is inevitably depreciated by the money managers. Trust can never be restored with a paper currency.

A New Attitude

The final severance of our currency's link to gold in 1971 ushered in a new attitude among Americans unknown previously in our history.

Even though there were short periods during wartime when an inflationary psychology existed, it never persisted for an indefinite period and it has never been as pervasive as we are experiencing now. Associated with this inflationary psychology is a general attitude toward government and life in general. Pessimism has replaced our traditional optimism. Scheming, speculation, and sophisticated tax avoidance have replaced productive efforts, savings, and planning for the future.

Trading in currencies can now be more rewarding to banks than the conventional business of brokering loans from savings. The futures and options market has turned into a giant gambling game. The new markets that have developed since the dollar lost its precise definition reflect the ingenuity of man. Now we see futures sold in currencies, betting on the monetary inflation of various governments. Instead of buying a bond or treasury bill and holding it, we now can speculate on a daily and massive basis.

Just this winter, futures and options began to be sold on stock indexes. One is able to buy futures on large CD's as well. Outstanding European rate futures and GNMA options (GNMA futures started in 1975) will be offered also. Billions of dollars are now used in industry for the purpose of "takeovers" of other industries with no real signs of developing new industries or re-capitalizing old industries. The dollar amount involved in the speculation is into the trillions of dollars from these various ventures. All this is a result of unsound money. Ten years ago, most of the futures and options markets did not exist.

With a sound currency there would be no speculation and trading in U.S. government bonds. Speculation would be minimal as compared with today. Their value would be predictable and betting on their day-to-day value would be meaningless. Yet in 1980, on the Chicago Board of Trade, far more U.S. Treasury Bond futures contracts than cattle contracts were traded. The options market is also growing by leaps and bounds and becoming more sophisticated and more complex every day. The frenzy with which the speculation is growing is literally incomprehensible and immeasureable. This tendency will continue so long as we are operating with an unsound currency that is being deliberately depreciated on a regular basis.

The speculation has spilled over into the fiscal arena as well. In 1980, $2,107,325,000 was collected by state-run lotteries. It is illegal for most citizens to gamble, but it is legal for governments to operate lotteries to raise revenues.

In the past decade the definition of money has undergone continuous change, reflecting the new rules of a fiat monetary system. In 1970 the

Federal Reserve had a single monetary aggregate. In 1971 the concepts of M1, M2, and M3 were introduced. By 1975 it became necessary to define two new aggregates, M4 and M5. The more chaotic money management became after the dollar-gold linkage broke down, the more the definition of money was changed. After the mid-1970s "demand" deposits were virtually impossible to calculate due to interest-bearing transaction accounts. This prompted the temporary use of a measurement called M1+ in 1978.

By 1980 a major redefinition of all the monetary aggregates was required. The turbulent international monetary crisis of 1979 convinced many that current definitions and money management were totally inadequate. Five new definitions were introduced: M1-A, M1-B, M2, M3, and L. Even these did not suffice. In 1981 the Fed started publishing a "shift-adjusted" measure of M1B to account for the new nationwide NOW accounts. By 1982, this adjusted measure of M1B was dropped, and M1A and M1B became M1.

It's probably safe to predict that new definitions will be invented in hopes that the impossible task of managing a fiat monetary system will be miraculously achieved by new measurements. This problem of measuring monetary aggregates would not exist under a gold standard, for there would be no purpose in it.

This decade has taught Americans to accept for the first time that their standard of living, over a period of years, is more likely to go down than up. It is also recognized by many Americans that conditions caused by inflation and the tax code are achieving a transfer of wealth from the large middle class and the working poor to both the rich and the welfare poor. Average people can no longer buy houses, cars are smaller for the shrinking number who are still able to buy one, most people pump their own gas, and household help and other services are on the wane. These have all led to a sense of frustration and anger.

More and more Americans have resorted to the underground economy to compensate for losses they see as unfair. Lawbreakers have replaced lawabiders. Fear of the unknown has prompted a whole subculture of survivalists—convinced by their own analysis that the government in the foreseeable future will not adopt a sound monetary system. This group no longer depends on conventional news services for their information and relies on expensive newsletters for what is considered accurate information regarding what is happening to the monetary system. It is easy to write them off as speculators, but compared with "speculating" in five percent-per-year losses with a government bond, it seems that their existence and their success are a reflection of our inflationary monetary policy. There is a sincere attempt by a growing number of Americans to preserve assets that have been earned over a period of time and whose value is threatened by inflation. For this reason, tens of thousands have attended hard money conferences in the past 10 years in the hope that they can learn how to protect themselves from the destructiveness of a government-caused inflation. This is a new phenomenon and is directly related to the breakdown of the Bretton Woods and Smithsonian Agreements. Prior to 1974, the conferences were virtually unheard of.

In 1968 and 1971 a vocal minority decried the abandonment of gold convertibility and predicted the subsequent events of the 1970s. A remnant throughout the period of the dissolution of the gold standard (1913 to 1971) steadfastly proclaimed that one day a gold standard would be required to stop inflation and restore order to monetary policy and to the financial markets. The number of Americans insisting on a sound currency is multiplying rapidly. Today's events dramatize the urgent need to lay plans for establishing a modern gold standard. A growing number of free-market economists defend the wisdom of the gold standard. Their voices may not have been heard by the officials, but their impact has been felt.

The need for something better than we have today is conceded by almost everyone. The past 10 years have taken a heavy toll with general confidence shattered. Most agree that this country and the Western nations appear hopelessly enmeshed in the problems of persistent inflation, high interest rates, weak economies, and high unemployment. No one expects these conditions to improve without a significant change in monetary policy. It is our purpose in this report to offer and to lay out the plans for a sound monetary system.

II. A History of Money and Banking in the United States Before the 20th Century

As an outpost of Great Britain, colonial America of course used British pounds, pence, and shillings as its money. Great Britain was officially on a silver standard, with the shilling defined as equal to 86 pure Troy grains of silver, and with silver as so defined legal tender for all debts (i.e., creditors were compelled to accept silver at that rate). However, Britain also coined gold and maintained a bimetallic standard by fixing the gold guinea, weighing 129.4 grains of gold, as equal in value to a certain weight of silver. In that way, gold became, in effect, legal tender as well. Unfortunately, by establishing bimetallism, Britain became perpetually subject to the evils known as Gresham's Law, which states that when government compulsorily overvalues one money and undervalues another, the undervalued money will leave the country or disappear into hoards, while the overvalued money will flood into circulation. Hence, the popular catchphrase of Gresham's Law: "Bad money drives out good." But the important point to note is that the triumph of "bad" money is the result, *not* of perverse free-market competition, but of government using the compulsory legal tender power to privilege one money above another.

In 17th-and 18th-century Britain, the government maintained a mint ratio between gold and silver that consistently overvalued gold and undervalued silver in relation to world market prices, with the resultant disappearance and outflow of full-bodied silver coins, and an influx of gold, and the maintenance in circulation of only eroded and "light-weight" silver coins. Attempts to rectify the fixed bimetallic ratios were always too little and too late.[1]

In the sparsely settled American colonies, money, as it always does, arose in the market as a useful and scarce commodity and began to serve as a general medium of exchange. Thus, beaver fur and wampum

---

[1] In the late 17th and early 18th centuries, the British maintained fixed mint ratios of from 15.1:1 of silver grains in relation to gold grains, to about 15.5:1. Yet the world market ratio of weight, set by forces of supply and demand, was about 14.9:1. Thus, silver was consistently undervalued and gold overvalued. In the 18th century, the problem got even worse, for increasing gold production in Brazil and declining silver production in Peru brought the market ratio down to 14.1:1 while the mint ratios fixed by the British government continued to be the same.

were used as money in the North for exchanges with the Indians, and fish and corn also served as money. Rice was used as money in South Carolina, and the most widespread use of commodity money was tobacco, which served as money in Virginia. The pound-of-tobacco was the currency unit in Virginia, with warehouse receipts in tobacco circulating as money backed 100 percent by the tobacco in the warehouse.

While commodity money continued to serve satisfactorily in rural areas, as the colonial economy grew, Americans imported gold and silver coins to serve as monetary media in urban centers and in foreign trade. English coins were imported, but so too were gold and silver coins from other European countries. Among the gold coins circulating in America were the French guinea, the Portuguese "joe," the Spanish doubloon, and Brazilian coins, while silver coins included French crowns and livres.

It is important to realize that gold and silver are international commodities, and that therefore, when not prohibited by government decree, foreign coins are perfectly capable of serving as standard moneys. There is no need to have a national government monopolize the coinage, and indeed foreign gold and silver coins constituted much of the coinage in the United States until Congress outlawed the use of foreign coins in 1857. Thus, if a free market is allowed to prevail in a country, foreign coins will circulate naturally. Silver and gold coins will tend to be valued in proportion to their respective weights, and the ratio *between* silver and gold will be set by the market in accordance with their relative supply and demand.

Shilling/Dollar Manipulations

By far the leading specie coin circulating in America was the Spanish silver dollar, defined as consisting of 387 grains of pure silver. The dollar was divided into "pieces of eight," or "bits," each consisting of one-eighth of a dollar. Spanish dollars came into the North American colonies through the lucrative trade with the West Indies. The Spanish silver dollar had been the world's outstanding coin since the early 16th century, and was spread partially by dint of the vast silver output of the Spanish colonies in Latin America. More important, however, was the fact that the Spanish dollar, from the 16th to the 19th century, was relatively the most stable and least debased coin in the Western world.[2]

[2]The name "dollar" came from the "thaler," the name given to the coin of similar weight, the "Joachimsthaler" or "schlicken thaler," issued since the early 16th century by the Count of Schlick in Joachimsthal in Bohemia. The Joachimsthalers weigh 451 Troy grains of silver. So successful were these coins that similar thalers were minted in Bur-

18

Since the Spanish silver dollar consisted of 387 grains, and the English shilling consisted of 86 grains of silver, this meant the natural, free-market ratio between the two coins would be 4 shillings 6 pence per dollar.[3]

Constant complaints, both by contemporaries and by some later historians, arose about an alleged "scarcity of money," especially of specie, in the colonies, allegedly justifying numerous colonial paper money schemes to remedy that "shortage." In reality, there was no such shortage. It is true that England, in a mercantilist attempt to hoard specie, kept minting for its own prerogative and outlawed minting in the colonies; it also prohibited the export of English coin to America. But this did not keep specie from America, for, as we have seen, Americans were able to import Spanish and other foreign coin, including English, from other countries. Indeed, as we shall see, it was precisely paper money issues that led, by Gresham's Law, to outflows and disappearance of specie from the colonies.

In their own mercantilism, the colonial governments early tried to hoard their own specie by debasing their shilling standards in terms of Spanish dollars. Whereas their natural weights dictated a ratio of 4 shillings per 6 pence to the dollar, Massachusetts, in 1642, began a general colonial process of competitive debasement of shillings. Massachusetts arbitrarily decreed that the Spanish dollar be valued at 5 shillings; the idea was to attract an inflow of Spanish silver dollars into that colony, and to subsidize Massachusetts exports by making their prices cheaper in terms of dollars. Soon, Connecticut and other colonies followed suit, each persistently upping the ante of debasement. The result was to increase the supply of nominal units of account by debasing the shilling, inflating domestic prices and thereby bringing the temporary export stimulus to a rapid end. Finally, the English government brought a halt to this futile and inflationary practice in 1707.

But the colonial governments had already found another, and far more inflationary, arrow for their bow: the invention of government fiat paper money.

---

gundy, Holland, France; most successful of these was the Maria Theresa thaler, which began being minted in 1751, and formed a considerable portion of American currency after that date. The Spanish "pieces of eight" adopted the name "dollar" after 1690.

[3]Since 20 shillings make £1, this meant that the natural ratio between the two currencies was £1 = $4.44.

Government Paper Money

Apart from medieval China, which invented both paper and printing centuries before the West, the world had never seen government paper money until the colonial government of Massachusetts emitted a fiat paper issue in 1690.[4,5] Massachusetts was accustomed to launching plunder expeditions against the prosperous French colony in Quebec. Generally, the expeditions were successful, and would return to Boston, sell their booty, and pay off the soldiers with the proceeds. This time, however, the expedition was beaten back decisively, and the soldiers returned to Boston in ill-humor, grumbling for their pay. Discontented soldiers are ripe for mutiny, so the Massachusetts government looked around in concern for a way to pay the soldiers. It tried to borrow 3–4,000 pounds from Boston merchants, but evidently the Massachusetts credit rating was not the best. Finally, Massachusetts decided in December 1690 to print £ 7,000 in paper notes and to use them to pay the soldiers. Suspecting that the public would not accept irredeemable paper, the government made a twofold pledge when it issued the notes: that it would redeem them in gold or silver out of tax revenue in a few years and that absolutely no further paper notes would be issued. Characteristically, however, both parts of the pledge went quickly by the board: The issue limit disappeared in a few months, and all the bills continued unredeemed for nearly 40 years. As early as February 1691, the Massachusetts government proclaimed that its issue had fallen "far short" and so it proceeded to emit £ 40,000 of new money to repay all of its outstanding debt, again pledging falsely that this would be the absolutely final note issue.

But Massachusetts found that the increase in the supply of money, coupled with a fall in the demand for paper because of growing lack of confidence in future redemption in specie, led to a rapid depreciation of new money in relation to specie. Indeed, in a year after the initial issue, the new paper pound had depreciated on the market by 40 percent against specie.

[4]Government paper redeemable in gold began in the early 9th century, and after three centuries the government escalated to irredeemable fiat paper, with the usual consequence of boom-bust cycles, and runaway inflation. See Gordon Tullock, "Paper Money—A Cycle in Cathay," *Economic History Review*, vol. IX, no. 3 (1957), pp. 393–396.

[5]The only exception was a curious form of paper money issued five years earlier in Quebec, to become known as Card Money. The governing *intendant* of Quebec, Monsieur Mueles, divided some playing cards into quarters, marked them with various monetary denominations, and then issued them to pay for wages and materials sold to the government. He ordered the public to accept the cards as legal tender, and this particular issue was later redeemed in specie sent from France.

By 1692, the government moved against this market evaluation by use of force, making the paper money compulsory legal tender for all debts at par with specie, and by granting a premium of five percent on all payment of debts to the government made in paper notes. This legal tender law had the unwanted effect of Gresham's Law: the disappearance of specie circulation in the colony. In addition, the expanding paper issues drove up prices and hampered exports from the colony. In this way, the specie "shortage" became the creature rather than the cause of the fiat paper issues. Thus, in 1690, before the orgy of paper issues began, £ 200,000 of silver money was available in New England; by 1711 however, with Connecticut and Rhode Island having followed suit in paper money issue, £ 240,000 of paper money had been issued in New England but the silver had almost disappeared from circulation.

Ironically, then, Massachusetts' and her sister colonies' issue of paper created rather than solved any "scarcity of money." The new paper drove out the old specie. The consequent driving up of prices and depreciation of paper scarcely relieved any alleged money scarcity among the public. But since the paper was issued to finance government expenditures and pay public debts, the *government*, not the public, benefited from the fiat issue.

After Massachusetts had emitted another huge issue of £ 500,000 in 1711 to pay for another failed expedition against Quebec, not only was the remainder of the silver driven from circulation, but despite the legal tender law, the paper pound depreciated 30 percent against silver. Massachusetts pounds, officially seven shillings to the silver ounce, had now fallen on the market to nine shillings per ounce. Depreciation proceeded in this and other colonies despite fierce governmental attempts to outlaw it, backed by fines, imprisonment, and total confiscation of property for the high crime of not accepting the paper at par.

Faced with a further "shortage of money" due to the money issues, Massachusetts decided to press on; in 1716, it formed a government "land bank" and issued £ 100,000 in notes to be loaned on real estate in the various counties of the province.

Prices rose so dramatically that the tide of opinion in Massachusetts began to turn against paper, as writers pointed out that the result of the issues was a doubling of prices in the past 20 years, depreciation of paper, and the disappearance of Spanish silver through the operation of Gresham's Law. From then on, Massachusetts, pressured by the Crown, tried intermittently to reduce the bills in circulation and return to a specie currency, but was hampered by its assumed obligations to honor the paper notes at par of its sister New England colonies.

In 1744, another losing expedition against the French led Massachusetts to issue an enormous amount of paper money over the next several years. From 1744 to 1748, paper money in circulation expanded from £ 300,000 to £ 2.5 million, and the depreciation of Massachusetts was such that silver had risen on the market to 60 shillings an ounce, 10 times the price at the beginning of an era of paper money in 1690.

By 1740, every colony but Virginia had followed suit in fiat paper money issues, and Virginia succumbed in the late 1750s in trying to finance part of the French and Indian War against the French. Similar consequences—dramatic inflation, shortage of specie, massive depreciation despite compulsory par laws—ensued in each colony. Thus, along with Massachusetts' depreciation of 11:1 of its notes against specie compared to the original par, Connecticut's notes had sunk to 9:1 and the Carolinas' at 10:1 in 1740, and the paper of virulently inflationist Rhode Island had sunk to 23:1 against specie. Even the least-inflated paper, that of Pennsylvania, had suffered an appreciation of specie to 80 percent over par.

A detailed study of the effects of paper money in New Jersey shows how it creatd a boom-bust economy over the colonial period. When new paper money was injected into the economy, an inflationary boom would result, to be followed by a deflationary depression when the paper money supply contracted.[6]

At the end of King George's War with France in 1748, Parliament began to pressure the colonies to retire the mass of paper money and return to a specie currency. In 1751, Great Britain prohibited all further issues of legal tender paper in New England and ordered a move toward redemption of existing issues in specie. Finally, in 1764, Parliament extended the prohibition of new issues to the remainder of the colonies and required the gradual retirement of outstanding notes.

Following the lead of Parliament, the new England colonies, apart from Rhode Island, decided to resume specie payment and retire their paper notes rapidly at the current depreciated market rate. The panicky opponents of specie resumption and monetary contraction made the usual predictions in such a situation: that the result would be a virtual absence of money in New England and the consequent ruination of all trade. Instead, however, after a brief adjustment, the resumption and retirement led to a far more prosperous trade and production—the harder money and lower prices attracting an inflow of specie. In fact,

[6]Donald L. Kemmerer, "Paper Money in New Jersey, 1668–1775," New Jersey Historical Society, *Proceedings* 74 (April 1956): 107–144.

with Massachusetts on specie and Rhode Island still on depreciated paper, the result was that Newport, which had been a flourishing center for West Indian imports for Western Massachusetts, lost its trade to Boston and languished in the doldrums.[7,8]

In fact, as one student of colonial Massachusetts has pointed out, the return to specie occasioned remarkably little dislocation, recession, or price deflation. Indeed, wheat prices fell by less in Boston than in Philadelphia, which saw no such return to specie in the early 1750s. Foreign exchange rates, after the resumption of specie, were highly stable, and "the restored specie system operated after 1750 with remarkable stability during the Seven Years War and during the dislocation of international payments in the last years before the Revolution."[9]

Not being outlawed by government decree, specie remained in circulation throughout the colonial period, even during the operation of paper money. Despite the inflation, booms and busts, and shortages of specie caused by paper issues, the specie system worked well overall: "Here was a silver standard. . . in the absence of institutions of the central government intervening in the silver market, and in the absence of either a public or private central bank adjusting domestic credit or managing a reserve of specie or foreign exchange with which to stabilize exchange rates. The market. . . kept exchange rates remarkably close to the legislated par. . . . What is most remarkable in this context is the

[7]Before Massachusetts went back to specie, it was committed to accept the notes of the other New England colonies at par. This provided an incentive for Rhode Island to inflate its currency wildly, for this small colony, with considerable purchases to make in Massachusetts, could make these purchases in inflated money at par. Thereby Rhode Island could export its inflation to the larger colony, but make its purchases with the new money before Massachusetts prices could rise in response. In short, Rhode Island could expropriate wealth from Massachusetts and impose the main cost of its inflation on the latter colony.

[8]If Rhode Island was the most inflationary of the colonies, Maryland's monetary expansion was the most bizarre. In 1733, Maryland's public land bank issued £ 70,000 of paper notes, of which £ 30,000 was *given away* in a fixed amount to each inhabitant of the province. This was done to universalize the circulation of the new notes, and is probably the closest approximation in history of Milton Friedman's "helicopter" model, in which a magical helicopter lavishes new paper money in fixed amounts of proportions to each inhabitant. The result of the measure, of course, was rapid depreciation of new notes. However, the inflationary impact of the notes was greatly lessened by tobacco still being the major money of the new colony. Tobacco was legal tender in Maryland and the paper was not receivable for all taxes.

[9]Roger W. Weiss, "The Colonial Monetary Standard of Massachusetts," *Economic History Review* 27 (November 1974): 589.

continuity of the specie system through the seventeenth and eighteenth centuries."[10]

Private Bank Notes

In contrast to government paper, private bank notes and deposits, redeemable in specie, had begun in Western Europe in Venice in the 14th century. Firms granting credit to consumers and businesses had existed in the ancient world and in medieval Europe, but these were "money lenders" who loaned out their own savings. "Banking" in the sense of lending out the savings of others only began in England with the "scriveners" of the early 17th century. The scriveners were clerks who wrote contracts and bonds and were therefore in a position to learn of mercantile transactions and engage in money lending and borrowing.[11]

There were, however, no banks of deposit in England until the Civil War in the mid-17th century. Merchants had been in the habit of storing their surplus gold in the King's Mint for safekeeping. The habit proved to be unfortunate, for when Charles I needed money in 1638, shortly before the outbreak of the Civil War, he confiscated the huge sum of £200,000 of gold, calling it a "loan" from the owners. Although the merchants finally got their gold back, they were understandably shaken by the experience, and foresook the Mint, depositing their gold instead in the coffers of private goldsmiths, who, like the Mint, were accustomed to storing the valuable metal. The warehouse receipts of the goldsmiths soon came to be used as a surrogate for the gold itself. By the end of the Civil War, in the 1660s, the goldsmiths fell prey to the temptation to print pseudo-warehouse receipts not covered by gold and lend them out; in this way fractional-reserve banking came to England.[12]

[10]Ibid., p. 591.

[11]During the 16th century, before the rise of the scriveners, most English money-lending was not even conducted by specialized firms, but by wealthy merchants in the clothing and woollen industries, as outlets for their surplus-capital. See J. Milnes Holden, *The History of Negotiable Instruments in English Law* (London: The Athlone Press, 1955), pp. 205–206.

[12]Once again, ancient China pioneered in deposit banking, as well as in fractional-reserve banking. Deposit banking *per se* began in the 8th century A.D., when shops would accept valuables, in return for warehouse receipts, and receive a fee for keeping them safe. After a while, the deposit receipts of these shops began to circulate as money. Finally, after two centuries, the shops began to issue and lend out more receipts than they had on deposit; they had caught on to fractional reserve banking. (Tullock, "Paper Money," p. 396.)

Very few private banks existed in colonial America, and they were shortlived. Most prominent was the Massachusetts Land Bank of 1740, issuing notes and lending them out on real estate. The Land Bank was launched as an inflationary alternative to government paper, which the royal governor was attempting to restrict. The land bank issued frankly irredeemable notes, and fear of its unsound issue generated a competing private silver Bank, which emitted notes redeemable in silver. The Land Bank promptly issued over £49,000 in irredeemable notes, which depreciated very rapidly. In six months' time the public was almost universally refusing to accept the bank's notes and Land Bank sympathizers vainly accepting the notes. The final blow came in 1741, when Parliament, acting at the request of several Massachusetts merchants and the royal governor, outlawed both the law and the silver banks.

One intriguing aspect of both the Massachusetts Land Bank and other inflationary colonial schemes is that they were advocated and lobbied for by some of the wealthiest merchants and land speculators in the respective colonies. Debtors benefit from inflation and creditors lose; realizing this fact, older historians assumed that debtors were largely poor agrarians and creditors were wealthy merchants and that therefore the former were the main sponsors of inflationary nostrums. But, of course, there are no rigid "classes" of debtors and creditors; indeed, wealthy merchants and land speculators are often the heaviest debtors. Later historians have demonstrated that members of the latter group were the major sponsors of inflationary paper money in the colonies.[13,14]

[13]On the Massachusetts Land Bank, see the illuminating study by George Athan Billias, "The Massachusetts Land Bankers of 1740." *University of Maine Bulletin* LXI (April 1959). On merchant enthusiasm for inflationary banking in Massachusetts, see Herman J. Belz, "Paper Money in Colonial Massachusetts," Essex Institute, *Historical Collections* 101 (April 1965): 146–163; and Belz, "Currency Reform in Colonial Massachusetts, 1749–1750." Essex Institute, *Historical Collections* 103 (January 1967): 66–84. On the forces favoring colonial inflation in general, see Bray Hammond, *Banks and Politics in America* (Princeton University Press, 1957), Chap. 1; Joseph Dorfman, *The Economic Mind in American Civilization, 1606–1865* (New York: Viking Press, 1946), p. 142.

[14]For an excellent bibliographical essay on colonial money and banking, see Jeffrey Rogers Hummel, "The Monetary History of America to 1789: A Historiographical Essay," *Journal of Libertarian Studies* 2 (Winter 1978): 373–389. For a summary of colonial monetary experience, see Murray N. Rothbard, *Conceived in Liberty, Vol. II, Salutary Neglect, The American Colonies in the First Half of the 18th Century* (New Rochelle, N.Y.: Arlington House, 1975), pp. 123–140. A particularly illuminating analysis is in the classic work by Charles Jesse Bullock, *Essays on the Monetary History of the United States* (1900, New York: Greenwood Press, 1969), pp. 1–59. Up-to-date data on the period is in Roger W. Weiss, "The Issue of Paper Money in the American Colonies, 1720–1774," *Journal of Economic History* 30 (December 1970): 770–784.

Revolutionary War Finance

To finance the Revolutionary War, which broke out in 1775, the Continental Congress early hit on the device of issuing fiat paper money. The leader in the drive for paper money was Gouverneur Morris, the highly conservative young scion of the New York landed aristocracy. There was no pledge to redeem the paper, even in the future, but it was supposed to be retired in seven years by taxes levied pro rata by the separate states. Thus, a heavy future tax burden was supposed to be added to the inflation brought about the new paper money. The retirement pledge, however, was soon forgotten, as Congress, enchanted by this new, seemingly costless form of revenue, escalated its emissions of fiat paper. As a historian has phrased it, "such was the beginning of the 'federal trough,' one of America's most imperishable institutions."[15]

The total money supply of the United States at the beginning of the Revolution has been estimated at $12 million. Congress launched its first paper issue of $2 million in late June 1775, and before the notes were printed it had already concluded that another $1 million was needed. Before the end of the year, a full $6 million in paper issues were issued or authorized, a dramatic increase of 50 percent in the money supply in one year.

The issue of this fiat "continental" paper rapidly escalated over the next few years. Congress issued $6 million in 1775, $19 million in 1776, $13 million in 1777, $64 million in 1778, and $125 million in 1779. This was a total issue of over $225 million in five years superimposed upon preexisting money supply of $12 million. The result was, as could be expected, a rapid price inflation in terms of the paper notes, and a corollary accelerating depreciation of the paper in terms of specie. Thus, by the end of 1776, the Continentals were worth $1 to $1.25 in specie; by the fall of the following year, its value had fallen to 3 to 1; by December 1778 the value was 6.8 to 1; and by December 1779 to the negligible 42 to 1. By the spring of 1781, the Continentals were virtually worthless, exchanging on the market at 168 paper dollars to one dollar in specie. This collapse of the Continental currency gave rise to the phrase, "not worth a Continental."

To top this calamity, the several states issued their own paper money, and each depreciated at varying rates. Virginia and the Carolinas led

---

[15]Edmund Cody Burnett, *The Continental Congress* (New York: W.W. Norton, 1964), p. 83.

the inflationary move, and by the end of the war, state issues added a total of 210 million depreciated dollars to the nation's currency.

In an attempt to stem the inflation and depreciation, various states levied maximum price controls and compulsory par laws. The result was only to create shortages and impose hardships on large sections of the public. Thus, soldiers were paid in Continentals, but farmers understandably refused to accept payment in paper money despite legal coercion. The Continental Army then moved to "impress" food and other supplies, seizing the supplies and forcing the farmers and shopkeepers to accept depreciated paper in return. By 1779, with Continental paper virtually worthless, the Continental Army stepped up its impressments, "paying" for them in newly issued paper tickets or "certificates" issued by the army quartermaster and commissary departments. The states followed suit with their own massive certificate issues. It understandably took little time for these certificates, federal and state, to depreciate in value to nothing; by the end of the war, federal certificate issues alone totalled $200 million.

The one redeeming feature of this monetary calamity was that the federal and state governments at least allowed these paper issues to sink into worthlessness without insisting that taxpayers shoulder another grave burden by being forced to redeem these issues specie at par, or even to redeem them at all.[16] Continentals were not redeemed at all, and state paper was only redeemed at depreciating rates, some at the greatly depreciated market value.[17] By the end of the war, all the wartime state paper had been withdrawn from circulation.

Unfortunately, the same policy was not applied to another important device that Congress turned to after its Continental paper had become almost worthless in 1779: loan certificates. Technically, loan certificates were public debt, but they were scarcely genuine loans. They were simply notes issued by the government to pay for supplies and accepted by the merchants because the government would not pay anything else. Hence, the loan certificates became a form of currency, and rapidly depreciated. As early as the end of 1779, they had depreciated to 24 to

[16]As one historian explained, "Currency and certificates were the 'common debt' of the Revolution, most of which at war's end had been sunk at its depreciated value. Public opinion. . .tended to grade claims against the government according to their real validity. Paper money had the least status. . . ." E. James Ferguson, *The Power of the Purse: A History of American Public Finance, 1776–1790* (Chapel Hill, N.C.: University of North Carolina Press, 1961), p. 68.

[17]In Virginia and Georgia, the state paper was redeemed at the highly depreciated market rate of 1,000 to 1 in specie.

1 in specie. By the end of the war, $600 million of loan certificates had been issued. Some of the later loan certificate issues were liquidated at a depreciated rate, but the bulk remained after the war to become the substantial core of the permament, peacetime federal debt.

The mass of federal and state debt could have depreciated and passed out of existence by the end of the war, but the process was stopped and reversed by Robert Morris, wealthy Philadelphia merchant and virtual economic and financial czar of the Continental Congress in the last years of the war. Morris, leader of the nationalist forces in American politics, moved to make the depreciated federal debt ultimately redeemable in par and also agitated for federal assumption of the various state debts. The reason was twofold: (a) to confer a vast subsidy on speculators who had purchased the public debt at highly depreciated values, by paying interest and principal at par in specie;[18] and (b) to build up the agitation for taxing power in the Congress, which the Articles of Confederation refused to allow to the federal government. The decentralist policy of the states' raising taxes or issuing new paper money to pay off the *pro rata* federal debt as well as their own was thwarted by the adoption of the Constitution, which brought about the victory of the nationalist program, led by Morris's youthful disciple and former aide, Alexander Hamilton.

The Bank of North America

Robert Morris's nationalist vision was not confined to a strong central government, the power of the federal government to tax, and a massive public debt fastened permanently upon the taxpayers. Shortly after he assumed total economic power in Congress in the spring of 1781, Morris introduced a bill to create the first commercial bank, as well as the first central bank, in the history of the new Republic. This bank, headed by Morris himself, the Bank of North America, was not only the first fractional-reserve commercial bank in the U.S.; it was to be a privately owned central bank, modelled after the Bank of England. The money system was to be grounded upon specie, but with a controlled monetary inflation pyramiding an expansion of money and credit upon a reserve of specie.

The Bank of North America, which quickly received a federal charter and opened its doors at the beginning of 1782, received the privilege

---

[18]As Morris candidly put it, this windfall to the public debt speculators at the expense of the taxpayers would cause wealth to flow "into those hands which could render it most productive." (Ferguson, *Power of the Purse*, p. 124).

from the government of its notes being receivable in all duties and taxes to all governments, at par with specie. In addition, no other banks were to be permitted to operate in the country. In return for its monopoly license to issue paper money, the bank would graciously lend most of its newly created money to the federal government to purchase public debt and be reimbursed by the hapless taxpayer. The Bank of North America was made the depository for all congressional funds. The first central bank in America rapidly loaned $1.2 million to the Congress, headed also by Robert Morris.[19]

Despite Robert Morris's power and influence, and the monopoly privileges conferred upon his bank, it was perceived in the market that the Bank's notes were being inflated compared with specie. Despite the nominal redeemability of the Bank of North America's notes in specie, the market's lack of confidence in the inflated notes led to their depreciation outside its home base in Philadelphia. The Bank even tried to shore up the value of its notes by hiring people to urge redeemers of its notes not to ruin everything by insisting upon specie—a move scarcely calculated to improve ultimate confidence in the Bank.

After a year of operation, however, Morris, his political power slipping after the end of the war, moved quickly to end his Bank's role as a central bank and to shift it to the status of a private commercial bank chartered by the state of Pennsylvania. By the end of 1783, all of the federal government's stock in the Bank of North America, which had the previous year amounted to 5/8 of its capital, had been sold by Morris into private hands, and all the U.S. government debt to the bank had been repaid. The first experiment with a central bank in the United States had ended.[20]

At the end of the Revolutionary War, the contraction of the swollen mass of paper money, combined with the resumption of imports from Great Britain, combined to cut prices by more than half in a few years.

---

[19]When Morris failed to raise the legally required specie capital to launch the Bank of North America, Morris, in an act tantamount to embezzlement, simply appropriated specie loaned to the U.S. by France and invested it for the government in his own Bank. In this way, the bulk of specie capital for his Bank was appropriated by Morris out of government funds. A multiple of these funds was then borrowed back from Morris's bank by Morris as government financier for the pecuniary benefit of Morris as banker; and finally, Morris channeled most of the money into war contracts for his friends and business associates. Murray N. Rothbard, *Conceived in Liberty, Vol. IV, The Revolutionary War, 1775–1784* (New Rochelle, N.Y.: Arlington House, 1979), p. 392.

[20]See Rothbard, *The Revolutionary War*, pp. 409–410. On the Bank of North America and on Revolutionary War finance generally, see Curtis P. Nettels, *The Emergence of a National Economy, 1775–1815* (New York: Holt, Rinehart, and Winston, 1962), pp. 23–34.

Vain attempts by seven state governments, in the mid-1780s, to cure the "shortage of money" and reinflate prices were a complete failure. Part of the reason for the state paper issues was a frantic attempt to pay the wartime public debt, state and *pro rata* federal, without resorting to crippling burdens of taxation. The increased paper issues merely added to the "shortage" by stimulating the export of specie and the import of commodities from abroad. Once again, Gresham's Law was at work. State paper issues—despite compulsory par laws—merely depreciated rapidly, and aggravated the shortage of specie. A historian discusses what happened to the paper issues of North Carolina:

> In 1787-1788 the specie value of the paper had shrunk by more than 50 percent. Coin vanished, and since the paper had practically no value outside the state, merchants could not use it to pay debts they owed abroad; hence they suffered severe losses when they had to accept it at inflated values in the settlement of local debts. North Carolina's performance warned merchants anew of the menace of depreciating paper money which they were forced to receive at par from their debtors but which they could not pass on to their creditors.[21]

Neither was the situation helped by the expansion of banking following the launching of the Bank of North America in 1782. The Bank of New York and the Massachusetts Bank (Boston) followed two years later, with each institution enjoying a monopoly of banking in its region.[22] Their expansion of bank notes and deposits helped to drive out specie, and in the following year the expansion was succeeded by a contraction of credit, which aggravated the problems of recession.[23]

The United States: Bimetallic Coinage

Since the Spanish silver dollar was the major coin circulating in North America during the colonial and Confederation periods, it was generally agreed that the "dollar" would be the basic currency unit of the new United States of America.[24] Article I, section 8 of the new Constitution gave to Congress the power "to coin money, regulate the value thereof, and of foreign coin"; the power was exclusive because the state

---

[21]Nettels, *National Economy*, p. 82.

[22]See Hammond, *Banks and Politics*, pp. 67, 87–88.

[23]Nettels, *National Economy*, pp. 61–62. Also see ibid; pp. 77–80, 85.

[24]As Jefferson put it at the time: "The unit or dollar is a known coin, and the most familiar of all to the mind of the public. It is already adopted from South to North, has identified our currency, and therefore happily offers itself a unit already introduced." Cited in J. Laurence Laughlin, *The History of Bimetallism in the United States*, 4th ed. (New York: D. Appleton and Co., 1901), p. 11n.

governments were prohibited, in Article I, section 10, from coining money, emitting paper money, or making anything but gold and silver coin legal tender in payment of debts. (Evidently the Founding Fathers were mindful of the bleak record of colonial and revolutionary paper issues and provincial juggling of the weights and denominations of coin.) In accordance with this power, Congress passed the Coinage Act of 1792 on the recommendation of Secretary of Treasury Alexander Hamilton's *Report on the Establishment of a Mint* of the year before.[25]

The Coinage Act established a bimetallic dollar standard for the United States. The dollar was defined as *both* a weight of 371.25 grains of pure silver *and/or* a weight of 24.75 grains of pure gold—a fixed ratio of 15 grains of silver to 1 grain of gold.[26] Anyone could bring gold and silver bullion to the Mint to be coined, and silver and gold coins were both to be legal tender at this fixed ratio of 15:1. The basic silver coin was to be the silver dollar, and the basic gold coin the 10-dollar eagle, containing 247.5 grains of pure gold.[27]

The 15:1 fixed bimetallic ratio almost precisely corresponded to the market gold/silver ration of the early 1790s,[28] but of course the tragedy of any bimetallic standard is that the fixed mint ratio must always come a cropper against inevitably changing market ratios, and that Gresham's Law will then come inexorably into effect. Thus, Hamilton's express desire to keep both metals in circulation in order to increase the supply of money was doomed to failure.[29]

Unfortunately for the bimetallic goal, the 1780s saw the beginning of a steady decline in the ratio of the market values of silver to gold, largely due to the massive increases over the next three decades of silver production from the mines of Mexico. The result was that the market ratio fell to 15.5:1 by the 1790s, and after 1805 fell to approximately 15.75:1. The latter figure was enough of a gap between the market and mint ratios to set Gresham's Law into operation so that by

[25]The text of the Coinage Act of 1792 may be found in Laughlin, *History of Bimetallism*, pp. 300–301. Also see ibid; pp. 21–23; Hepburn, *History of Currency*, pp. 43–45.

[26]The current Spanish silver dollars in use were lighter than the earlier dollars weighing 387 grains. See Laughlin, *History of Bimetallism*, pp. 16–18.

[27]Golden half-eagles (worth $5) and quarter-eagles (worth $2.50) were also to be coined, of corresponding proportional weights, and, for silver coins, half-dollars, quarter-dollars, dimes, and half-dimes of corresponding weights.

[28]Silver had declined in market value from the 14.1:1 ratio of 1760, largely due to the declining production of gold from Russian mines in this period and therefore the rising relative value of gold.

[29]See Laughlin, *History of Bimetallism*, p. 14.

1810 gold coins began to disappear from the United States and silver coins to flood in. The fixed government ratio now significantly overvalued silver and undervalued gold, and so it paid people to bring in silver to exchange for gold, melt the gold coins into bullion and ship it abroad. From 1810 until 1834, only silver coin, domestic and foreign, circulated in the United States.[30]

Originally, Congress in 1793 provided that all foreign coins circulating in the United States be legal tender. Indeed, foreign coins have been estimated to form 80 percent of American domestic specie circulation in 1800. Most of the foreign coins were Spanish silver, and while the legal tender privilege was progressively cancelled for various foreign coins by 1827, Spanish silver coins continued as legal tender and to predominate in circulation.[31] Spanish dollars however, soon began to be heavier in weight by one to five percent over their American equivalents, even though they circulated at face value here, and so the American mint ratio overvalued American more than Spanish dollars. As a result, the Spanish silver dollars were re-exported, leaving American silver dollars in circulation. On the other hand, fractional Spanish silver coins—half-dollars, quarter-dollars, dimes, and half dimes—were considerably over-valued in the U.S., since they circulated at face value and yet were far lighter weight. Gresham's Law again came into play, and the result was that American silver fractional coins were exported and disappeared, leaving Spanish silver fractional coins as the major currency. To make matters still more complicated, American silver dollars, though lighter weight than the Spanish, circulated equally by name in the West Indies. As a result, American silver dollars were exported to the Caribbean. Thus, by the complex workings of Gresham's Law, the United States was left, especially after 1820, with no gold coins and only Spanish fractional silver coin in circulation.[32]

---

[30]For a lucid explanation of the changing silver/gold ratios and how Gresham's Law operated in this period, see Laughlin, *History of Bimetallism*, pp. 10-51. Also see Laughlin, *A New Exposition of Money, Credit and Prices* (Chicago: University of Chicago Press, 1931), pp. 93-111.

[31]These "Spanish" coins were almost exclusively minted in the Spanish colonies of Latin America. After the Latin American nations achieved independence in the 1820s, the coins circulated freely in the United States without being legal tender.

[32]On the complex workings of fractional as against dollar coins in this period, see the excellent article by David A. Martin, "Bimetallism in the United States before 1850," *Journal of Political Economy* 76 (May-June 1968): 428-434.

The First Bank of the United States 1791-1811

A linchpin of the Hamiltonian financial program was a central bank, the First Bank of the United States, replacing the abortive Bank of North America experiment. Hamilton's *Report on a National Bank* of December 1790 urged such a bank, to be owned privately with the government owning one-fifth of the shares. Hamilton argued that the alleged "scarcity" of specie currency needed to be overcome by infusions of paper, and the new Bank was to issue such paper, to be invested in the assumed federal debt and in subsidy to manufacturers. The Bank notes were to be legally redeemable in specie on demand, and its notes were to be kept at par with specie by the federal government's accepting its notes in taxes—giving it a quasi-legal tender status. Also, the federal government would confer upon the Bank the prestige of being depository for its public funds.

In accordance with Hamilton's wishes, Congress quickly established the First Bank of the United States in February 1791. The charter of the Bank was for 20 years, and it was assured a monopoly of the privilege of having a national charter during that period. In a significant gesture of continuity with the Bank of North America, the latter's long-time president and former partner of Robert Morris, Thomas Willing of Philadelphia, was made president of the new Bank of the United States.

The Bank of the United States promptly fulfilled its inflationary potential by issuing millions of dollars in paper money and demand deposits, pyramiding on top of $2 million in specie. The Bank of the United States invested heavily in loans to the United States government. In addition to $2 million invested in the assumption of preexisting long-term debt assumed by the new federal government, the Bank of the United States engaged in massive temporary lending to the government, which reached $6.2 million by 1796.[33] The result of the outpouring of credit and paper money by the new Bank of the United States was an inflationary rise in prices. Thus, wholesale prices rose from an index of 85 in 1791 to a peak of 146 in 1796, an increase of 72

---

[33]Schultz and Caine are severely critical of these operations: "In indebting itself heavily to the Bank of the United States, the Federal Government was obviously misusing its privileges and seriously endangering the Bank's stability." They also charged that "the Federalists had saddled the government with a military and interest budget that threatened to topple the structure of federal finances. Despite the addition of tax after tax to the revenue system, the Federal Government's receipts through the decade of the 90's were barely able to cling to the skirts of its expenditures." William J. Schultz and M.R. Caine, "Federalist Finance," in G.R. Taylor, ed. *Hamilton and the National Debt* (Boston: D.C. Heath and Co., 1950), pp. 6-7.

percent.[34] In addition, speculation boomed in government securities and real estate values were driven upward.[35] Pyramiding on top of the Bank of the United States expansion and aggravating the paper money expansion and the inflation was a flood of newly created commercial banks. Whereas there were only three commercial banks before the founding of the United States, and only four by the establishment of the Bank of the United States, eight new banks were founded shortly thereafter, in 1791 and 1792, and 10 more by 1796. Thus, the Bank of the United States and its monetary expansion spurred the creation of 18 new banks in five years.[36]

The establishment of the Bank of the United States precipitated a grave constitutional argument, the Jeffersonians arguing that the Constitution gave the federal government no power to establish a bank. Hamilton, in turn, paved the way for virtually unlimited expansion of federal power by maintaining that the Constitution "implied" a grant of power for carrying out vague national goals. The Hamiltonian interpretation won out officially in the decision of Supreme Court Justice John Marshall in *McCulloch* v. *Maryland* (1819).[37]

Despite the Jeffersonian hostility to commercial and central banks, the Democratic-Republicans, under the control of quasi-Federalist moderates rather than militant Old Republicans, made no move to repeal the charter of the Bank of the United States before its expiration in 1811 and happily multiplied the number of state banks and bank credit in the next two decades.[38] Thus, in 1800 there were 28 state banks; by 1811, the number had escalated to 117, a fourfold increase. In 1804, there were 64 state banks, of which we have data on 13, or 20 percent

[34]Similar movements occurred in wholesale prices in Philadelphia, Charleston, and the Ohio River Valley. U.S. Department of Commerce, *Historical Statistics of the United States, Colonial Times to 1957* (Washington, D.C.: Government Printing Office, 1960), pp. 116, 119-121.

[35]Nettels, *National Economy*, pp. 121-122.

[36]J. Van Fenstermaker, "The Statistics of American Commercial Banking, 1782-1818," *Journal of Economic History* (September, 1965), p. 401.; Van Fenstermaker, *The Development of American Commercial Banking 1782-1837* (Kent, Ohio: Kent State University, 1965), pp. 111-183; William M. Gouge, *A Short History of Paper Money and Banking in the United States* (1833, New York: Augustus M. Kelley, 1968), p. 42.

[37]Marshall, a disciple of Hamilton, repeated some of Hamilton's arguments virtually word for word in the decision. See Gerald T. Dunne, *Monetary Decisions of the Supreme Court* (New Brunswick, N.J.: Rutgers University Press, 1960), p. 30.

[38]On the quasi-Federalists as opposed to the Old Republicans, on banking and on other issues, see Richard E. Ellis, *The Jeffersonian Crisis: Courts and Politics in the Young Republic* (New York: Oxford University Press, 1971), p. 277 and *passim*.

of the banks. These reporting banks had $0.98 million in specie, as against notes and demand deposits outstanding of $2.82 million, a reserve ratio of .35 (or, a notes + deposits pyramiding on top of specie of 2.88:1). By 1811, 26 percent of the 117 banks reported a total of $2.57 million; but the two-and-a-half fold increase in specie was more than matched by an emission of $10.95 million of notes and deposits, a nearly fourfold increase. This constituted a pyramiding of 4.26:1 on top of specie, or a reserve ratio of these banks of .23.[39]

As for the Bank of the United States, which acted in conjunction with the federal government and with the state banks, in January 1811 it had specie assets of $5.01 million, and notes and deposits outstanding of $12.87 million, a pyramid ratio of 2.57:1, or a reserve ratio of .39.[40]

Finally, when the time for rechartering the Bank of the United States came in 1811, the recharter bill was defeated by one vote each in the House and Senate. Recharter was fought for by the Madison administration aided by nearly all the Federalists in Congress, but was narrowly defeated by the bulk of the Democratic-Republicans, including the hard-money Old Republican forces. In view of the widely held misconception among historians that Central Banks serve, and are looked upon, as restraints upon state or private bank inflation, it is instructive to note that the major forces in favor of recharter were merchants, chambers of commerce, and most of the state banks. Merchants found that the Bank had expended credit at cheap rates and had eased the eternal complaint about a "scarcity of money." Even more suggestive is the support of the state banks, which hailed the Bank as "advantageous" and worried about the contraction of credit if the Bank were forced to liquidate. The Bank of New York, which had been founded by Alexander Hamilton, in fact lauded the Bank of the United States because it had been able "in case of any sudden pressure upon the

[39]Van Fenstermaker notes that there has been a tendency of historians to believe that virtually all bank emissions were in the form of notes, but that actually a large portion was in the form of demand deposits. Thus, in 1804, bank liabilities were $1.70 million in notes and $1.12 million in deposits; in 1811 they were $5.68 million and $5.27 respectively. He points out that deposits exceeded notes in the large cities such as Boston and Philadelphia, some times by two or threefold, whereas bank notes were used far more widely in rural areas for hand-to-hand transactions. Van Fenstermaker, "Statistics," pp. 406-411.

[40]Of Bank of the United States liabilities, bank notes totalled $5.04 million and demand deposits $7.83 million. John Jay Knox, *A History of Banking in the United States* (New York: Bradford Rhodes & Co., 1900), p. 39. There are no other reports for the Bank of the United States extant except for 1809. The others were destroyed by fire. John Thom Holdsworth, *The First Bank of the United States* (Washington, D.C.: National Monetary Commission, 1910), pp. 111ff., 138-144.

merchants to step forward to their aid in a degree which the state institutions were unable to do.''[41]

The War of 1812 and Its Aftermath

War has generally had grave and fateful consequences for the American monetary and financial system. We have seen that the Revolutionary War occasioned a mass of depreciated fiat paper, worthless Continentals, a huge public debt, and the beginnings of central banking in the Bank of North America. The Hamiltonian financial system, and even the Constitution itself, was in large part shaped by the Federalist desire to fund the federal and state public debt via federal taxation, and a major reason for the establishment of the First Bank of the United States was to contribute to the funding of the newly assumed federal debt. The Constitutional prohibition against state paper money, and the implicit rebuff to all fiat paper were certainly influenced by the Revolutionary War experience.

The War of 1812–15 had momentous consequences for the monetary system. An enormous expansion in the number of banks and in bank notes and deposits was spurred by the dictates of war finance. New England banks were more conservative than in other regions, and the region was strongly opposed to the war with England, so little public debt was purchased in New England. Yet imported goods, textile manufactures, and munitions had to be purchased in that region by the federal government. The government therefore encouraged the formation of new and recklessly inflationary banks in the Mid-Atlantic, Southern, and Western states, which printed huge quantities of new notes to purchase government bonds. The federal government thereupon used these notes to purchase manufactured goods in New England.

Thus, from 1811 to 1815 the number of banks in the country increased from 117 to 212; in addition, there had sprung up 35 private unincorporated banks, which were illegal in most states but were allowed to function under war conditions. Specie in the 30 reporting banks, 26 percent of the total number of 1811, amounted to $2.57 million in 1811;

---

[41]Holdsworth, *First Bank*, p. 83. Also see ibid., pp. 83-90. Holdsworth, the premier historian of the First Bank of the United States, saw the overwhelming support by the state banks, but still inconsistently clung to the myth that the Bank of the United States functioned as a restraint on their expansion: "The state banks, *though their note issues and discounts had been kept in check by the superior resources and power of the Bank of the United States*, favored the extension of the charter, and memorialized Congress to that effect." (italics added) Ibid., p. 90.

this figure had risen to $5.40 million in the 98 reporting banks in 1815, or 40 percent of the total. Notes and deposits, on the other hand, were $10.95 million in 1811 and had increased to $31.6 million in 1815 among the reporting banks.

If we make the heroic assumption that we can estimate the money supply for the country by multiplying by the proportion of unreported banks and we then add in the BUS totals for 1811, specie in all banks would total $14.9 million in 1811 and $13.5 million in 1815, or a 9.4 percent decrease. On the other hand, total bank notes and deposits aggregated to $42.2 million in 1811, and $79.0 million four years later, so that an increase of 87.2 percent, pyramided on top of a 9.4 percent decline in specie. If we factor in the Bank of the United States, then, the bank pyramid ratio was 3.70:1 and the reserve ratio .27 in 1811; while the pyramid ratio four years later was 5.85:1 and the reserve ratio .17.

But the aggregates scarcely tell the whole story since, as we have seen, the expansion took place solely outside of New England, while New England banks continued on their relatively sound basis and did not inflate their credit. The record expansion of the number of banks was in Pennsylvania, which incorporated no less than 41 new banks in the month of March 1814, contrasting to only four banks which had existed in that state—all in Philadelphia—until that date. It is instructive to compare the pyramid ratios of banks in various reporting states in 1815: only 1.96:1 in Massachusetts, 2.7:1 in New Hampshire, and 2.42:1 in Rhode Island, as contrasted to 19.2:1 in Pennsylvania, 18.46:1 in South Carolina, and 18.73:1 in Virginia.[42]

This monetary situation meant that the United States government was paying for New England manufactured goods with a mass of inflated bank paper outside the region. Soon, as the New England banks called upon the other banks to redeem their notes in specie, the mass of inflating banks faced imminent insolvency.

It was at this point that a fateful decision was made by the U.S. government and concurred in by the governments of the states outside New England. As the banks all faced failure, the governments, in August 1814, permitted all of them to suspend specie payments—that is to stop all redemption of notes and deposits in gold or silver—and

---

[42]Van Fenstermaker, "Statistics," pp. 401–409. For the list of individual incorporated banks, see Van Fenstermaker, "Development," pp. 112–183, with Pennsylvania on pp. 169–173.

yet to continue in operation. In short, in one of the most flagrant violations of property rights in American history, the banks were permitted to waive their contractual obligations to pay in specie while they themselves could expand their loans and operations and force their own debtors to repay their loans as usual.

Indeed, the number of banks, and bank credit, expanded rapidly during 1815 as a result of this governmental carte blanche. It was precisely during 1815 when virtually all the private banks sprang up, the number of banks increasing in one year from 208 to 246. Reporting banks increased their pyramid ratios from 3.17:1 in 1814 to 5.85:1 the following year, a drop of reserve ratios from .32 to .17. Thus, if we measure bank expansion by pyramiding and reserve ratios, we see that a major inflationary impetus during the War of 1812 came during the year 1815 after specie payments had been suspended throughout the country by government action.

Historians dedicated to the notion that central banks restrain state or private bank inflation have placed the blame for the multiplicity of banks and bank credit inflation during the War of 1812 on the absence of a central bank. But as we have seen, both the number of banks and bank credit grew apace during the period of the First BUS, pyramiding on top of the latter's expansion, and would continue to do so under the Second Bank, and, for that matter, the Federal Reserve System in later years. And the federal government, not the state banks themselves, is largely to blame for encouraging new, inflated banks to monetize the war debt. Then, in particular, it allowed them to suspend specie payment in August 1814, and to continue that suspension for two years after the war was over, until February 1817. Thus, for two and a half years banks were permitted to operate and expand while issuing what was tantamount to fiat paper and bank deposits.

Another neglected responsibility of the U.S. government for the wartime inflation was its massive issue of treasury notes to help finance the war effort. While this treasury paper was interest-bearing and was redeemable in specie in one year, the cumulative amount outstanding functioned as money, as they were used in transactions among the public and were also employed as reserves or "high-powered money" by the expanding banks. The fact that the government received the treasury notes for all debts and taxes gave the notes a quasi-legal tender status. Most of the treasury notes were issued in 1814 and 1815, when their outstanding total reached $10.65 million and $15.46 million respectively. Not only did the treasury notes fuel the bank inflation, but their quasi-legal tender status brought Gresham's Law into operation and specie flowed out of the banks and public circulation outside of New England, and into New England and out of the country.[43]

The expansion of bank money and treasury notes during the war drove up prices in the United States. Wholesale price increases from 1811 to 1815 averaged 35 percent, with different cities experiencing a price inflation ranging from 28 percent to 55 percent. Since foreign trade was cut off by the war, prices of imported commodities rose far more, averaging 70 percent.[44] But more important than this inflation, and at least as important as the wreckage of the monetary system during and after the war, was the precedent that the two-and-a-half year-long suspension of specie payment set for the banking system for the future. From then on, every time there was a banking crisis brought on by inflationary expansion and demands for redemption in specie, state and federal governments looked the other way and permitted general suspension of specie payments while bank operations continued to flourish. It thus became clear to the banks that in a general crisis they would not be required to meet the ordinary obligations of contract law or of respect for property rights, so their inflationary expansion was permanently encouraged by this massive failure of government to fulfill its obligation to enforce contracts and defend the rights of property.

Suspensions of specie payments informally or officially permeated the economy outside of New England during the Panic of 1819, occurred everywhere outside of New England in 1837, and in all states south and west of New Jersey in 1839. A general suspension of specie payments occurred throughout the country once again in the panic of 1857.[45]

It is important to realize, then, in evaluating the American banking system before the Civil War, that even in the later years when there was no central bank, the system was not "free" in any proper economic sense. "Free" banking can only refer to a system in which banks are treated as any other business, and that therefore failure to obey contractual obligations—in this case, prompt redemption of notes and

[43]For a perceptive discussion of the nature and consequences of treasury note issue in this period, see Richard H. Timberlake, Jr., *The Origins of Central Banking in the United States* (Cambridge: Harvard University Press, 1978), pp. 13–18. The Gresham Law effect probably accounts for the startling decline of specie held by the reporting banks, from $9.3 million to $5.4 million, from 1814 to 1815. Van Fenstermaker, "Statistics," p. 405.

[44]*Historical Statistics*, pp. 115–124; Murray N. Rothbard, *The Panic of 1819: Reactions and Policies* (New York: Columbia University Press, 1962), p. 4.

[45]On the suspensions of specie payments, and on their importance before the Civil War, see Vera C. Smith, *The Rationale of Central Banking* (London: P.S. King & Son, 1936), pp. 38–46. Also see Dunne, *Monetary Decisions*, p. 26.

deposits in specie—must incur immediate insolvency and liquidation. Burdened by the tradition of allowing general suspensions that arose in the United States in 1814, the pre-Civil War banking system, despite strong elements of competition when not saddled with a central bank, must rather be termed in the phrase of one economist, as "Decentralization without Freedom."[46]

From the 1814–17 experience on, the notes of state banks circulated at varying rates of depreciation, depending on public expectations of how long they would be able to keep redeeming their obligations in specie. These expectations, in turn, were heavily influenced by the amount of notes and deposits issued by the bank as compared with the amount of specie held in its vaults.

In that era of poor communications and high transportation cost, the tendency for a bank note was to depreciate in proportion to its distance from the home office. One effective, if time-consuming, method of enforcing redemption on nominally specie-paying banks was the emergence of a class of professional "money brokers." These brokers would buy up a mass of depreciated notes of nominally specie-paying banks, and then travel to the home office of the bank to demand redemption in specie. Merchants, money brokers, bankers, and the general public were aided in evaluating the various state bank notes by the development of monthly journals known as "bank note detectors." These "detectors" were published by money brokers and periodically evaluated the market rate of various bank notes in relation to specie.[47]

---

[46]Smith, *Rationale*, p. 36. Smith properly defines "free banking" as "a regime where note-issuing banks are allowed to set up in the same way as any other type of business enterprise, so long as they comply with the general company law. The requirement for their establishment is not special conditional authorization from a government authority, but the ability to raise sufficient capital, and public confidence, to gain acceptance for their notes and ensure the profitability of the undertaking. Under such a system all banks would not only be allowed the same rights, but would also be subjected to the same responsibilities as other business enterprises. If they failed to meet their obligations they would be declared bankrupt and put into liquidation, and their assets used to meet the claims of their creditors, in which case the shareholders would lose the whole or part of their capital, and the penalty for failure would be paid, at least for the most part, by those responsible for the policy of the bank. Notes issued under this system would be 'promises to pay,' and such obligations must be met on demand in the generally accepted medium which we will assume to be gold. No bank would have the right to call on the government or on any other institution for special help in time of need. . . . A general abandonment of the gold standard is inconceivable under these conditions, and with a strict interpretation of the bankruptcy laws any bank suspending payments would at once be put into the hands of a receiver." Ibid., pp. 148–149.

[47]See Richard H. Timberlake, Jr., *Money,Banking and Central Banking* (New York: Harper & Row, 1965), p. 94.

40

"Wildcat" banks were so named because in that age of poor transportation, banks hoping to inflate and not worry about redemption attempted to locate in "wildcat" country where money brokers would find it difficult to travel. It shold be noted that if it were not for periodic suspension, there would have been no room for wildcat banks or for varying degrees of lack of confidence in the genuineness of specie redemption at any given time.

It can be imagined that the advent of the money broker was not precisely welcomed in the town of an errant bank, and it was easy for the townspeople to blame the resulting collapse of bank credit on the sinister stranger rather than on the friendly neighborhood banker. During the panic of 1819, when banks collapsed after an inflationary boom lasting until 1817, obstacles and intimidation were often the lot of those who attempted to press the banks to fulfill their contractual obligation to pay in specie.

Thus, Maryland and Pennsylvania, during the panic of 1819, engaged in almost bizarre inconsistency in this area. Maryland, on February 15, 1819, enacted a law "to compel . . . banks to pay specie for their notes, or forfeit their charters." Yet two days after this seemingly tough action, it passed another law relieving banks of any obligation to redeem notes held by money brokers, "the major force ensuring the people of this state from the evil arising from the demands made on the banks of this state for gold and silver by brokers." Pennsylvania followed suit a month later. In this way, these states could claim to maintain the virtue of enforcing contract and property rights while moving to prevent the most effective method of ensuring such enforcement.

During the 1814–1817 general suspension, noteholders who sued for specie payment seldom gained satisfaction in the courts. Thus, Isaac Bronson, a prominent Connecticut banker in a specie-paying region, sued various New York banks for payment of notes in specie. He failed to get satisfaction, and for his pains received only abuse in the New York press as an agent of "misery and ruin."[48]

The banks south of Virginia largely went off specie payment during the panic of 1819, and in Georgia at least general suspension continued almost continuously down to the 1830s. One customer complained

---

[48]Hammond, *Banks and Politics*, p. 179–180. Even before the suspension, in 1808, a Bostonian named Hireh Durkee who attempted to demand specie for $9,000 in notes of the state-owned Vermont State Bank, was met by an indictment for an attempt by this "evil-disposed person" to "realize a filthy gain" at the expense of the resources of the state of Vermont and the ability of "good citizens thereof to obtain money." Ibid., p. 179. Also see Gouge, *Short History*, p. 84.

during 1819 that in order to collect in specie from the largely state-owned Bank of Darien, Georgia, he was forced to swear before a justice of the peace in the bank that each and every note he presented to the bank was his own and that he was not a money broker or an agent for anyone else; he was forced to swear to the oath in the presence of at least five bank directors and the bank's cashier; and he was forced to pay a fee of $1.36 on each note in order to acquire specie on demand. Two years later, when a noteholder demanded $30,000 in specie at the Planters' Bank of Georgia, he was told he would be paid in pennies only, while another customer was forced to accept pennies handed out to him at the rate of $60 a day.[49]

During the panic, North Carolina and Maryland in particular moved against the money brokers in a vain attempt to prop up the depreciated notes of their states' banks. In North Carolina, banks were not penalized by the legislature for suspending specie payments to "brokers," while maintaining them to others. Backed by government, the three leading banks of the state met and agreed, in June 1819, not to pay specie to brokers or their agents. Their notes immediately fell to a 15 percent discount outside the state. However, the banks continued to require—ignoring the inconsistency—that their own debtors pay them at par in specie. Maryland, during the same year, moved to require a license of $500 per year for money brokers, in addition to an enormous $20,000 bond to establish the business.

Maryland tried to bolster the defense of banks and the attack on brokers by passing a compulsory par law in 1819, prohibiting the exchange of specie for Maryland bank notes at less than par. The law was readily evaded, however, the penalty merely adding to the discount as compensation for the added risk. Specie furthermore was driven out of the state by the operation of Gresham's Law.[50]

In Kentucky, Tennessee, and Missouri, stay laws were passed requiring creditors to accept depreciated and inconvertible bank paper in payment of debts, else suffer a stay of execution of the debt. In this way, quasi-legal tender status was conferred on the paper.[51] Many states permitted banks to suspend specie payment, and four Western

---

[49]Gouge, *Short History*, pp. 141–142. Secretary of the Treasury William H. Crawford, a Georgia politician, tried in vain to save the Bank of Darien from failure by depositing Treasury funds there during the panic. Rothbard, *The Panic of 1819*, p. 62.

[50]Rothbard, *Panic of 1819,* pp. 64–68. Other compulsory par laws were passed by Ohio and Delaware.

[51]The most extreme proposal was that of Tennessee politician Felix Grundy's scheme, never adopted, to compel creditors to accept bank notes of the state bank or forfeit the

states—Tennessee, Kentucky, Missouri, and Illinois—established state-owned banks to try to overcome the depression by issuing large issues of inconvertible paper money. In all states trying to prop up inconvertible bank paper, a quasi-legal status was also conferred on the paper by agreeing to receive the notes in taxes or debts due to the state. The result of all the inconvertible paper schemes was rapid and massive depreciation, disappearance of specie, succeeded by speedy liquidation of the new state-owned banks.[52]

An amusing footnote on the problem of banks being protected against their contractual obligations to pay in specie occurred in the course of correspondence between one of the earliest economists in America, the young Philadelphia State Senator Condy Raguet, and the eminent English economist David Ricardo. Ricardo had evidently been bewildered by Raguet's statement that banks technically required to pay in specie were often not called upon to do so. On April 18, 1821, Raguet replied, explaining the power of banks in the United States:

> You state in your letter that you find it difficult to comprehend, why persons who had a right to demand coin from the Banks in payment of their notes, so long forebore to exercise it. This no doubt appears paradoxical to one who resides in a country where an act of parliament was necessary to protect a bank, but the difficulty is easily solved. The whole of our population are either stockholders of banks or in debt to them. It is not the *interest* of the first to press the banks and the rest are *afraid*. This is the whole secret. An independent man who was neither a stockholder or debtor, who would have ventured to compel the banks to do justice, would have been persecuted as an enemy of society. . . .[53]

The Second Bank of the United States, 1816-1833

The United States emerged from the War of 1812 in a chaotic monetary state, with banks multiplying and inflating ad lib, checked only by

---

debt: that would have conferred full legal tender status on the bank. Rothbard, *Panic of 1819*, p. 91; Joseph H. Parks, "Felix Grundy and the Depression of 1819 in Tennessee," *Publications of the East Tennessee Historical Society* X (1938): 22.

[52]Only New England, New York, New Jersey, Virginia, Mississippi, and Louisiana were comparatively untouched by the inconvertible paper contagion, either in the form of suspended specie banks continuing in operation or new state-owned banks emitting more paper. For an analysis of the events and controversies in each state, see Rothbard, *Panic of 1819*, pp. 57–111.

[53]Rague to Ricardo, April 18, 1821, in David Ricardo, *Minor Papers on the Currency Question, 1809–23*, J. Hollander, ed. (Baltimore: Johns Hopkins Press, 1932), pp. 199–201; Rothbard, *Panic of 1819*, pp. 10–11. Also see Hammond, *Banks and Politics*, p. 242.

the varying rates of depreciation of their notes. With banks freed from redeeming their obligations in specie, the number of incorporated banks increased during 1816, from 212 to 232.[54] Clearly, the nation could not continue indefinitely with the issue of fiat money in the hands of discordant sets of individual banks. It was apparent that there were two ways out of the problem: one was the hard-money path, advocated by the Old Republicans and, for their own purposes, the Federalists. The federal and state governments would have sternly compelled the rollicking banks to redeem promptly in specie, and, when most of the banks outside of New England could not, to force them to liquidate. In that way, the mass of depreciated and inflated notes and deposits would have been swiftly liquidated, and specie would have poured back out of hoards and into the country to supply a circulating medium. The inflationary experience would have been over.

Instead, the Democratic-Republican establishment in 1816 turned to the old Federalist path: a new central bank, a Second Bank of the United States. Modelled closely after the First Bank, the Second Bank, a private corporation with one-fifth of the shares owned by the federal government, was to create a national paper currency, purchase a large chunk of the public debt, and receive deposits of Treasury funds. The BUS notes and deposits were to be redeemable in specie, and they were given quasi-legal tender status by the federal government's receiving them in payment of taxes.

That the purpose of establishing the BUS was to support the state banks in their inflationary course rather than crack down on them is seen by the shameful deal that the BUS made with the state banks as soon as it opened its doors in January 1817. At the same time it was establishing the BUS in April 1816, Congress passed the resolution of Daniel Webster, at that time a Federalist champion of hard money, requiring that after February 20, 1817, the United States should accept in payments for debts or taxes only specie, Treasury notes, BUS notes, or state bank notes redeemable in specie on demand. In short, no irredeemable state bank notes would be accepted after that date. Instead of using the opportunity to compel the banks to redeem, however, the BUS, in a meeting with representatives from the leading urban banks, excluding Boston, agreed to issue $6 million worth of credit in New York, Philadelphia, Baltimore, and Virginia before insisting on specie

---

[54]New note issue series by banks reached a heavy peak in 1815 and 1816 in New York and Pennsylvania. D.C. Wismar, *Pennsylvania Descriptive List of Obsolete State Bank Notes, 1782–1866* (Frederick, Md.: J.W. Stovell Printing Co., 1933); and idem, *New York Descriptive List of Obsolete Paper Money* (Frederick, Md.: J.W. Stovell Printing Co., 1931).

payments from debts due to it from the state banks. In return for that agreed-upon massive inflation, the state banks graciously consented to resume specie payments.[55] Moreover, the BUS and the state banks agreed to mutually support each other in any emergency, which of course meant in practice that the far stronger BUS was committed to the propping up of the weaker state banks.

The BUS was pushed through Congress by the Madison administration and particularly by Secretary of the Treasury Alexander J. Dallas, whose appointment was lobbied for, for that purpose. Dallas, a wealthy Philadelphia lawyer, was a close friend, counsel, and financial associate of Philadelphia merchant and banker Stephen Girard, reputedly one of the two wealthiest men in the country. Toward the end of its term, Girard was the largest stockholder of the first BUS, and during the War of 1812 Girard became a very heavy investor in the war debt of the federal government. Both as a prospective large stockholder and as a way to unload his public debt, Girard began to agitate for a new BUS. Dallas's appointment as Secretary of Treasury in 1814 was successfully engineered by Dallas and his close friend, wealthy New York merchant and fur trader John Jacob Astor, also a heavy investor in the war debt. When the BUS was established, Stephen Girard purchased the $3 million of the $28 million that remained unsubscribed, and he and Dallas managed to secure for the post of president of the new bank their good friend William Jones, former Philadelphia merchant.[56]

Much of the opposition to the founding of the BUS seems keenly prophetic. Thus, Senator William H. Wells, Federalist from Delaware, in arguing against the Bank bill, said that it was "ostensibly for the purpose of correcting the diseased state of our paper currency by restraining and curtailing the overissue of bank paper, and yet it came prepared to inflict upon us the same evil, being itself nothing more than simply a paper-making machine."[57] In fact, the result of the deal

[55]On the establishment of the BUS and on the deal with the state banks, see Ralph C.H. Catterall, *The Second Bank of the United States* (Chicago: University of Chicago Press, 1902), pp. 9–26, 479–490. Also see Hammond, *Banks and Politics*, pp. 230–248; David R. Dewey, *The Second United States Bank* (Washington, D.C.: National Monetary Commission, 1910), pp. 148–176.

[56]On the Girard-Dallas connection, see Hammond, *Banks and Politics*, pp. 231–246, 252; Philip H. Burch, Jr., *Elites in American History, Vol. I The Federalist Years to the Civil War* (New York: Holmes & Meier, 1981), pp. 88, 97, 116–117, 119–121; Kenneth L. Brown, "Stephen Girard, Promoter of the Second Bank of the United States." *Journal of Economic History*, November 1942, pp. 125–132.

[57]*Annals of Congress*, 14 Cong., 1 sess., April 1, 1816, pp. 267–270. Also see ibid., pp. 1066, 1091, 1110ff. Cited in Murray N. Rothbard, *The Case for a 100 Percent Gold Dollar*

with the state banks was that their resumption of specie payments after 1817 was more nominal than real, thereby setting the stage for the widespread suspensions of the 1819-21 depression. As Bray Hammond writes:

> . . . specie payments were resumed, with substantial shortcomings. Apparently the situation was better than it had been, and a pretense was maintained of its being better than it was. But redemption was not certain and universal; there was still a premium on specie and still a discount on bank notes, with considerable variation in both from place to place. Three years later, February 1820, Secretary [of the Treasury] Crawford reported to Congress that during the greater part of the time that had elapsed since the resumption of specie payments, the convertibility of bank notes into specie had been nominal rather than real in the largest portion of the Union.[58]

One problem is that the BUS lacked the courage to insist on payment of its notes from the state banks. As a result, state banks had large balances piled up against them at the BUS, totalling over $2.4 million during 1817 and 1818, remaining on the books as virtual interest-free loans. As Catterall points out, "so many influential people were interested in the [state banks] as stockholders that it was not advisable to give offense by demanding payment in specie, and borrowers were anxious to keep the banks in the humor to lend." When the BUS did try to collect on state bank notes in specie, President Jones reported, "the banks, our debtors, plead inability, require unreasonable indulgence, or treat our reiterated claims and expostulations with settled indifference."[59]

From its inception, the Second BUS launched a spectacular inflation of money and credit. Lax about insisting on the required payment of its capital in specie, the Bank failed to raise the $7 million legally supposed to have been subscribed in specie; instead, during 1817 and 1818, its specie held never rose above $2.5 million. At the peak of its initial expansion, in July 1818, BUS specie totalled $2.36 million, and its aggregate notes and deposits totalled $21.8 million. Thus, in a scant

(Washington, D.C.: Libertarian Review Press, 1974), p. 18n. Also see Gouge, *Short History*, pp. 79–83.

[58]Hammond, *Banks and Politics*, p. 248. Also see Condy Raguet, *A Treatise on Currency and Banking* (2nd ed., 1840, New York: Augustus M. Kelley, 1967), pp. 302–303; Catterall, *Second Bank*, pp. 37–39; Walter Buckingham Smith, *Economic Aspects of the Second Bank of the United States* (Cambridge: Harvard University Press, 1953), p. 104.

[59]Catterall, *Second Bank*, p. 36.

year-and-a-half of operation, the BUS had added a net of $19.2 million to the nation's money supply, for a pyramid ratio of 9.24, or a reserve ratio of .11.

Outright fraud abounded at the BUS, especially at the Philadelphia and Baltimore branches, particularly the latter. It is no accident that three-fifths of all of the BUS loans were made at these two branches.[60] Also, the BUS attempt to provide a uniform currency throughout the nation floundered on the fact that the western and southern branches could inflate credit and bank notes and that the inflated notes would wend their way to the more conservative branches in New York and Boston, which would be obligated to redeem the inflated notes at par. In this way, the conservative branches were stripped of specie while the western branches could continue to inflate unchecked.[61]

The expansionary operations of the BUS, coupled with its laxity toward insisting on specie payment by the state banks, impelled a further inflationary expansion of state banks on top of the spectacular enlargement of the central bank. Thus, the number of incorporated state banks rose from 232 in 1816 to 338 in 1818. Kentucky alone chartered 40 new banks in the 1817-18 legislative session. The estimated total money supply in the nation rose from $67.3 million in 1816 to $94.7 million in 1818, a rise of 40.7% in two years. Most of this increase was supplied by the BUS.[62]

The huge expansion of money and credit impelled a full-scale inflationary boom throughout the country. Import prices had fallen in 1815, with the renewal of foreign trade after the war, but domestic prices were another story. Thus, the index of export staples in Charleston rose from 102 in 1815 to 160 in 1818; the prices of Louisiana staples at

[60]On the expansion and fraud at the BUS, see Catterall, *Second Bank*, pp. 28–50, 503. The main culprits were James A. Buchanan, president of the Baltimore mercantile firm of Smith & Buchanan, and the Baltimore BUS cashier James W. McCulloch, who was simply an impoverished clerk at the mercantile house. Smith, an ex-Federalist, was a senator from Maryland and a powerful member of the national Democrat-Republican establishment.

[61]As a result of the contractionary influence on the Boston branch of the BUS, the notes of the Massachusetts banks actually declined in this period, from $1 million in June 1815 to $850,000 in June 1818. See Rothbard, *Panic of 1819*, p. 8.

[62]Total notes and deposits of 39 percent of the nation's reporting state banks was $26.3 million in 1816, while 38 percent of the banks had total notes and deposits of $27.7 million two years later. Converting this pro rata to 100 percent of the banks gives an estimated $67.3 million in 1816, and $72.9 million in 1818. Add to the latter figure $21.8 million for BUS notes and deposits, and this yields $94.7 million in 1818, or a 40.7 percent increase. Adapted from tables in Van Fenstermaker, "Statistics," pp. 401, 405, 406.

New Orleans rose from 178 to 224 in the same period. Other parts of the economy boomed; exports rose from $81 million in 1815 to a peak of $116 million in 1818. Prices rose greatly in real estate, land, farm improvement projects, and slaves, much of it fueled by the use of bank credit for speculation in urban and rural real estate. There was a boom in turnpike construction, furthered by vast federal expenditures on turnpikes. Freight rates rose on steamboats, and shipbuilding shared in the general prosperity. Also, general boom conditions expanded stock trading so rapidly that traders, who had been buying and selling stocks on the curbs on Wall Street for nearly a century, found it necessary to open the first indoor stock exchange in the country, the New York Stock Exchange, in March 1817. Also, investment banking began in the United States during this boom period.[63]

Starting in July 1818, the government and the BUS began to see what dire straits they were in; the enormous inflation of money and credit, aggravated by the massive fraud, had put the BUS in real danger of going under and illegally failing to sustain specie payments. Over the next year, the BUS began a series of heroic contractions, forced curtailment of loans, contractions of credit in the south and west, refusal to provide uniform national currency by redeeming its shaky branch notes at par, and seriously enforcing the requirement that its debtor banks redeem in specie. In addition, it purchased millions of dollars of specie from abroad. These heroic actions, along with the ouster of President William Jones, managed to save the BUS, but the massive contraction of money and credit swiftly brought the United States its first widespread economic and financial depression. The first nationwide "boom-bust" cycle had arrived in the United States, impelled by rapid and massive inflation, quickly succeeded by contraction of money and credit. Banks failed, and private banks curtailed their credits and liabilities and suspended specie payments in most parts of the country.

Contraction of money and credit by the BUS was almost unbelievable, total notes and deposits falling from $21.9 million in June 1818 to $11.5 million only a year later. The money supply contributed by the BUS was thereby contracted by no less than 47.2 percent in one year. The number of incorporated banks at first remained the same, and then fell rapidly from 1819 to 1822, falling from 341 in mid-1819 to 267 three years later. Total notes and deposits of state banks fell from an esti-

[63]Rothbard, *Panic of 1819*, pp. 6–10; *Historical Statistics*, pp. 120, 122, 563. Also see George Rogers Taylor, *The Transportation Revolution, 1815–1860* (New York: Rinehart & Co., 1951), pp. 334–336.

mated $72.0 million in mid-1818 to $62.7 million a year later, a drop of 14.0 percent in one year. If we add in the fact that the U.S. Treasury contracted total treasury notes from $8.81 million to zero during this period, we get the following estimated total money supply: in 1818, $103.5 million; in 1819, $74.2 million, a contraction in one year of 28.3 percent.[64]

The result of the contraction was a massive rash of defaults, bankruptcies of business and manufacturers, and liquidation of unsound investments during the boom. There was a vast drop in real estate values and rents and in the prices of freight rates and of slaves. Public land sales dropped greatly as a result of the contraction, declining from $13.6 million in 1818 to $1.7 million to 1820.[65] Prices in general plummeted: The index of export staples fell from 158 in November 1818 to 77 in June 1819, an annualized drop of 87.9 percent during those seven months. South Carolina export staples dropped from 160 to 96 from 1818 to 1819, and commodity prices in New Orleans dropped from 200 in 1818 to 119 two years later.

Falling money incomes led to a precipitous drop in imports, which fell from $122 million in 1818 to $87 million the year later. Imports from Great Britain fell from $43 million in 1818 to $14 million in 1820, and cotton and woolen imports from Britain fell from over $14 million each in the former year to about $5 million in the latter.

The great fall in prices aggravated the burden of money debts, reinforced by the contraction of credit. Bankruptcies abounded, and one observer estimated that $100 million of mercantile debts to Europe were liquidated by bankruptcy during the crisis. Western areas, shorn of money by the collapse of the previously swollen paper and debt, often returned to barter conditions, and grain and whiskey were used as media of exchange.[66]

In the dramatic summing up of the hard-money economist and historian William Gouge, by its precipitous and dramatic contraction "the Bank was saved, and the people were ruined."[67]

---

[64]These estimates are adapted from the tables in Van Fenstermaker, "Statistics," pp. 401–406; Van Fenstermaker, *Development*, pp. 66–68. The data for 38 percent of incorporated banks in 1818, and for 54 percent in 1819, are converted pro rata to 100 percent figures. BUS figures are in Catterall, *Second Bank*, p. 502. On the contraction by the BUS see ibid., pp. 51–72.

[65]On Treasury note contraction in this period, see Timberlake, *Origins*, pp. 21–26.

[66]See Rothbard, *Panic of 1819*, pp. 11–16.

[67]Gouge, *Short History*, p. 110.

The Jacksonian Movement and the Bank War

Out of the bitter experiences of the Panic of 1819 emerged the beginnings of the Jacksonian movement, dedicated to hard money, the eradication of fractional-reserve banking in general, and of the Bank of the United States in particular. Andrew Jackson himself, Senator Thomas Hart ("Old Bullion") Benton of Missouri, future President James K. Polk of Tennessee, and Jacksonian economists Amos Kendall of Kentucky and Condy Raguet of Philadelphia, were all converted to hard money and 100 percent reserve banking by the experience of the Panic of 1819.[68] The Jacksonians adopted, or in some cases pioneered in, the Currency School analysis, which pinned the blame for boom-bust cycles on inflationary expansions followed by contractions of bank credit. Far from being the ignorant bumpkins that most historians have depicted, the Jacksonians were steeped in the knowledge of sound economics, particularly of the Ricardian Currency School.

Indeed, no movement in American politics has been as flagrantly misunderstood by historians as the Jacksonians. They were emphatically *not*, as historians until recently have depicted, either "ignorant anti-capitalist agrarians," or "representatives of the rising entrepreneurial class," or "tools of the inflationary state banks," or embodiments of an early proletarian anti-capitalist movement or a non-ideological power group or "electoral machine." The Jacksonians were libertarians, plain and simple. Their program and ideology were libertarian; they strongly favored free enterprise and free markets, but they just as strongly opposed special subsidies and monopoly privileges conveyed by government to business or to any other group. They favored absolutely minimal government, certainly at the federal level, but also at the state level. They believed that government should be confined to upholding the rights of private property. In the monetary sphere, this meant the separation of government from the banking system and a shift from inflationary paper money and fractional-reserve banking to pure specie and banks confined to 100 percent reserves.

In order to put this program into effect, however, the Jacksonians faced the grueling task of creating a new party out of what had become a one-party system after the War of 1812, in which the Democrat-Republicans had ended up adopting the Federalist program, including the reestablishing of the Bank of the United States. The new party, the Democratic Party, was largely forged in the mid-1820s by New York political leader, Martin Van Buren, newly converted by the aging Thomas

---

[68]Rothbard, *Panic of 1819*, p. 188.

Jefferson to the laissez-faire cause. Van Buren cemented an alliance with Thomas Hart Benton of Missouri and the Old Republicans of Virginia, but he needed a charismatic leader to take the Presidency away from Adams and what was becoming known as the National Republican Party. He found that leader in Andrew Jackson, who was elected President under the new Democratic banner in 1828.

The Jacksonians eventually managed to put into effect various parts of their free-market and minimal-government economic program, including a drastic lowering of tariffs, and for the first and probably the last time in American history, paying off the federal debt. But their major concentration was on the issue of money and banking. Here they had a coherent program, which they proceeded to install in rapidly succeeding stages.

The first important step was to abolish central banking, in the Jacksonian view the major inflationary culprit. The object was not to eliminate the BUS in order to free the state banks for inflationary expansion, but, on the contrary, to eliminate the major source of inflation before proceeding, on the state level, to get rid of fractional reserve banking. The BUS charter was up for renewal in 1836, but Jackson denounced the Bank in his first annual message, in 1829. The imperious Nicholas Biddle,[69] head of the BUS, decided to precipitate a showdown with Jackson before his reelection effort, so Biddle filed for renewal early, in 1831. The host of National Republicans and non-Jacksonian Democrats proceeded to pass the recharter bill, but Jackson, in a dramatic message, vetoed the bill, and Congress failed to pass it over his veto.

Triumphantly reelected on the Bank issue in 1832, President Jackson lost no time in disestablishing the BUS as a central bank. The critical action came in 1833, when Jackson removed the public Treasury deposits from the BUS and placed them in a number of state banks (soon labelled as "pet banks") throughout the country. The original number of pet banks was seven, but the Jacksonians were not interested in creating a privileged bank oligarchy to replace the previous monopoly; so the number of pet banks had increased to 91 by the end of 1836.[70] In that year, Biddle managed to secure a Pennsylvania charter for his bank, and the new United States Bank of Pennsylvania functioned as a much reduced but still influential state bank for a few years thereafter.

[69]Biddle continued the chain of control over both BUSs by the Philadelphia financial elite, from Robert Morris and William Bingham, to Stephen Girard and William Jones. See Burch, *Elites*, p. 147. Also see Thomas P. Govan, *Nicholas Biddle: Nationalist and Public Banker, 1786–1844* (Chicago: University of Chicago Press, 1959), pp. 45, 74–75, 79.

[70]Hammond, *Banks and Politics*, p. 420.

Orthodox historians have long maintained that by his reckless act of destroying the BUS and shifting government funds to the numerous pet banks, Andrew Jackson freed the state banks from the restraints imposed on them by a central bank. Thus, the banks were supposedly allowed to pyramid notes and deposits rashly on top of existing specie and precipitate a wild inflation that was later succeeded by two bank panics and a disastrous deflation.

Recent historians, however, have totally reversed this conventional picture.[71] In the first place, the record of bank inflation under the regime of the BUS was scarcely ideal. From the depth of the post-1819 depression in January 1820 to January 1823, under the regime of the conservative Langdon Cheves, the BUS increased its notes and deposits at an annual rate of 5.9 percent. The nation's total money supply remained about the same in that period. Under the far more inflationist regime of Nicholas Biddle, however, BUS notes and deposits rose, after January 1823, from $12 million to $42.1 million, an annual rate increase of 27.9 percent. As a consequence of this base of the banking pyramid inflating so sharply, the total money supply during this period vaulted from $81 million to $155 million, an annual increase of 10.2 percent. It is clear that the driving force for monetary expansion was the BUS, which acted as an inflationary rather than restraining force upon the state banks. Looking at the figures another way, the 1823 data represented a pyramid ratio of money liabilities to specie of 3.86:1 on the part of the BUS and 4:1 of the banking system as a whole, or respective reserve ratios of .26 and .25. By 1832, in contrast, the BUS reserve ratio had fallen to .17 and the country as a whole to .15. Both sets of institutions had inflated almost precisely proportionately on top of specie.[72]

The fact that wholesale prices remained about the same over this period is no indication that the monetary inflation was not improper and dangerous. As "Austrian" business cycle theory has pointed out, any bank credit inflation sets up conditions for boom-and-bust; there is no need for prices actually to rise. The reason that prices did not rise was that the increased production of goods and services sufficed to offset the monetary expansion during this period. But similar conditions of the 1920s precipitated the great crash of 1929, an event which

[71]For an excellent bibliographical essay and critique of historical interpretations of Jacksonism and the Bank War, see Jeffrey Rogers Hummel, "The Jacksonians, Banking, and Economic Theory: A Reinterpretation," *Journal of Libertarian Studies* 2 (Summer 1978): 151–165.

[72]For the BUS data, see Catterall, *Second Bank*, p. 503; for total money supply, see Peter Temin, *The Jacksonian Economy* (New York: W.W. Norton, 1969), p. 71.

shocked most economists, who had adopted the proto-monetarist position of Irving Fisher and other economists of the day that a stable
wholesale price level cannot, by definition, be inflationary. In reality,
the unhampered free-market economy will usually increase the supply
of goods and services and thereby bring about a gently falling price
level, as happened in most of the 19th century except during wartime.

What, then, of the consequences of Jackson's removal of the deposits? What of the fact that wholesale prices rose from 84 in April 1834,
to 131 in February 1837, a remarkable increase of 52 percent in a little
less than three years? Wasn't that boom due to the abolition of central
banking?

An excellent reversal of the orthodox explanation of the boom of the
1830s, and indeed of the ensuing panic, has been provided by Professor
Temin.[73] First, he points out that the price inflation really began earlier,
when wholesale prices reached a trough of 82 in July 1830 and then
rose by 20.7 percent in three years to reach 99 in the fall of 1833. The
reason for the price rise is simple: The total money supply had risen
from $109 million in 1830 to $159 million in 1833, an increase of 45.9
percent or an annual rise of 15.3 percent. Breaking the figures down
further, the total money supply had risen from $109 million in 1830 to
$155 million a year and a half later, a spectacular expansion of 35
percent. Unquestionably, this monetary expansion was spurred by the
still flourishing BUS, which increased its notes and deposits from January 1830 to January 1832, from a total of $29 million to $42.1 million,
a rise of 45.2 percent.

Thus, the price and money inflation in the first few years of the 1830s
were again sparked by the expansion of the still dominant central bank.
But what of the notable inflation after 1833? There is no doubt that the
cause of the price inflation was the remarkable monetary inflation
during the same period. For the total money supply rose from $150
million at the beginning of 1833 to $267 million at the beginning of
1837, an astonishing rise of 84 percent, or 21 percent per annum.

But as Temin points out, this monetary inflation was not caused by
the liberated state banks expanding to a fare-thee-well. If it were true
that the state banks used their freedom and their new federal government deposits to pyramid wildly on the top of specie, then their pyramid ratio would have risen a great deal, or, conversely, their reserve

[73]Temin, *Jacksonian Economy*, passim. Also see Hugh Rockoff, "Money, Prices, and Banks
in the Jacksonian Era," in R. Fogel and S. Engerman, eds., *The Reinterpretation of American
Economic History* (New York: Harper & Row, 1971), pp. 448–458.

ratio of specie to notes and deposits would have fallen sharply. Yet the banks' reserve ratio was .16 at the beginning of 1837. During the intervening years, the reserve ratio was never below this figure. But this means that the state banks did no more pyramiding after the demise of the BUS as a central bank than they had done before.[74]

Conventional historians, believing that the BUS *must* have restrained the expansion of state banks, naturally assumed that they were hostile to the central bank. But now Jean Wilburn has discovered that the state banks overwhelmingly supported the BUS:

> We have found that Nicholas Biddle was correct when he said, "state banks in the main are friendly." Specifically, only in Georgia, Connecticut, and New York was there positive evidence of hostility. A majority of state banks in some states of the South, such as North Carolina and Alabama, gave strong support to the Bank as did both the Southwest states of Louisiana and Mississippi. Since Virginia gave some support, we can claim that state banks in the South and Southwest for the most part supported the Bank. New England, contrary to expectations, showed the banks of Vermont and New Hampshire behind the Bank, but support of Massachusetts was both qualitatively and quantitatively weak. The banks of the Middle states all supported the Second Bank except for those of New York.[75]

What, then, was the cause of the enormous monetary expansion of the 1830s? It was a tremendous and unusual expansion of the stock of specie in the nation's banks. The supply of specie in the country had remained virtually constant at about $32 million, from the beginning of 1823 until the beginning of 1833. But the proportion of specie to bank notes, held by the public as money, dropped during this period from 23 percent to 5 percent, so that more specie flowed from the public into the banks to fuel the relatively moderate monetary expansion of the 1820s. But starting at the beginning of 1833, the total specie in the country rose swiftly from $31 million to $73 million at the beginning of 1837, for a rise of 141.9 percent or 35.5 percent per annum. Hence, even though increasing distrust of banks led the public to withdraw some specie from them, so that the public now held 13 percent of its money in specie instead of 5 percent, the banks were able to increase their notes and deposits at precisely the same rate as the expansion of specie flowing into their coffers.

[74]Temin, *Jacksonian Economy*, pp. 68–74.

[75]Jean Alexander Wilburn, *Biddle's Bank: The Crucial Years* (New York: Columbia University Press, 1970), pp. 118–119, Quoted in Hummel, "Jacksonians," p. 155.

Thus, the Jackson administration is absolved from blame for the 1833–37 inflation. In a sense, the state banks are as well; certainly, they scarcely acted as if being "freed" by the demise of the BUS. Instead, they simply increased their money issues proportionately with the huge increase of specie. Of course, the basic fractional reserve banking system is scarcely absolved from responsibility, since otherwise the monetary expansion in absolute terms would not have been as great.[76]

The enormous increase in specie was the result of two factors: first and foremost, a large influx of silver coin from Mexico, and secondly, the sharp cut in the usual export of silver to the Orient. The latter was due to the substantial increases in China's purchase of opium instead of silver from abroad. The influx of silver was the result of paper money inflation by the Mexican government, which drove Mexican silver coins into the United States, where they circulated as legal tender. The influx of Mexican coin has been attributed to a possible increase in the productivity of the Mexican mines, but this makes little sense, since the inflow stopped permanently as soon as 1837. The actual cause was an inflation of the Mexican currency by the Santa Anna regime, which financed its deficits during this period by minting highly debased copper coins. Since the debased copper grossly overvalued copper and undervalued gold and silver, both of the later metals proceeded to flow rapidly out of Mexico until they virtually disappeared. Silver, of course, and not gold, was flowing into the United States during this period. Indeed, the Mexican government was forced to rescind its actions in 1837 by shifting the copper coinage to its proper ratio. The influx of Mexican silver into the U.S. promptly ceased.[77]

A bank credit inflation of the magnitude of the 1830s is bound to run into shoals that cause the banks to stop the expansion and begin to contract. As the banks expand, and prices rise, specie is bound to flow out of the country and into the hands of the domestic public, and the pressure on the banks to redeem in specie will intensify, forcing cessation of the boom and even monetary contraction. In a sense, the immediate precipitating cause is of minor importance. Even so, the Jackson administration has been unfairly blamed for precipitating the Panic of 1837 by issuing the Specie Circular in 1836.

[76]Moreover, if the Jacksonians had been able to move more rapidly in returning the banking system to a 100 percent specie basis, they could have used the increase in specie to ease the monetary contraction required by a return to a pure specie money.

[77]Mexico was pinpointed as the source of the inflow of specie by Temin, *Jacksonian Economy*, p. 80, while the disclosure of the cause in Mexican copper inflation came in Rockoff, "Money, Prices, and Banks," p. 454.

In 1836 the Jackson administration decided to stop the enormous speculation in Western public lands that had been fueled during the past two years by the inflation of bank credit. Hence, Jackson decreed that public land payments would have to be made in specie. This had the healthy effect of stopping public land speculation, but recent studies have shown that the Specie Circular had very little impact in putting pressure on the banks to pay specie.[78] From the point of view of the Jacksonian program, however, it was as important as moving toward putting the U.S. government finances on a purely specie basis.

Another measure advancing the Jacksonian program was also taken in 1836. Jackson, embarrassed at the government having amassed a huge budget surplus during his eight years in office, ordered the Treasury to distribute the surplus proportionately to the states. The distribution was made in notes presumably payable in specie. But again, Temin has shown that the distribution had little impact on movements of specie between banks and therefore in exerting contractionist pressure upon them.[79]

What, then, was the precipitating factor in triggering the Panic of 1837? Temin plausibly argues that the Bank of England, worried about inflation in Britain, and the consequent outflow of gold, tightened the money supply and raised interest rates in the latter half of 1836. As a result, credit contraction severely restricted the American cotton export trade in London, exports declined, cotton prices fell, capital flowed into England, and contractionist pressure was put upon American trade and the American banks. Banks throughout the United States—including the BUS—promptly suspended specie payments in May 1837, their notes depreciated at varying rates, and interregional trade within the country was crippled.

While banks were able to evade specie payments and continue operations, they were still obliged to contract credit in order to go back on specie eventually, since they could not hope to be creating fiat money

---

[78]Public land sales by the federal government, which had been going steadily at approximately $4–6 million per year, suddenly spurted upward in 1835 and 1836, to $16.2 million and $24.9 million respectively. The latter was the largest sale of public lands in American history, and the 1835 figure was the second largest. Temin, *Jacksonian Economy*, p. 124. The first demonstration of the negligible impact of the Specie Circular on the position of the banks was Richard H. Timberlake, Jr., "The Specie Circular and Distribution of the Surplus," *Journal of Political Economy* 68 (April 1960): 109–117, reprinted in Timberlake, *Origins*, pp. 50–62. Timberlake defended his thesis in idem, "The Specie Circular and the Sale of Public Lands: A Comment," *Journal of Economic History* 25 (September 1965): 414–416.

[79]Temin, *Jacksonian Economy*, pp. 128–136.

indefinitely and be allowed to remain in business. Finally, the New York banks were compelled by law to resume paying their contractual obligations, and the other banks followed in the fall of 1838. During the year 1837, the money supply fell from $276 million to $232 million, a large drop of 15.6 percent in one year. Total specie in the country continued to increase in 1837, up to $88 million, but increased public distrust of the banks (reflected in an increased proportion of money held as specie from 13 to 23 percent) put enough pressure upon the banks to force the contraction. The banks' reserve ratio rose from .16 to .20. In response to the monetary contraction, wholesale prices fell precipitately, by over 30 percent in seven months, declining from 131 in February 1837 to 98 in September of that year.

In 1838 the economy revived. Britain resumed easy credit that year, cotton prices rose, and a short-lived boomlet began. Public confidence in the banks unwisely returned as they resumed specie payment, and as a result, the money supply rose slightly during the year, and prices rose by 25 percent, increasing from 98 in September 1837 to 125 in February 1839.

Leading the boom of 1838 were state governments, who, finding themselves with the unexpected windfall of a distributed surplus from the federal government, proceeded to spend the money wildly and borrow even more extravagantly on public works and other uneconomic forms of "investment." But the state governments engaged in rashly optimistic plans that their public works would be financed heavily from Britain and other countries, and the cotton boom on which these hopes depended again collapsed in 1839. The states had to abandon their projects en masse. Cotton prices declined, and severe contractionist pressure was put on trade. Furthermore, the Philadelphia-based BUS had heavily invested in cotton speculation, and the falling price of cotton forced the BUS, once again, to suspend payments in October 1839. This touched off a wave of general bank suspensions in the South and West, but this time the banks of New York and New England continued to redeem their obligations in specie. Finally, the Bank of the United States, having for the last time played a leading role in generating a recession and monetary crisis, was forced to close its doors two years later.

With the crisis of 1839 there ensued four years of massive monetary and price deflation. Unsound banks were finally eliminated; unsound investments generated in the boom were liquidated. The number of banks during these four years fell by 23 percent. The money supply fell from $240 million at the beginning of 1839 to $158 million in 1843, a seemingly cataclysmic drop of 34 percent, or 8.5 percent per annum. Prices fell even further, from 125 in February 1839 to 67 in March 1843, a tremendous drop of 42 percent or 10.5 percent per year.

During the boom, as we have indicated, state governments went heavily into debt, issuing bonds to pay for wasteful public works. In 1820, the total indebtedness of American states was a modest $12.8 million; by 1830, it rose to $26.5 million. But then it started to escalate, reaching $66.5 million in 1835 and skyrocketing to $170 million by 1839. The collapse of money, credit banking, and prices after 1839 brought these state debts into jeopardy. At this point, the Whigs, taking a leaf from their forebearers, the Federalists, agitated for the federal government to bail out the states and assume their debts.[80] After the crisis of 1839 arrived, some of the southern and western states were clearly in danger of default, their plight made worse by the fact that the bulk of the debt was held by British and Dutch capitalists and that specie would have to be sent abroad to meet the heavy interest payments. The Whigs pressed further for federal assumption of the debt, with the federal government to issue $200 million worth of bonds in payment. Furthermore, British bankers put severe pressure on the United States to assume the state debts if it expected to float further loans abroad.

The American people, however, spurned federal aid, including even the citizens of the states in difficulty, and the advent of the Polk administration ended any prospects for federal assumption. The British noted in wonder that the average American was far more concerned about his personal debts to other individuals and banks than about the debts of his state. In fact, the people were quite willing to have the states repudiate their debts outright. Demonstrating an astute perception of the reckless course the states had taken, the typical American response to the problem: "Suppose foreign capitalists did not lend any more to the states?" was the sharp retort: "Well who cares if they don't? We are now as a community heels over head in debt and can scarcely pay the interest."[81] The implication was that the disappearance of foreign credit to the states would have the healthy effect of cutting off their wasteful spending—as well as avoiding the imposition of a crippling tax burden to pay for the interest and principal. There was in this response an awareness by the public that they and their government

---

[80]See Reginald C. McGrane, *Foreign Bondholders and American State Debts* (New York: Macmillan, 1935), pp. 6–7, 24ff.

[81]McGrane, *Foreign Bondholders*, pp. 39–40.

were separate and sometimes even hostile entities rather than one and the same organism.[82]

By 1847, four western and southern states (Mississippi, Arkansas, Michigan, and Florida) had repudiated all or part of their debts. Six other states (Maryland, Illinois, Indiana, Louisiana, Arkansas, and Pennsylvania) had defaulted from three to six years before resuming payment.

It is evident, then, that the 1839–43 contraction was healthful for the economy in liquidating unsound investments, debts and banks, including the pernicious Bank of the United States. But didn't the massive deflation have catastrophic effects—on production, trade, and employment, as we have been led to believe? In a fascinating analysis and comparison with the deflation of 1929–33 a century later, Professor Temin shows that the percentage of deflation over the comparable four years (1839–43, and 1929–33) was almost the same.[83] Yet the effects on real production of the two deflations were very different. Whereas in 1929–33 real gross investment fell catastrophically by 91 percent, real consumption by 19 percent, and real GNP by 30 percent; in 1839–43, investment fell by 23 percent, but real consumption *increased* by 21 percent and real GNP also rose by 16 percent. The interesting problem is to account for the enormous fall in production and consumption in the 1930s, as contrasted to the rise in production and consumption in the 1840s. It seems that only the initial months of the contraction worked a hardship on the American public and that most of the earlier deflation was a period of economic growth. Temin properly suggests that the reason can be found in the downward flexibility of prices in the 19th century, so that massive monetary contraction would lower prices but not particularly cripple the world of real production or standards of living. In contrast, in the 1930s government placed massive roadblocks on the downward fall of prices and wage rates and hence brought about severe and continuing depression of production and living standards.

---

[82]The Americans also pointed out that the banks, including the Bank of the United States, who were presuming to denounce repudiation of state debt, had already suspended specie payments and were largely responsible for the contraction. "Let the bondholders look to the United States Bank and to the other banks for their payment declared the people." McGrane, *Foreign Bankholders*, p. 48.

[83]From 1839–43, the money supply, as we have seen, fell by 34 percent, wholesale prices by 42 percent, and the number of banks by 23 percent. In 1929–33, the money supply fell by 27 percent, prices by 31 percent, and the number of banks by 42 percent. Temin, *Jacksonian Economy*, pp. 155ff.

The Jacksonians had no intention of leaving a permanent system of pet banks, and so after the retirement of Jackson, his successor, Martin Van Buren, fought to establish the Independent Treasury System, in which the federal government conferred no special privilege or inflationary prop on any bank; instead of a central bank or pet banks, the government was to keep its funds purely in specie, in its own treasury vaults—or its "subtreasury" branches—and simply take in and spend funds from there. Van Buren finally managed to establish the Independent Treasury System, which would last until the Civil War. At long last, the Jacksonians had achieved their dream of severing the federal government totally from the banking system and placing its finances on a purely hard-money, specie basis.

The Jacksonians and the Coinage Legislation of 1834

We have seen that the Coinage Act of 1792 established a bimetallic system in which the dollar was defined as equaling both 371.25 grains of pure silver and 24.75 grains of pure gold—a fixed weight ratio of 15 grains of silver to 1 grain of gold. But bimetallism foundered on Gresham's Law. After 1805, the world market value of silver fell to approximately 15.75 to 1, so that the U.S. fixed mint ratio greatly undervalued gold and overvalued silver. As a result gold flowed out of the country and silver flowed in, so that after 1810 only silver coin, largely overvalued Spanish-American fractional silver coin, circulated within the United States. The rest of the currency was inflated bank paper in various stages of depreciation.

The Jacksonians, as we have seen, were determined to eliminate inflationary paper money and substitute a hard money consisting of specie—or, at the most—of paper 100 percent-backed by gold or silver. On the federal level, this meant abolishing the Bank of the United States and establishing the Independent Treasury. The rest of the fight would have to be conducted, during the 1840s and later, at the state level where the banks were chartered. But one thing the federal government could do was readjust the specie coinage. In particular, the Jacksonians were anxious to eliminate small denomination bank notes ($20 and under) and substitute gold and silver coins for them. They reasoned that the average American largely used these coins, and they were the ones bilked by inflated paper money. For a standard to be really gold and silver, it was vital that gold or silver coins circulate and be used as a medium of exchange by the average American.

To accomplish this goal, the Jacksonians set about to establish a comprehensive program. As one vital step, one of the Coinage Acts of 1834 readjusted the old mint ratio of 15:1 that had undervalued gold and driven it out of circulation. The Coinage Act devalued the definition of the gold dollar from the original 24.75 grains to 23.2 grains, a debasement of gold by 6.26 percent. The silver dollar was left at the old weight of 371.25 grains, so that the mint ratio between silver and gold was now fixed at a ratio of 16:1, replacing the old 15:1. It was unfortunate that the Jacksonians did not appreciate silver (to 396 grains) instead of debasing gold, for this set a precedent for debasement that was to plague America in 1933 and after.[84]

The new ratio of 16:1, however, now undervalued silver and overvalued gold, since the world market ratio had been approximately 15.79:1 in the years before 1834. Until recently, historians have assumed that the Jacksonians deliberately tried to bring in gold and expel silver and establish a monometallic gold standard by the back door. Recent study has shown, however, that the Jacksonians only wanted to give gold inflow a little push through a slight undervaluation and that they anticipated a full coin circulation of both gold and silver.[85] In 1833, for example, the world market ratio was as high as 15.93:1. Indeed, it turns out that for two decades the Jacksonians were right, and that the slight one percent premium of silver over gold was not enough to drive the former coins out of circulation.[86] Both silver and gold were imported from then on, and silver and gold coins both circulated successfully side-by-side until the early 1850s. Lightweight Spanish fractional silver remained overvalued even at the mint ratio, so it flourished in circulation, replacing depreciated small notes. Even American silver dollars were now retained in circulation since they were "shielded" and kept

[84]Probably the Jacksonians did so in order to preserve the illusion that the original silver dollar, the "dollar of our fathers" and the standard currency of the day, remained fixed in value. Laughlin, *History of Bimetallism*, p. 70.

[85]For the illuminating discovery that the Jacksonians were interested in purging small bank notes by bringing in gold, see Paul M. O'Leary, "The Coinage Legislation of 1834," *Journal of Political Economy* 45 (February 1937): 80–94. For the development of this insight by Martin, who shows that the Jacksonians anticipated a coinage of both gold and silver, and reveals the comprehensive Jacksonian coinage program, see David A. Martin, "Metallism, Small Notes, and Jackson's War with the B.U.S.," *Explorations in Economic History*, 11 (Spring 1974): 227–247.

[86]For the next 16 years, from 1835–1850, the market ratio averaged 15.8:1, a silver premium of only 1 percent over the 16:1 mint ratio. For the data, see Laughlin, *History of Bimetallism*, p. 291.

circulating by the presence of new, heavyweight Mexican silver dollars, which were exported instead.[87]

In order to stimulate the circulation of both gold and silver coin instead of paper notes, the Jacksonians also passed two companion Coinage Acts in 1834. The Jacksonians were not monetary nationalists; specie was specie, and they saw that there was no reason that foreign gold or silver coins should not circulate with the same full privileges as American-minted coins. Hence, the Jacksonians, in two separate measures, legalized the circulation of all foreign silver and gold coins, and they flourished in circulation until the 1850s.[88,89]

A third plank in the Jacksonian coinage platform was to establish branch U.S. mints so as to coin the gold found in newly-discovered mines in Georgia and North Carolina. The Jackson administration finally succeeded in getting Congress to do so in 1835 when it set up branch mints to coin gold in North Carolina and Georgia, and silver and gold at New Orleans.[90]

Finally, on the federal level, the Jacksonians sought to levy a tax on small bank notes and to prevent the federal government from keeping its deposits in state banks, issuing small notes, or from accepting small bank notes in taxes. They were not successful, but the Independent Treasury eliminated public deposit in state banks and the Specie Circular, as we have seen, stopped the receipt of bank notes for public land sales. From 1840 on, the hard-money battle would be waged at the state level.

---

[87]Martin, "Bimetallism," pp. 435–437. Spanish fractional silver coins were from 5 to 15 percent underweight, and so their circulation in the U.S. at par by name (or "tale") meant that they were still considerably overvalued.

[88]As Jackson's Secretary of the Treasury Levi Woodbury explained the purpose of this broad legalization of foreign coins: "to provide a full supply and variety of coins, instead of bills below five and ten dollars," for this would be "particularly conducive to the security of the poor and middling classes, who, as they own but little in, and profit but little by, banks, should be subjected to as small risk as practicable by their bills." Quoted in Martin, "Metallism," p.242.

[89]In 1837 another Coinage Act made a very slight adjustment in the mint ratios. In order to raise the alloy composition of gold coins to have them similar to silver, the definition of the gold dollar was raised slightly from 23.2 to 23.22 grains. With the weight of the silver dollar remaining the same, the silver/gold ratio was now very slightly lowered from 16.002:1 to 15.998:1. Further slight adjustments in valuations of foreign coins in another Coinage Act of 1843 resulted in the undervaluation of many foreign coins and their gradual disappearance. The major ones—Spanish fractional silver—continued, however, to circulate widely. Martin, "Bimetallism," p. 436.

[90]Martin, "Metallism," p. 240.

In the early 1850s, Gresham's Law finally caught up with the bimetallist idyll that the Jacksonians had forged in the 1830s, replacing the earlier de facto silver monometallism. The sudden discovery of extensive gold mines in California, Russia, and Australia greatly increased gold production, reaching a peak in the early 1850s. From the 1720s through the 1830s, annual world gold production averaged $12.8 million, never straying very far from that norm. Then, world gold production increased to an annual average of $38.2 million in the 1840s, and spurted upward to a peak of $155 million in 1853. World gold production then fell steadily from that peak to an annual average of $139.9 million in the 1850s and to $114.7 million from 1876–1890. It was not to surpass this peak until the 1890s.[91]

The consequence of the burst in gold production was, of course, a fall in the price of gold relative to silver in the world market. The silver/gold ratio declined from 15.97 in January 1849 to an average of 15.70 in 1850 to 15.46 in 1851 and to an average of 15.32:1 in the eight years from 1853 to 1860.[92] As a result, the market premium of American silver dollars over gold quickly rose above the one-percent margin, which was the estimated cost of shipping silver coin abroad. That premium, which had hovered around one percent since the mid-1830s, suddenly rose to 4.5 percent at the beginning of 1851, and after falling back to about 2 percent at the turn of 1852, bounced back up and remained at the 4-5 percent level.

The result was a rapid disappearance of silver from the country, the heaviest and therefore most undervalued coins vanishing first. Spanish-milled dollars, which contained 1 percent to 5 percent more silver than American dollars, commanded a premium of 7 percent and went first. Then went the full-weight American silver dollars and after that, American fractional silver coins, which were commanding a 4 percent premium by the fall of 1852. The last coins left were the worn Spanish and Mexican fractions, which were depreciated by 10 to 15 percent. By the beginning of 1851, however, even these worn foreign silver fractions had gone to a one-percent premium, and were beginning to go.

It was clear that America was undergoing a severe small coin crisis. Gold coins were flowing into the country, but they were too valuable

[91]On gold production, see Laughlin, *History of Bimetallism*, pp. 283–286; David A. Martin, "1853: The End of Bimetallism in the United States," *Journal of Economic History* 33 (December 1973): 830.

[92]The silver/gold ratio began to slide sharply in October and November 1850. Laughlin, *History of Bimetallism*, pp. 194, 291.

to be technically usable for small denomination coins. The Democratic Pierce administration saw with horror a flood of millions of dollars of unauthorized private small notes flood into circulation in early 1853 for the first time since the 1830s. The Jacksonians were in grave danger of losing the fight for hard-money coinage, at least for the smaller and medium denominations. Something had to be done quickly.[93]

The ultimate breakdown of bimetallism had never been clearer. If bimetallism is in the long run not viable, this leaves two free-market, hard-money alternatives: (a) silver monometallism with the dollar defined as a weight of silver only, and gold circulating freely by weight at freely-fluctuating market rates; or (b) gold monometallism with the dollar defined only as a weight of gold, with silver circulating by weight. Each of these is an example of what has been called "parallel standards" or "free metallism," in which two or more metal coins are allowed to fluctuate freely within the same area and exchange at free-market prices. As we have seen, colonial America was an example of such parallel standards, since foreign gold and silver coins circulated freely and at fluctuating market prices.[94]

The United States could have taken this opportunity of monetary crisis to go on either version of a parallel standard.[95] Apparently, how-

---

[93]Martin, "Metallism," p. 240

[94]For an account of how parallel standards worked in Europe from the medieval period through the 18th century, see Luigi Einaudi, "The Theory of Imaginary Money from Charlemagne to the French Revolution," in F. Lane and J. Riemersma, eds., *Enterprise and Secular Change* (Homewood, Ill.: Irwin, 1953), pp. 229–261. Robert Lopez contrasts the ways in which Florence and Genoa each returned to gold coinage in the mid-13th century, after a gap of half a millenium: "Florence, like most medieval states, made bimetallism and trimetallism a base of its monetary policy . . . it committed the government to the Sysiphean labor of readjusting the relations between different coins as the ratio between the different metals changes, or as one or another coin was debased . . . Genoa on the contrary, *in conformity with the principle of restricting state intervention as much as possible* [italics ours], did not try to enforce a fixed relation between coins of different metals . . . Basically, the gold coinage of Genoa was not meant to integrate the silver and bullion coinages but to form an independent system." Robert Sabatino Lopez, "Back to Gold, 1252," *Economic History Review,* April 1956, p.224. Also see James Rolph Edwards, "Monopoly and Competition in Money," *Journal of Libertarian Studies* IV (Winter 1980): 116. For an analysis of parallel standards, see Ludwig von Mises, *The Theory of Money and Credit* 3rd ed. (Indianapolis: Liberty Classics, 1980), pp. 87, 89–91, 205–207.

[95]Given parallel standards, the ultimate, admittedly remote solution would be to eliminate the term "dollar" altogether, and simply have both gold and silver coins circulate by regular units of weight: "Grain," "Ounce," or "Gram." If that were done, all problems of bimetallism, debasement, Gresham's Law, etc., would at last disappear. While such a

64

ever, few thought of doing so. Another viable though inferior solution to the problem of bimetallism was to establish a monometallic system, either de facto or de jure, with the other metal circulating in the form of lightweight, and therefore overvalued, or "token" coinage. Silver monometallism was immediately unfeasible since it was rapidly flowing out of the country, and because gold, being far more valuable than silver, could not technically function easily as a lightweight, subsidiary coin. The only feasible solution, then, within a monometallic framework, was to make gold the basic standard and let highly overvalued, essentially token, silver coins function as subsidiary small coinage. Certainly if a parallel standard was not to be adopted, the latter solution would be far better than allowing depreciated paper notes to function as small currency.

Under pressure of the crisis, Congress decided, in February 1853, to keep the de jure bimetallic standard but to adopt a de facto gold monometallic standard, with fractional silver coins circulating as a deliberately overvalued subsidiary coinage, legal tender up to a maximum of only five dollars. The fractional silver coins were debased by 6.91 percent. With silver commanding about a 4 percent market premium over gold, this meant that fractional silver was debased 3 percent below gold. At that depreciated rate, fractional silver was not overvalued in relation to gold, and remained in circulation. By April, the new subsidiary quarter dollars proved to be popular and by early 1854 the problem of the shortage of small coins in America was over.

In rejecting proposals either to go over completely to de jure gold monometallism, or to keep the existing bimetallic system, Congress was choosing a gold standard temporarily, but keeping its options open. The fact that it continued the old full-bodied silver dollar, the "dollar of our fathers," demonstrates that an eventual return to de facto bimetallism was by no means being ruled out—albeit Gresham's Law could not then maintain the American silver dollar in circulation.[96]

---

pure free-market solution seems remote today, the late 19th century saw a series of important international monetary conferences trying to move toward a universal gold or silver gram, with each national currency beginning as a simple multiple of each other, and eventually only units of weight being used. Before the conferences foundered on the gold/silver problem, such a result was not as remote or Utopian as we might now believe. See the fascinating account of these conferences in Henry B. Russell, *International Monetary Conferences* (New York: Harper & Bros., 1898).

[96]For an excellent portrayal of the congressional choice in 1853, see Martin, "1853," pp. 825–844.

In 1857, an important part of the Jacksonian coinage program was repealed, as Congress, in an exercise of monetary nationalism, eliminated all legal tender power of foreign coins.[97]

Decentralized Banking from the 1830s to the Civil War

After the central bank was eliminated in the 1830s, the battle for hard money largely shifted to the state governmental arena. During the 1830s, the major thrust was to prohibit the issue of small notes, which was accomplished for notes under five dollars in 10 states by 1832, and subsequently, five others restricted or prohibited such notes.[98]

The Democratic Party became ardently hard-money in the various states after the shock of the financial crisis of 1837 and 1839. The Democratic drive was toward the outlawry of all fractional reserve bank paper. Battles were fought, also, in the late 1840s, at constitutional conventions of many states, particularly in the West. In some western states the Jacksonians won temporary success, but soon the Whigs would return and repeal the bank prohibition. The Whigs, trying to find some way to overcome the general revulsion against banks after the crisis of the late 1830s, adopted the concept of "free" banking, which had been enacted by New York and Michigan in the late 1830s. From New York, the idea spread outward to the rest of the country and triumphed in 15 states by the early 1850s. On the eve of the Civil War, 18 out of the 33 states in the Union had adopted "free" banking laws.[99]

It must be realized that "free" banking, as it came to be known in the United States before the Civil War, was unrelated to the philosophic concept of free banking analyzed by economists. As we have seen earlier, genuine free banking is a system where entry into banking is totally free, the banks are neither subsidized nor regulated, and at the first sign of failure to redeem in specie payments, the bank is forced to declare insolvency and close its doors.

"Free" banking before the Civil War, on the other hand, was very different.[100] As we have pointed out, the government allowed periodic

[97]Only Spanish-American fractional silver coins were to remain legal tender, and they were to be received quickly at government offices and immediately reminted into American coins. Hepburn, *History of Currency*, pp. 66–67.

[98]See Martin, "Metallism," pp. 242–243.

[99]Hugh Rockoff, *The Free Banking Era: A Re-Examination* (New York: Arno Press, 1975), pp. 3–4.

[100]Rockoff goes so far as to call free banking the "antithesis of *laissez-faire* banking laws." Hugh Rockoff, "Varieties of Banking and Regional Economic Development in the United

general suspensions of specie payments whenever the banks over-expanded and got into trouble—the latest episode was in the Panic of 1857. It is true that bank incorporation was now more liberal since any bank which met the legal regulations could become incorporated automatically without lobbying for special legislative charters, as had been the case before. But the banks were not subject to a myriad of regulations, including edicts by state banking commissioners and high minimum capital requirements which greatly restricted entry into the banking business. But the most pernicious aspect of "free" banking was that the expansion of bank notes and deposits was directly tied to the amount of state government securities which the bank had invested in and posted as bond with the state. In effect, then, state government bonds became the reserve base upon which the banks were allowed to pyramid a multiple expansion of bank notes and deposits. Not only did this system provide explicitly or implicitly for fractional reserve banking; but the pyramid was tied rigidly to the amount of government bonds purchased by the banks. This provision deliberately tied banks and bank credit expansion to the public debt; it meant that the more public debt the banks purchased, the more they could create and lend out new money. Banks, in short, were encouraged to monetize the public debt, state governments were thereby encouraged to go into debt, and hence, government and bank inflation were intimately linked.

In addition to allowing periodic suspension of specie payments, federal and state governments conferred upon the banks the privilege of their notes being accepted in taxes. Moreover, the general prohibition of interstate branch banking—and often of intrastate branches as well—greatly inhibited the speed by which one bank could demand payment from other banks in specie. In addition, state usury laws, pushed by the Whigs and opposed by the Democrats, made credit excessively cheap for the riskiest borrowers and encouraged inflation and speculative expansion of bank lending.

Furthermore, the desire of state governments to finance internal improvements was an important factor in subsidizing and propelling expansion of bank credit. As Hammond admits: "The wild-cats lent no money to farmers and served no farmer interest. They arose to meet the credit demands not of farmers (who were too economically astute

States, 1840–1860," *Journal of Economic History* 35 (March 1975): 162. Quoted in Hummel, "Jacksonians," p. 157.

to accept wildcat money) but of states engaged in public improvements."[101]

Despite the flaws and problems, the decentralized nature of the pre-Civil War banking system meant that banks were free to experiment on their own with improving the banking system. The most successful such device was the creation of the Suffolk system.

A Free-Market "Central Bank"

It is a fact, almost never recalled, that there once existed an American private bank that brought order and convenience to a myriad of privately issued banknotes. Further, the Suffolk Bank restrained the over-issuance of these notes. In short, it was a private central bank that kept the other banks honest. As such, it made New England an island of monetary stability in an America contending with currency chaos.

Chaos was, in fact, that condition in which New England found herself just before the Suffolk Bank was established. There were a myriad of banknotes circulating in the area's largest financial center, Boston. Some were issued by Boston banks which all in Boston knew to be solvent. But others were issued by state-chartered banks. These could be quite far away, and in those days such distance impeded both general knowledge about their solvency and easy access in bringing the banks' notes in for redemption into gold or silver. Thus, while at the beginning these country notes were accepted in Boston at par value, this just encouraged some far-away banks to issue far more notes than they had gold to back them. So country bank notes began to be generally traded at discounts to par, of from 1 percent to 5 percent.

City banks finally refused to accept country bank notes altogether. This gave rise to the money brokers mentioned earlier in this chapter. But it also caused hardship for Boston merchants, who had to accept country notes whose real value they could not be certain of. When they exchanged the notes with the brokers, they ended up assuming the full cost of discounting the bills they had accepted at par.

A False Start

Matters began to change in 1814. The New England Bank of Boston announced it too would go into the money broker business, accepting

---

[101]Hammond, *Banks and Politics*, p. 627. On free banking, see Hummel, "Jacksonians," pp. 154–160; Smith, *Rationale*, pp. 44–45; and Hugh Rockoff, "American Free Banking Before the Civil War: A Reexamination," *Journal of Economic History* 32 (March 1972): 417–420. On the effect of usury laws, see William Graham Sumner, *A History of American Currency* (New York: Henry Holt & Co., 1876), p. 125. On the Jacksonians versus their

country notes from holders and turning them over to the issuing bank for redemption. The note holders, though, still had to pay the cost. In 1818, a group of prominent merchants formed the Suffolk Bank to do the same thing. This enlarged competition brought the basic rate of country note discount down from three percent in 1814 to one percent in 1818 and finally to a bare one-half of one percent in 1820. But this did not necessarily mean that country banks were behaving more responsibly in their note creation. By the end of 1820 the business had become clearly unprofitable, and both banks stopped competing with the private money brokers. The Suffolk became just another Boston bank.

Operation Begins

During the next several years city banks found their notes representing an ever smaller part of the total New England money supply. Country banks were simply issuing far more notes in proportion to their capital (i.e., gold and silver) than were the Boston banks.

Concerned about this influx of paper money of lesser worth, both Suffolk and New England Bank began again in 1824 to purchase country notes. But this time they did so not to make a profit on redemption, but simply to reduce the number of country notes in circulation in Boston. They had the foolish hope that this would increase the use of their (better) notes, thus increasing their own loans and profits.

But the more they purchased country notes, the more notes of even worse quality (particularly from far-away Maine banks) would replace them. Buying these latter involved more risk, so the Suffolk proposed to six other city banks a joint fund to purchase and send these notes back to the issuing bank for redemption. These seven banks, known as the Associated Banks, raised $300,000 for this purpose. With the Suffolk acting as agent and buying country notes from the other six, operations began March 24, 1824. The volume of country notes bought in this way increased greatly, to $2 million per month by the end of 1825. By then, Suffolk felt strong enough to go it alone. Further, it now had the leverage to pressure country banks into depositing gold and

opponents on the state level after 1839, see William G. Shade, *Banks or No Banks: The Money Issue in Western Politics, 1832–1865* (Detroit: Wayne State University Press, 1972); Herbert Ershkowitz and William Shade, "Consensus or Conflict? Political Behavior in the State Legislatures During the Jacksonian Era," *Journal of American History* 58 (December 1971): 591–621; and James Roger Sharp, *Jacksonians versus the Banks: Politics in the States After the Panic of 1837* (New York: Columbia University Press, 1970).

silver with the Suffolk, to make note redemption easier. By 1838, almost every bank in New England did so, and were redeeming their notes through the Suffolk Bank.

The Suffolk ground rules from beginning (1825) to end (1858) were as follows: Each country bank had to maintain a permanent deposit of specie of at least $2,000 for the smallest bank, plus enough to redeem all its notes that Suffolk received. These gold and silver deposits did not have to be at Suffolk, so long as they were at some place convenient to Suffolk, so that the notes would not have to be sent home for redemption. But in practice, nearly all reserves were at Suffolk. (City banks had only to deposit a fixed amount, which decreased to $5,000 by 1835.) No interest was paid on any of these deposits. But, in exchange, the Suffolk began performing an invaluable service: It agreed to accept at par all the notes it received as deposits from other New England banks in the system, and credit the depositor banks' accounts on the following day.

With the Suffolk acting as a "clearing bank," accepting, sorting, and crediting bank notes, it was now possible for any New England bank to accept the notes of any other bank, however far away, and at face value. This drastically cut down on the time and inconvenience of applying to each bank separately for specie redemption. Moreover, the certainty spread that the notes of the Suffolk member banks would be valued at par: It spread at first among other bankers and then to the general public.

The Country Banks Resist

How did the inflationist country banks react to this? Not very well, for as one can see the Suffolk system put limits on the amount of notes they could issue. They resented par redemption and detested systematic specie redemption because that forced them to stay honest. But the country banks knew that any bank that did not play by the rules would be shunned by the banks that did (or at least see their notes accepted only at discount, and not in a very wide area, at that). All legal means to stop Suffolk failed: The Massachusetts Supreme Court upheld in 1827 Suffolk's right to demand gold or silver for country bank notes, and the state legislature refused to charter a clearing bank run by country banks; probably rightly assuming that these banks would run much less strict operations. Stung by these setbacks, the country banks played by the rules, bided their time, and awaited their revenge.

Suffolk's Stabilizing Effects

Even though Suffolk's initial objective had been to increase the circulation of city banks, this did not happen. In fact, by having their notes redeemed at par, country banks gained a new respectability. This came, naturally, at the expense of the number of notes issued by the worst former inflationists. But at least in Massachusetts, the percentage of city bank notes in circulation fell from 48.5 percent in 1826 to 35.8 percent in 1833.

Circulation of the Notes of Massachusetts Banks (in Thousands)

Date	All Banks	Boston Banks	Boston Percentage
1823	$3,129	$1,354	43.3
1824	3,843	1,797	46.8
1825	4,091	1,918	46.9
1826	4,550	2,206	48.5
1827	4,936	2,103	42.6
1828	4,885	2,067	42.3
1829	4,748	2,078	43.8
1830	5,124	2,171	42.3
1831	7,139	3,464	44.8
1832	7,123	3,060	43.0
1833	7,889	2,824	35.8

Source: Wilfred S. Lake, *The End of the Suffolk System*, p. 188.

The biggest, most powerful weapon Suffolk had to keep stability was the power to grant membership into the system. It accepted only banks whose notes were sound. While Suffolk could not prevent a bad bank from inflating, denying it membership ensured that the notes would not enjoy wide circulation. And the member banks which were mismanaged could be stricken from the list of Suffolk-approved New England banks in good standing. This caused the offending banks' notes to trade at a discount at once, even though the bank itself might be still redeeming its notes in specie.

In another way, Suffolk exercised a stabilizing influence on the New England economy. It controlled the use of overdrafts in the system. When a member bank needed money, it could apply for an overdraft, that is, a portion of the excess reserves in the banking system. If Suffolk decided that a member bank's loan policy was not conservative enough, it could refuse to sanction that bank's application to borrow reserves at Suffolk. The denial of overdrafts to profligate banks thus forced those banks to keep their assets more liquid. (Few government central banks today have succeeded in that.) This is all the more remarkable when one considers that Suffolk—or any central bank—could have earned extra interest income by issuing overdrafts irresponsibly.

But Dr. George Trivoli, whose excellent monograph, *The Suffolk Bank*, we rely on in this study, states that by providing stability to the New England banking system "it should not be inferred that the Suffolk bank was operating purely as public benefactor." Suffolk, in fact, made handsome profits. At its peak in 1858, the last year of existence, it was redeeming $400 million in notes, with a total annual salary cost of only $40,000. The healthy profits were derived primarily from loaning out those reserve deposits which Suffolk itself, remember, did not pay interest on. These amounted to over $1 million in 1858. The interest charged on overdrafts augmented that. Not surprisingly, Suffolk stock was the highest priced bank stock in Boston, and by 1850, regular dividends were 10 percent.

The Suffolk Difference

That the Suffolk system was able to provide note redemption much more cheaply than the U.S. government was stated by a U.S. Comptroller of the Currency. John Jay Knox compared the two systems from a vantage point of half a century: ". . . in 1857 the redemption of notes by the Suffolk Bank was almost $400,000,000 as against $137,697,696 in 1875, the highest amount ever reported under the National Banking system. The redemptions in 1898 were only $66,683,476 at a cost of $1.29 per thousand. The cost of redemption under the Suffolk system was ten cents per $1,000, which does not appear to include transportation. If this item is deducted from the cost of redeeming National Bank notes, it would reduce it to about ninety-four cents. This difference is accounted for by the relatively small amount of redemptions by the Treasury, and the increased expense incident to the necessity of official checks by the Government, and by the higher salaries paid. But allowing for these differences, the fact is established that private enterprise could be entrusted with the work of redeeming the circulating notes of the banks, and it could thus be done as safely and much more economically than the same services can be performed by the Government."[102]

[102]John Jay Knox, *A History of Banking in the United States* (New York: Augustus M. Kelley, 1969 [1900]), pp. 368–69.

The volume of redemptions was much larger under Suffolk than under the National Banking system. During Suffolk's existence (1825–57) they averaged $229 million per year. The average of the National system from its start in 1863 to about 1898 is put by Mr. Knox at only $54 million. Further, at its peak in 1858, $400 million was redeemed. But the New England money supply was only $40 million. This meant that, astoundingly, the average note was redeemed 10 times per year, or once every five weeks.

Bank capital, note circulation, and deposits, considered together as "banking power," grew in New England on a per capita basis much faster than in any other region of the country from 1803 to 1850. And there is some evidence that New England banks were not as susceptible to disaster during the several banking panics during that time. In the Panic of 1837 not one Connecticut bank failed, nor did any suspend specie payments. All remained in the Suffolk system. And when in 1857 specie payment was suspended in Maine, all but three banks remained in business. As the Bank Commission of Maine stated, "The Suffolk system, though not recognized in banking law, has proved to be a great safeguard to the public; whatever objections may exist to the system in theory, its practical operation is to keep the circulation of our banks within the bounds of safety."

The Suffolk's Demise

The extraordinary profits—and power—that the Suffolk had by 1858 attained spawned competitors. The only one to become established was a Bank for Mutual Redemption in 1858. This bank was partially a response to the somewhat arrogant behavior of the Suffolk by this time, after 35 years of unprecedented success. But further, and more importantly, the balance of power in the state legislature had shifted outside of Boston, to the country bank areas. The politicians were more amenable to the desires of the overexpanding country banks. Still, it must be said that Suffolk acted toward the Bank of Mutual Redemption with spite where conciliation would have helped. Trying to force Mutual Redemption out of business, Suffolk, starting October 9, 1858, refused to honor notes of banks having deposits in the newcomer. Further, Suffolk in effect threatened any bank withdrawing deposits from it. But country banks rallied to the newcomer, and on October 16, Suffolk announced that it would stop clearing any country bank notes, thus becoming just another bank.

Only the Bank for Mutual Redemption was left, and though it soon had half the New England banks as members, it was much more lax toward overissuance by country banks. Perhaps the Suffolk would have returned amid dissatisfaction with its successor, but in 1861, just over two years after Suffolk stopped clearing, the Civil War began and all specie payments were stopped. As a final nail in the coffin, the National Banking System Act of 1863 forbade the issuance of any state bank notes, giving a monopoly to the government that has continued ever since.

While it lasted, though, the Suffolk banking system showed that it is possible in a free-market system to have private banks competing to establish themselves as efficient, safe, and inexpensive clearing houses limiting overissue of paper money.

The Civil War

The Civil War exerted an even more fateful impact on the American monetary and banking system than had the War of 1812. It set the United States, for the first time except for 1814–17, on an irredeemable fiat currency that lasted for two decades and led to reckless inflation of prices. This "greenback" currency set a momentous precedent for the post-1933 United States, and even more particularly for the post-1971 experiment in fiat money.

Perhaps an even more important consequence of the Civil War was the permanent change wrought in the American banking system. The federal government in effect outlawed the issue of state bank notes, and created a new, quasi-centralized, fractional reserve national banking system which paved the way for the return of outright central banking in the Federal Reserve System. The Civil War, in short, ended the separation of the federal government from banking, and brought the two institutions together in an increasingly close and permanent symbiosis. In that way, the Republican Party, which inherited the Whig admiration for paper money and governmental control and sponsorship of inflationary banking, was able to implant the soft-money tradition permanently in the American system.

Greenbacks

The Civil War led to an enormous ballooning of federal expenditures, which skyrocketed from $66 million in 1861 to $1.30 billion four years later. To pay for these swollen expenditures, the Treasury initially attempted, in the fall of 1861, to float a massive $150 million bond issue, to be purchased by the nation's leading banks. However, Secretary of the Treasury Salmon P. Chase, a former Jacksonian, tried to require the banks to pay for the loan in specie that they did not have. This massive pressure on their specie, as well as an increased public demand for specie due to a well-deserved lack of confidence in the banks, brought about a general suspension of specie payments a few months later, at the end of December 1861. This suspension was followed swiftly by the Treasury itself, which suspended specie payments on its Treasury notes.

The U.S. government quickly took advantage of being on an inconvertible fiat standard. In the Legal Tender Act of February 1862, Congress authorized the printing of $150 million in new "United States Notes" (soon to be known as "greenbacks") to pay for the growing war deficits. The greenbacks were made legal tender for all debts, public and private, except that the Treasury continued its legal obligation of paying the interest on its outstanding public debt in specie.[103] The greenbacks were also made convertible at par into U.S. bonds, which remained a generally unused option for the public, and was repealed a year later.

In creating greenbacks in February, Congress resolved that this would be the first and last emergency issue. But printing money is a heady wine, and a second $150 million issue was authorized in July, and still a third $150 million in early 1863. Greenbacks outstanding reached a peak in 1864 of $415.1 million.

Greenbacks began to depreciate in terms of specie almost as soon as they were issued. In an attempt to drive up the price of government bonds, Secretary Chase eliminated the convertibility of greenbacks in July 1863, an act which simply drove down their value further. Chase and the Treasury officials, instead of acknowledging their own premier responsibility for the continued depreciation of the greenbacks, conveniently placed the blame on anonymous "gold speculators." In March 1863, Chase began a determined campaign, which would last until he was driven from office, to stop the depreciation by controlling, assaulting, and eventually eliminating the gold market. In early March, he had Congress levy a stamp tax on gold sales and to forbid loans on a

---

[103]To be able to keep paying interest in specie, Congress provided that customs duties, at least, had to be paid in gold or silver. For a comprehensive account and analysis of the issue of greenbacks in the Civil War, see Wesley Clair Mitchell, *A History of the Greenbacks* (Chicago: University of Chicago Press, 1903). For a summary, see Paul Studenski and Herman E. Kross, *Financial History of the United States* (New York: McGraw-Hill, 1952), pp. 141–149.

collateral of coin above its par value. This restriction on the gold market had little effect, and when depreciation resumed its march at the end of the year, Chase decided to de facto repeal the requirement that customs duties be paid in gold. In late March 1864, Chase declared that importers would be allowed to deposit greenbacks at the Treasury and receive gold in return at a premium below the market. Importers could then use the gold to pay the customs duties. This was supposed to reduce greatly the necessity for importers to buy gold coin on the market and therefore to reduce the depreciation. The outcome, however, was that the greenback, at 59 cents in gold when Chase began the experiment, had fallen to 57 cents by mid-April. Chase was then forced to repeal his customs duties scheme.

With the failure of this attempt to regulate the gold market, Chase promptly escalated his intervention. In mid-April, he sold the massive amount of $11 million in gold in order to drive down the gold premium of greenbacks. But the impact was trifling, and the Treasury could not continue this policy indefinitely, because it had to keep enough gold in its vaults to pay interest on its bonds. At the end of the month, the greenback was lower than ever, having sunk to below 56 cents in gold.

Indefatigably, Chase tried yet again. In mid-May 1864, he sold foreign exchange in London at below-market rates in order to drive down pounds in relation to dollars, and, more specifically, to replace some of the U.S. export demand for gold in England. But this, too, was a failure, and Chase ended this experiment before the end of the month.

Finally, Secretary Chase decided to take off the gloves. He had failed to regulate the gold market; he would therefore end the depreciation of greenbacks by destroying the gold market completely. By mid-June, he had driven through Congress a truly despotic measure to prohibit under pain of severe penalties all futures contracts in gold, as well as all sales of gold by a broker outside his own office.

The result was disaster. The gold market was in chaos, with wide ranges of prices due to the absence of an organized market. Businessmen clamored for repeal of the "gold bill," and, worst of all, the object of the law—to lower the depreciation of the paper dollar—had scarcely been achieved. Instead, public confidence in the greenback plummeted, and its depreciation in terms of gold got far worse. At the beginning of June, the greenback dollar was worth over 52 cents in gold. Apprehensions about the emerging gold bill drove the greenback down slightly to 51 cents in mid-June. Then, after the passage of the bill, the greenback plummeted, reaching 40 cents at the end of the month.

The disastrous gold bill was hastily repealed at the end of June, and perhaps not coincidentally, Secretary Chase was ousted from office at the same time. The war against the speculators was over.[104,105]

As soon as greenbacks depreciated to less than 97 cents in gold, fractional silver coins became undervalued and so were exported to be exchanged for gold. By July 1862, in consequence, no coin higher than the copper/nickel penny remained in circulation. The U.S. government then leaped in to fill the gap with small tickets, first issuing postage stamps for the purpose, then bits of unglued paper, and finally, after the spring of 1863, fractional paper notes.[106] A total of $28 million in postage currency and fractional notes was issued by the middle of 1864. Even the nickel/copper pennies began to disappear from circulation, as greenbacks depreciated, and the nickel/copper coin began to move toward being undervalued. The expectation and finally the reality of undervaluation drove the coins into hoards and then into exports. Postage and fractional notes did not help matters, because their lowest denominations were 5 cents and 3 cents respectively. The penny short-age was finally alleviated when a debased and lighter weight penny was issued in the spring of 1864, consisting of bronze instead of nickel and copper.[107]

As soon as the nation's banks and the Treasury itself suspended specie payments at the end of 1861, Gresham's Law went into operation and gold coin virtually disappeared from circulation, except for the government's interest payments and importers' customs duties. The

[104]Chase and the administration should have heeded the advice of Sen. Jacob Collamer (R-Vt.): "Gold does not fluctuate in price . . . because they gamble in it; but they gamble in it because it fluctuates . . . . But the fluctuation is not in the gold; the fluctuation is in the currency, and it is a fluctuation utterly beyond the control of individuals." Mitchell, *History of Greenbacks*, pp. 229–230.

[105]On the war against the gold speculators, see Mitchell, *History of Greenbacks*, pp. 223–235. The greenbacks fell further to 35 cents in mid-July on news of military defeats for the North. Military victories, and consequently rising prospects of possible future gold redemption of the greenbacks, caused a rise in greenbacks in terms of gold, particularly after the beginning of 1865. At war's end the greenback dollar was worth 69 cents in gold. Ibid., pp. 232–238, 423–428.

[106]Some of the greenbacks had been decorated with portraits of President Lincoln ($5) and Secretary Chase ($1). However, when Spencer Clark, chief clerk of the Treasury's National Currency Division, put his own portrait on 5-cent fractional notes, the indignant Rep. Martin R.Thayer (R-Pa.) put through a law, still in force, making it illegal to put the picture of any living American on any coin or paper money. See Gary North, "Greenback Dollars and Federal Sovereignty, 1861–1865," in H. Sennholz, ed., *Gold Is Money* (Westport, Conn.: Greenwood Press, 1975), pp. 124, 150.

[107]See Mitchell, *History of Greenbacks*, pp. 156–163.

swift issuance of legal tender greenbacks, which the government forced creditors to accept at par, insured the continued disappearance of gold from then on.

The fascinating exception was California. There were very few banks during this period west of Nebraska, and in California the absence of banks was insured by the fact that note-issuing banks, at least, were prohibited by the California constitution of 1849.[108] The California gold discoveries of the late 1840s insured a plentiful supply for coinage.

Used to a currency of gold coin only, with no intrusion of bank notes, California businessmen took steps to maintain gold circulation and avoid coerced payment in greenbacks. At first, the merchants of San Francisco, in November 1862, jointly agreed to refrain from accepting or paying out greenbacks at any but the (depreciated) market value, and to keep gold as the monetary standard. Any firms that refused to abide by the agreement would be blacklisted and required to pay gold in cash for any goods which they might purchase in the future.

Voluntary efforts did not suffice to overthrow the federal power standing behind legal tender, however, and so California merchants obtained the passage in the California legislature of a "specific contracts act" at the end of April 1863. The specific contract provided that contracts for the payment of specific kinds of money would be enforceable in the courts. After passage of that law, California businessmen were able to protect themselves against tenders of greenbacks by inserting gold coin payment clauses in all their contracts. Would that the other states, and even the federal government, had done the same![109] Furthermore, the private banks of deposit in California refused to accept greenbacks on deposit, newspapers used their influence to warn citizens about the dangers of greenbacks, and the state government refused to accept greenbacks in payment of taxes. In that way, all the major institutions in California joined in refusing to accept or give their imprimatur to federal inconvertible paper.

Judicial institutions also helped maintain the gold standard and repel the depreciated U.S. paper. Not only did the California courts uphold

[108]Banks of deposit existed in California, but of course they could not supply the public's demand for cash. See John Jay Knox, *A History of Banking in the United States* (New York: Bradford Rhodes & Co., 1900), pp. 843–845.

[109]This experience illustrates a continuing problem in contract law: It is not sufficient for government to allow contracts to be made in gold or gold coin. It is necessary for government to enforce *specific performance* of the contracts so that debtors must pay in the weight or value of the gold (or anything else) required in the contract, and not in some paper dollar equivalent decided by law or the courts.

the constitutionality of the specific contracts act, but the California Supreme Court ruled in 1862 that greenbacks could not be accepted in state or county taxes, since the state constitution prohibited any acceptance of paper money for taxes.

The state of Oregon was quick to follow California's lead. Oregon's constitution had also outlawed banks of issue, and gold had for years been the exclusive currency. Two weeks after the agreement of the San Francisco merchants, the merchants of Salem, Oregon, unanimously backed gold as the monetary standard and refused to accept greenbacks at par. Two months later, the leading merchants of Portland agreed to accept greenbacks only at rates current in San Francisco; the merchants in the rest of the state were quick to follow suit. The Portland merchants issued a circular warning of a blacklist of all customers who insisted on settling their debts in greenbacks, and they would be quickly boycotted, and dealings with them would only be in cash.

Oregon deposit banks also refused to accept greenbacks, and the Oregon legislature followed California a year and a half later in passing a specific performance law. Oregon, too, refused to accept greenbacks in taxes and strengthened the law in 1864 by requiring that "all taxes levied by state, counties, or municipal corporations therein, shall be collected and paid in gold and silver coin of the United States and not otherwise."[110]

In the same year, the Oregon Supreme Court followed California in ruling that greenbacks could not constitutionally be received in payment of taxes.

The banking story during the Civil War is greatly complicated by the advent of the national banking system in the latter part of the war. But it is clear that the state banks, being able to suspend specie and to pyramid money and credit on top of the federal greenbacks, profited greatly by being able to expand during this period. Thus, total state bank notes and deposits were $510 million in 1860, and by 1863 the amount rose to $743 million, an increase in state bank demand liabilities in those three years of 15.2 percent per year.[111]

---

[110]Cited in Richard A. Lester, *Monetary Experiments* (1939, London: David & Charles Reprints, 1970), p. 166. On the California and Oregon maintenance of the gold standard during this period, see ibid., pp. 161–171. On California, see Bernard Moses, "Legal Tender Notes in California," *Quarterly Journal of Economics*, (October 1892): 1–25; Mitchell, *History of Greenbacks*, pp. 142–144. On Oregon, see James H. Gilbert, *Trade and Currency in Early Oregon* (New York: Columbia University Press, 1907), pp. 101–122.

[111]*Historical Statistics*, pp. 625, 648–649.

It is no wonder, then, that contrary to older historical opinion, many state banks were enthusiastic about the greenbacks, which provided them with legal tender that could function as a reserve base upon which they could expand. As Hammond puts it, "Instead of being curbed (as some people supposed later), the powers of the banks were augmented by the legal tender issues. As the issues increased, the deposits of the banks would increase."[112] Indeed, Sen. Sherman (R-Ohio) noted that the state banks favored greenbacks. And the principal author of the greenback legislation, Rep. Elbridge G. Spaulding (R-N.Y.), the chairman of the House Ways and Means subcommittee that introduced the bill, was himself a Buffalo banker.

The total money supply of the country (including gold coin, state bank notes, subsidiary silver, U.S. currency including fractional and greenbacks) amounted to $745.4 million in 1860. By 1863, the money supply had skyrocketed to $1.435 billion, an increase of 92.5 percent in three years, or 30.8 percent per annum. By the end of the war, the money supply, which now included national bank notes and deposits, totalled $1.773 billion, an increase in two years of 23.6 percent or 11.8 percent per year. Over the entire war, the money supply rose from $45.4 million to $1.773 billion, an increase of 137.9 percent, or 27.69 percent per annum.[113]

The response to this severe monetary inflation was a massive inflation of prices. It is no wonder that the greenbacks, depreciating rapidly in terms of gold, depreciated in terms of goods as well. Wholesale prices rose from 100 in 1860, to 210.9 at the end of the war, a rise of 110.9 percent or 22.2 percent per year.[114]

The Republican administration argued that their issue of greenbacks was required by stern wartime "necessity." The spuriousness of this argument is seen by the fact that greenbacks were virtually not issued after the middle of 1863. There were three alternatives to the issuance of legal tender fiat money. 1) The government could have issued paper

[112]Bray Hammond, *Sovereignty and an Empty Purse: Banks and Politics in the Civil War* (Princeton: Princeton University Press, 1970), pp. 246, 249–250. Also see North, "Greenback Dollars," pp. 143–148.

[113]*Historical Statistics*, pp. 625, 648–649. In a careful analysis North estimates the total money supply at approximately $2 billion, and also points out that counterfeit notes in the Civil War have been estimated to amount to no less than one-third of the total currency in circulation. North, "Greenback Dollars," p. 134. The counterfeiting estimates are in William P. Donlon, *United States Large Size Paper Money, 1861 to 1923*, 2nd ed. (Iola, Wis.: Krause, 1970), p. 15.

[114]Ralph Andreano, ed., *The Economic Impact of the American Civil War* (Cambridge, Mass: Schenckman, 1961), p. 178.

money but not made it legal tender; it would have depreciated even more rapidly. At any rate, they would have had quasi-legal tender status by being receivable in federal dues and taxes. 2) It could have increased taxes to pay for the war expenditures. 3) It could have issued bonds and other securities and sold the debt to banks and non-bank institutions. In fact, the government employed both the latter alternatives, and after 1863 stopped issuing greenbacks and relied on them exclusively, especially a rise in the public debt. The accumulated deficit piled up during the war was $2.614 billion, of which the printing of greenbacks only financed $431.7 million. Of the federal deficits during the war, greenbacks financed 22.8 percent in fiscal 1862, 48.5 percent in 1863, 6.3 percent in 1864, and none in 1865.[115] This is particularly striking if we consider that the peak deficit came in 1865, totalling $963.8 million. All the rest was financed by increased public debt. Taxes also increased greatly, revenues rising from $52 million in 1862 to $333.7 million in 1865. Tax revenues as a percentage of the budget rose from the miniscule 10.7 percent in fiscal 1862 to over 26 percent in 1864 and 1865.

It is clear, then, that the argument from "necessity" in the printing of greenbacks was specious, and indeed the greenback advocates conceded that it was perfectly possible to issue public debt, provided that the administration was willing to see the prices of its bonds rise and its interest payments rise considerably. At least for most of the war, they were not willing to take their chances in the competitive bond market.[116]

---

[115]The Confederacy, on the other hand, financed virtually all of its expenditures through mammoth printing of fiat paper, the Southern version of the greenback. Confederate notes, which were first issued in June 1861 to a sum of $1.1 million, skyrocketed until the total supply of confederate notes in January 1864 was no less than $826.8 million, an increase of 750.6 percent for three and a half years, or 214.5 percent per year. Bank notes and deposits in the Confederacy rose from $119.3 million to $268.1 million in this period, so that the total money supply rose from $120.4 million to $1.095 billion, or an increase of 1,060 percent—302.9 percent per year. Prices in the Eastern Confederacy rose from 100 in early 1861 to no less than over 4,000 in 1864, and 9,211 at the end of the war in April 1865. Thus, in four year, prices rose by 9,100 percent or an average of 2,275 percent per annum. See Eugene M. Lerner, "Inflation in the Confederacy, 1862–65," in M. Friedman, ed., *Studies in the Quantity Theory of Money* (Chicago: University of Chicago Press, 1956), pp. 163–175; Lerner, "Money, Prices and Wages in the Confederacy, 1861–65," in Andreano, *Economic Impact*, pp. 11–40.

[116]Mitchell, *History of the Greenbacks*, pp. 61–74; 119f., 128–131. Also see Don C. Barrett, *The Greenbacks and Resumption of Specie Payments, 1862–1879* (Cambridge: Harvard University Press, 1931), pp. 25–57.

The Public Debt and the National Banking System

The public debt of the Civil War brought into American financial history the important advent of one Jay Cooke. The Ohio-born Cooke had joined the moderately successful Philadelphia investment banking firm of Clark and Dodge as a clerk at the age of 18. In a few years, Cooke worked himself up to the status of junior partner, and, in 1857, he left the firm to branch out on his own in canal and railroad promotion and other business ventures. There he doubtless would have remained, except for the lucky fact that he and his brother Henry, editor of the leading Republican newspaper in Ohio, the *Ohio State Journal*, were close friends of U.S. Sen. Salmon P. Chase. Chase, a veteran leader of the anti-slavery movement, fought for and lost the Republican Presidential nomination in 1860 to Abraham Lincoln. At that point, the Cookes determined that they would feather their nest by lobbying to make Salmon Chase Secretary of the Treasury. After heavy lobbying by the Cookes, the Chase appointment was secured, so Jay Cooke quickly set up his own investment banking house of Jay Cooke & Co.

Everything was in place; it now remained to seize the opportunity. As the Cooke's father wrote of Henry: "I took up my pen principally to say that H.S.'s [Henry's] plan in getting Chase into the Cabinet and [John] Sherman into the Senate is accomplished, and that now is the time for making money, by honest contracts out of the government."[117]

Now indeed was their time for making money, and Cooke lost no time in doing so. It did not take much persuasion, including wining and dining, for Cooke to induce his friend Chase to take an unprecedented step in the fall of 1862: granting the House of Cooke a monopoly on the underwriting of the public debt. With enormous energy, Cooke hurled himself into the task of persuading the mass of public to buy U.S. government bonds. In doing so, Cooke perhaps invented the art of public relations and of mass propaganda; certainly, he did so in the realm of selling bonds. As Kirkland writes:

> With characteristic optimism, he [Cooke] flung himself into a bond crusade. He recruited a small army of 2,500 subagents among bankers, insurance men, and community leaders and kept them inspired and informed by mail and telegraph. He taught the American people to buy bonds, using lavish advertising in newspapers, broadsides, and

[117]In Henrietta Larson, *Jay Cooke, Private Banker* (Cambridge: Harvard University Press, 1936), p. 103. Also see Edward C. Kirkland, *Industry Comes of Age: Business, Labor and Public Policy, 1860–1897* (New York: Holt, Rinehart and Winston, 1961), p. 20.

posters. God, destiny, duty, courage, patriotism—all summoned "Farmers, Mechanics, and Capitalists" to invest in loans. . .[118]

—loans which of course they had to purchase from Jay Cooke.

And purchase the loans they did, for Cooke's bond sales soon reached the enormous figure of one to two million dollars a day. Perhaps $2 billion in bonds were bought and underwritten by Jay Cooke during the war. Cooke lost his monopoly in 1864, under pressure of rival bankers; but a year later he was reappointed to keep that highly lucrative post until the House of Cooke crashed in the Panic of 1873.

In the Civil War, Jay Cooke began as a moderately successful promoter; he emerged at war's end a millionaire, a man who had spawned the popular motto, "as rich as Jay Cooke." Surely he must have counted the $100,000 he had poured into Salmon Chase's political fortunes by 1864 one of the most lucrative investments he had ever made.

It is not surprising that Jay Cooke acquired enormous political influence in the Republican administration of the Civil War and after. Hugh McCulloch, Secretary of the Treasury from 1865 to 1869, was a close friend of Cooke's and when McCulloch left office he assumed the post of head of Cooke's London office. The Cooke brothers were also good friends of General Grant, so they wielded great influence during the Grant administration.

No sooner had Cooke secured the monopoly of government bond underwriting than he teamed up with his associates, Secretary of the Treasury Chase and Ohio's Senator John Sherman, to drive through a measure which was destined to have far more fateful effects than greenbacks on the American monetary system: the National Banking Acts. The National Banking Acts destroyed the previously decentralized and fairly successful state banking system, and substituted a new, centralized, and far more inflationary banking system under the aegis of Washington and a handful of Wall Street banks. Whereas the effects of the greenbacks were finally eliminated by the resumption of specie payments in 1879, the effects of the National Banking System are still with us. Not only was this system in place until 1913, but it paved the way for the Federal Reserve System by instituting a quasi-central banking type of monetary system. The "inner contradictions" of the National Banking System were such that the nation was driven either to go onward to a frankly central bank or else to scrap centralized banking altogether and go back to decentralized state banking. Given the inner

[118]Kirkland, *Industry*, pp. 20–21.

dynamic of state intervention to keep intensifying, coupled with the almost universal adoption of statist ideology after the turn of the 20th century, which course the nation would take was unfortunately inevitable.

Chase and Sherman drove the new system through under cover of war necessity, but it was designed to alter the banking system permanently. The wartime ground was to set up national banks, which were so structured as to necessarily purchase large amounts of U.S. government bonds. Patterned after the "free" banking systems, this tied in the nation's banks with the federal government and the public debt in a close symbiotic relationship. The Jacksonian embarrassment of the independent treasury was de facto swept away, and the Treasury would now keep its deposits in a new series of "pets": the national banks, chartered directly by the federal government. In this way, the Republican Party was able to use the wartime emergency to fulfill the Whig-Republican dream of a federally-controlled centralized banking system able to inflate the supply of money and credit in a uniform manner. Meshing with this was a profound political goal: As Sherman expressly pointed out, a vital object of the National Banking System was to eradicate the embarrassing doctrine of state's rights and to nationalize American politics.[119]

As established in the Bank Acts of 1863 and 1864, the National Banking System provided for the chartering of national banks by the Comptroller of the Currency in Washington, D.C. The banks were "free" in the sense that any institution meeting the requirements could obtain a charter, but the requirements were so high (from $50,000 for rural banks to $200,000 in the bigger cities) that small national banks were ruled out, particularly in the large cities.[120]

---

[119]In his important work on Northern intellectuals and the Civil War, George Frederickson discusses an influential article by one Samuel Fowler written at the end of the war: " 'The Civil War which has changed the current of our ideas, and crowded into a few years the emotions of a lifetime,' Fowler wrote, 'has in measure given to the preceding period of our history the character of a remote state of political existence.' Fowler described the way in which the war, a triumph of nationalism and a demonstration of 'the universal tendency to combination,' had provided the *coup de grace* for the Jefferson philosophy of government with its emphasis on decentralization and the protection of local and individual liberties." George Frederickson, *The Inner Civil War: Northern Intellectuals and the Crisis of the Union* (New York: Harper & Row, 1965), p. 184. Also see Merrill D. Peterson, *The Jeffersonian Image in the American Mind* (New York: Oxford University Press, 1960), pp. 217–218.

[120]For a particularly lucid exposition of the structure of the national banking system, see John J. Klein, *Money and the Economy*, 2nd ed. (New York: Harcourt, Brace and World, 1970), pp. 140–147.

The National Banking System created three sets of national banks: *central reserve city*, which was only New York; *reserve city*, other cities with over 500,000 population; and *country*, which included all other national banks.

Central reserve city banks were required to keep 25 percent of their notes and deposits in reserve of vault cash or "lawful money," which included gold, silver, and greenbacks. This provision incorporated the "reserve requirement" concept which had been a feature of the "free" banking system. Reserve city banks, on the other hand, were allowed to keep one-half of their required reserves in vault cash, while the other half could be kept as demand deposits (checking deposits) in central reserve city banks. Finally, country banks only had to keep a minimum reserve ratio of 15 percent to their notes and deposits; and only 40 percent of these reserves had to be in the form of vault cash. The other 60 percent of the country banks' reserves could be in the form of demand deposits either at the reserve city or central reserve city banks.

The upshot of this system was to replace the individualized structure of the pre-Civil War state banking system by an inverted pyramid of country banks expanding on top of reserve city banks, which in turn expanded on top of New York City banks. Before the Civil War, every bank had to keep its own specie reserves, and any pyramiding of notes and deposits on top of that was severely limited by calls for redemption in specie by other, competing banks as well as by the general public. But now, reserve city banks could keep half of their reserves as deposits in New York City banks, and country banks could keep most of theirs in one or the other, so that as a result, all the national banks in the country could pyramid in two layers on top of the relatively small base of reserves in the New York banks. And furthermore, those reserves could consist of inflated greenbacks as well as specie.

A simplified schematic diagram can portray the essence of this revolution in American banking:

Figure 1

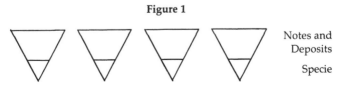

Notes and
Deposits

Specie

Figure 1 shows state banks in the decentralized system before the Civil War. Every bank must stand or fall on its bottom. It can pyramid notes and deposits on top of specie, but its room for such inflationary expansion is limited, because any bank's expansion will cause increased spending by its clients on the goods or services of other banks. Notes or checks on the expanding bank will go into the coffers of other banks, which will call on the expanding bank for redemption. This will put severe pressure on the expanding bank, which cannot redeem all of its liabilities as it is, and whose reserve ratio has declined, and so it will be forced to contract its loans and liabilities or else go under.

Figure 2

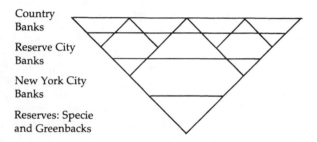

Country
Banks

Reserve City
Banks

New York City
Banks

Reserves: Specie
and Greenbacks

Figure 2 depicts the inverted pyramid of the National Banking System. New York City banks pyramid notes and deposits on top of specie and greenbacks; reserve city banks pyramid their notes and deposits on top of specie, greenbacks *and* deposits at New York City; and country banks pyramid on top of both. This means that, for example, if New York City banks inflate and expand their notes and deposits, they will not be checked by other banks calling upon them for redemption. Instead, reserve city banks will be able to expand their own loans and liabilities by pyramiding on top of their own increased deposits at New York banks. In turn, the country banks will be able to inflate their credit by pyramiding on top of their increased deposits at both reserve city and New York banks. The whole nation is able to inflate uniformly and relatively unchecked by pyramiding on top of a few New York City banks.

The national banks were not compelled to keep part of their reserves as deposits in larger banks, but they tended to do so—in the long run, so that they could expand uniformly on top of the larger banks, and in the short run because of the advantages of having a line of credit with a larger "correspondent" bank as well as earning interest on demand deposits at that bank.[121]

Let us illustrate in another way how the National Banking System pyramided by centralizing reserves. Let us consider the hypothetical balance sheets of the various banks.[122] Suppose that the country banks begin with $1 million in vault cash as their reserves. With the National Banking System in place, the country banks can now deposit three-fifths, or $600,000 of their cash in reserve city banks, in return for interest-paying demand deposits at those banks.

The balance-sheet changes are now as follows:

Country Banks

Assets		Liabilities + Equity
Reserves		
Vault cash	− $600,000	
Deposits at reserve city banks	+ $600,000	

Reserve City Banks

Assets		Liabilities + Equity
Reserves		
Vault cash	+ $600,000	Demand deposits due country banks + $600,000

Total reserves for the two sets of banks have not changed. But now because the country banks can use as their reserves deposits in reserve city banks, the same total reserves can now be used by the banks to expand far more of their credit. For now $400,000 in cash supports the same total of notes and deposits that the country banks had previously backed by $1 million, and the reserve city banks can now expand $2.4 million on top of the new $600,000 in cash—or rather, $1.8 million in addition to the $600,000 due to the city banks. In short, country bank

---

[121]Banks generally paid interest on demand deposits until the practice was outlawed in 1934.

[122]Adapted from Klein, *Money and the Economy*, pp. 144–145.

reserves have remained the same, but reserve city bank reserves have increased by $600,000, and they can engage in 4:1 pyramiding of credit on top of that.

But that is not all. For the reserve city banks can deposit half of their reserves at the New York banks. When they do that, the balance sheets of the respective banks change as follows:

Reserve City Banks

Assets		Liabilities + Equity	
Reserves			
Vault cash	+ $300,000		
Deposits at central reserve city banks	+ $300,000	Demand deposits due country banks	+ $600,000

Central Reserve City Banks

Assets		Liabilities + Equity	
Vault cash	+ $300,000	Demand deposits due reserve city banks	+ $300,000

Note that since the reserve city banks are allowed to keep half of their reserves in the central reserve city banks, the former can still pyramid $2.4 million on top of their new $600,000, and yet deposit $300,000 in cash at the New York banks. The latter, then, can expand another 4:1 on top of the new cash of $300,000, or increase their total notes and deposits to $1.2 million.

In short, not only did the national banking system allow pyramiding of the entire banking structure on top of a few large Wall Street banks, the very initiating of the system allowed a multiple expansion of all bank liabilities by centralizing a large part of the nation's cash reserves from the individual state banks into the hands of the larger, and especially the New York, banks. For the expansion of $1.2 million on top of the new $300,000 at New York banks served to expand the liabilities going to the smaller banks, which in turn could pyramid on top of their increased deposits. But even without that further expansion, $1 million which, we will assume, originally supported $6 million in notes and deposits, will now support, in addition to that $6 million, $2.4 million issued by the reserve city banks, and $1.2 million by the New York banks—to say nothing of further expansion by the latter two sets of banks which will allow country banks to pyramid more liabilities.

In June 1874, the fundamental structure of the National Banking System was changed when Congress, as part of an inflationist move after the Panic of 1873, eliminated all reserve requirements on notes, keeping them only on deposits. This released over $20 million of lawful money from bank reserves, and allowed a further pyramiding of demand liabilities.[123] In the long run, it severed the treatment of notes from deposits, with notes tied rigidly to bank holdings of government debt, and demand deposits pyramiding on top of reserve ratios in specie and greenbacks.

But this centralized inverse pyramiding of bank credit was not all. For, in a way modeled by the "free" banking system, every national bank's expansion of notes was tied intimately to its ownership of U.S. government bonds. Every bank could only issue notes if it deposited an equivalent of U.S. securities as collateral at the U.S. Treasury,[124] so that national banks could only expand their notes to the extent that they purchased U.S. government bonds. This provision tied the National Banking System intimately to the federal government, and more particularly, to its expansion of public debt. The federal government had an assured, built-in market for its debt, and the more the banks purchased that debt, the more the banking system could inflate. Monetizing the public debt was not only inflationary per se, it provided the basis—when done by the larger city banks—of other banks pyramiding on top of their own monetary expansion.

The tie-in and the pyramiding process were cemented by several other provisions. Every national bank was obliged to redeem the obligations of every other national bank at par. Thus, the severe market limitation on the circulation of inflated notes and deposits—depreciation as the distance from the bank increases—was abolished. And while the federal government could not exactly make the notes of a private bank legal tender, it conferred quasi-legal tender status on every national bank by agreeing to receive all its notes and deposits at par for dues and taxes.[125] It is interesting and even heartening to discover that

[123]See Hepburn, *History of Currency*, pp. 317–318.

[124]Originally, national banks could only issue notes to the value 90 percent of their U.S. government bonds. This limitation was changed to 100 percent in 1900.

[125]Except, of course, as we have seen with the greenbacks, for payment of customs duties, which had to be paid in gold, to build up a fund to pay interest on the government debt in gold.

despite these enormous advantages conferred by the federal government, national bank notes fell below par with greenbacks in the financial crisis of 1867, and a number of national banks failed the next year.[126]

Genuine redeemability, furthermore, was made very difficult under the National Banking System. Laxity was insured by the fact that national banks were required to redeem the notes and deposits of every other national bank at par, and yet it was made difficult for them to actually redeem those liabilities in specie; for one of the problems with the pre-Civil War state banking system is that interstate or even intrastate branches were illegal, thereby hobbling the clearing system for swiftly redeeming another bank's notes and deposits. One might think that a national banking system would at least eliminate this problem, but on the contrary, branch banking continued to be prohibited, and interstate branch banking is illegal to this day. A bank would only have to redeem its notes at its own counter in its home office. Furthermore, the redemption of notes was crippled by the fact that the federal government imposed a maximum limit of $3 million a month by which national bank notes could be contracted.[127]

Reserve requirements are now considered a sound and precise way to limit bank credit expansion, but the precision can work two ways. Just as government safety codes can *decrease* safety by setting a lower limit for safety measures and inducing private firms to reduce safety *downward* to that common level, so reserve requirements can and ordinarily do serve as lowest common denominators for bank reserve ratios. Free competition can and generally will result in banks voluntarily keeping higher reserve ratios. But a uniform legal requirement will tend to push all the banks down to that minimum ratio. And indeed we can see this now in the universal propensity of all banks to be "fully loaned up," that is, to expand as much as is legally possible up to the limits imposed by the legal reserve ratio. Reserve requirements of less than 100 percent are more an inflationary than a restrictive monetary device.

The National Banking System was intended to replace the state banks, but many state banks continued aloof and refused to join, despite the special privileges accorded to the national banks. The reserve and capital requirements were more onerous, and at that period, national banks were prohibited from making loans on real estate. With the state banks refusing to come to heel voluntarily, Congress, in March 1865,

[126]See Smith, *Rationale*, p. 48.
[127]See Smith, *Rationale*, p. 132.

completed the Civil War revolution of the banking system by placing a prohibitive 10 percent tax on all bank notes—which had the desired effect of virtually outlawing all note issues by the state banks. From 1865 on, the national banks had a legal monopoly on the issue of bank notes.

At first, the state banks contracted and disappeared under the shock, and it looked as if the United States would only have national banks. The number of state banks fell from 1,466 in 1863 to 297 in 1866, and total notes and deposits in state banks fell from $733 million in 1863 to only $101 million in 1866. After several years, however, the state banks readily took their place as an expanding element in the banking system, albeit subordinated to the national banks. In order to survive, the state banks had to keep deposit accounts at national banks, from whom they could "buy" national bank notes in order to redeem their deposits. In short, the state banks now became the fourth layer of the national pyramid of money and credit, on top of the country and other banks, for the reserves of the state banks became, in addition to vault cash, demand deposits at national banks, which they could redeem in cash. The multi-layered structure of bank inflation under the National Banking System was intensified.

In this new structure, the state banks began to flourish. By 1873, the total number of state banks had increased to 1,330, and their total deposits were $789 million.[128]

The Cooke-Chase connection with the new National Banking System was simple. As Secretary of the Treasury, Chase wanted an assured market for the government bonds that were being issued so heavily during the Civil War. And as the monopoly underwriter of U.S. government bonds for every year except one from 1862 to 1873, Jay Cooke was even more directly interested in an assured and expanding market for his bonds. What better method of obtaining such a market than creating an entirely new banking system, the expansion of which was directly tied to the banks' purchase of government bonds—from Jay Cooke?

The Cooke brothers played a major role in driving the National Banking Act of 1863 through a reluctant Congress. The Democrats, devoted to hard-money, opposed the legislation almost to a man. Only a majority of Republicans could be induced to agree on the bill. After John Sherman's decisive speech in the Senate for the measure, Henry Cooke—now head of the Washington Office of the House of Cooke—

---

[128]*Historical Statistics*, pp. 628–629.

wrote jubilantly to his brother: "It will be a great triumph, Jay, and one to which we have contributed more than any other living man. The bank had been repudiated by the House, and was without a sponsor in the Senate, and was thus virtually dead and buried when I induced Sherman to take hold of it, and we went to work with the newspapers."[129]

Going to work with the newspapers meant something more than mere persuasion for the Cooke brothers; as monopoly underwriter of government bonds, Cooke was paying the newspapers large sums for advertising, and so the Cookes thought—as it turned out correctly—that they could induce the newspapers to grant them an enormous amount of free space "in which to set forth the merits of the new national banking system." Such space meant not only publicity and articles, but even more important, the fervent editorial support of most of the nation's press. And so the press, implicitly bought for the occasion, kept up a drumfire of propaganda for the new National Banking System. As Cooke himself related: "For six weeks or more nearly all the newspapers in the country were filled with our editorials [written by the Cooke brothers] condemning the state bank system and explaining the great benefits to be derived from the national banking system now proposed." And every day the indefatigable Cookes put on the desks of every Congressman the relevant editorials from newspapers in their respective districts.[130]

While many state bankers, especially the conservative old-line New York bankers, opposed the National Banking System, Jay Cooke, once the system was in place, plunged in with a will. Not only did he sell the national banks their required bonds, he also set up new national banks which would have to buy his government securities. His agents formed national banks in the smaller towns of the South and West. Furthermore, he set up his own two large national banks, the First National Bank of Philadelphia and the First National Bank of Washington, D.C.

But the National Banking System was in great need of a mighty bank in New York City to serve as the base of the inflationary pyramid for a host of country and reserve city banks. Shortly after the inception of the system, three national banks had been organized in New York, but none of them was large or prestigious enough to serve as the key

---

[129]Quoted in Robert P. Sharkey, *Money, Class and Party: An Economic Study of Civil War and Reconstruction* (Baltimore: Johns Hopkins Press, 1959), p. 245.

[130]See Hammond, *Sovereignty*, pp. 289–290.

fulcrum of the new banking structure. Jay Cooke, however, was happy to oblige, and he quickly established the Fourth National Bank of New York, capitalized at a huge $5 million. After the war, Jay Cooke favored resumption of specie payments, but only if greenbacks could be replaced one-to-one by new national bank notes. In his unbounded enthusiasm for national bank notes and their dependence on the federal debt, Cooke urged repeal of the $300 million legal limit on national bank note issue. In 1865, he published a pamphlet proclaiming that in less than 20 years national bank note circulation would total $1 billion.[131]

The title of the pamphlet Cooke published is revealing: *How Our National Debt May Be A National Blessing. The Debt is Public Wealth, Political Union, Protection of Industry, Secure Basis for National Currency.*[132]

By 1866, it was clear that the National Banking System had replaced the state as the center of the monetary system of the United States. Only a year earlier, in 1865, state bank notes had totaled $142.9 million; by 1866 they had collapsed to $20 million. On the other hand, national bank notes grew from a mere $31.2 million in 1864, their first year of existence, to $276 million in 1866. And while, as we have seen, the number of state banks in existence was falling drastically from 1,466 to 297, the number of national banks grew from 66 in 1863 to 1,634 three years later.

The Post-Civil War Era: 1865-1879

The United States ended the war with a depreciated inconvertible greenback currency, and a heavy burden of public debt. The first question on the monetary agenda was what to do about the greenbacks. A powerful group of industrialists calling for continuation of greenbacks, opposing resumption and, of course, any contraction of money to prepare for specie resumption, was headed by the Pennsylvania iron and steel manufacturers. The Pennsylvania ironmasters, who had been in the forefront of the organized protective tariff movement since its beginnings in 1820,[133] were led here and instructed by their intellectual mentor—himself a Pennsylvania ironmaster—the elderly economist Henry C. Carey. Carey and his fellow iron manufacturers realized that

---

[131]Actually, Cooke erred, and national bank notes never reached that total. Instead, it was demand deposits that expanded, and reached the billion-dollar mark by 1879.

[132]See Sharkey, *Money, Class, and Party*, p. 247.

[133]The leader of the protectionists in Congress in 1820 was Rep. Henry Baldwin, a leading iron manufacturer from Pittsburgh. Rothbard, *Panic of 1819*, pp. 164ff.

during an inflation, since the foreign exchange market anticipates further inflation, domestic currency tends to depreciate faster than domestic prices are rising. A falling dollar and rising price of gold, they realized, make domestic prices cheaper and imported prices higher, and hence functions as a surrogate tariff. A cheap money, inflationist policy, then, could not only provide easy credit for manufacturing, it could also function as an extra tariff because of the depreciation of the dollar and the rise in the gold premium.

Imbibers of the Carey gospel of high tariffs and soft money were a host of attendees at the famous "Carey Vespers"—evenings of discussion of economics and politics. Influential Carey disciples included economist and Pennsylvania ironmaster Stephen Colwell; Eber Ward, president of the Iron and Steel Association; John A. Williams, editor of the Association's journal *Iron Age;* Rep. Daniel Morrell, Pennsylvania iron manufacturer; I. Smith Homans, Jr., editor of the *Bankers' Magazine;* and the powerful Rep. William D. Kelley of Pennsylvania, whose lifelong devotion to the interest of the ironmasters earned him the proud sobriquet of "Old Pig Iron." The Carey circle also dominated the American Industrial League and its successor, the Pennsylvania Industrial League, which spread the Carey doctrines of protection and paper money. Influential allies in Congress, if not precisely Carey followers, were the radical leader Rep. Thaddeus Stevens, himself a Pennsylvania ironmaster, and Rep. John A. Griswold, an ironmaster from New York.

Also sympathetic to greenbacks were many manufacturers who desired cheap credit, gold speculators who were betting on higher gold prices, and railroads, who as heavy debtors to their bondholders, realized that inflation benefits debtors by cheapening the dollar whereas it also tends to expropriate creditors by the same token. One of the influential Carey disciples, for example, was the leading railroad promoter, the Pennsylvanian Thomas A. Scott, leading entrepreneur of the Pennsylvania and Texas & Pacific Railroads.[134]

[134]On the Carey circle and its influence, see Irwin Unger, *The Greenback Era: A Social and Political History of American Finance, 1865–1879* (Princeton: Princeton University Press, 1964), pp. 53–59; and Joseph Dorfman, *The Economic Mind in American Civilization, Vol. III, 1864–1918* (New York: Viking Press, 1949), pp. 7–8. Dorfman notes that Kelley dedicated his collected *Speeches, Addresses and Letters* of 1872 to "The Great Master of Economic Science, the Profound Thinker, and the Careful Observer of Social Phenomena, My Venerable Friend and Teacher, Henry C. Carey." Ibid., p. 8. On the link between high tariffs and greenbacks for the Pennsylvania ironmasters, see Sharkey, *Money, Class and Party,* chap. 4.

One of the most flamboyant advocates of greenback inflation in the post-war era was the Wall Street stock speculator Richard Schell. In 1874, Schell became a member of Congress, where he proposed an outrageous pre-Keynesian scheme in the spirit of Keynes' later dictum that so long as money is *spent*, it doesn't matter what the money is spent on, be it pyramid-building or digging holes in the ground.[135] Schell seriously urged the federal government to dig a canal from New York to San Francisco, financed wholly by the issue of greenbacks. Schell's enthusiasm was perhaps matched only by the notorious railroad speculator and economic adventurer George Francis Train, who called repeatedly for immense issues of greenbacks. "Give us greenbacks we say," Train thundered in 1867, "and build cities, plant corn, open coal mines, control railways, launch ships, grow cotton, establish factories, open gold and silver mines, erect rolling mills. . . .Carry my resolution and there is sunshine in the sky."[136]

The Panic of 1873 was a severe blow to many overbuilt railroads, and it was railroad men who led in calling for more greenbacks to stem the tide. Thomas Scott, Collis P. Huntington, leader of the Central Pacific Railroad, Russel Sage, and other railroad men joined in the call for greenbacks. So strong was their influence that the *Louisville Courier-Journal*, in April 1874, declared: "The strongest influence at work in Washington upon the currency proceeded from the railroads. . . .The great inflationists after all, are the great trunk railroads."[137]

The greenback problem after the Civil War was greatly complicated by the massive public debt that lay over the heads of the American people. A federal debt, which had tallied only $64.7 million in 1860, amounted to the huge amount of $2.32 billion in 1866. Many ex-Jacksonian Democrats, led by Sen. George H. Pendleton of Ohio, began to agitate for further issue of greenbacks *solely* for the purpose of redeeming the principal of federal debts contracted in greenbacks during the war.[138] In a sense, then, hard-money hostility to both inflation and the public debt were now at odds. In a sense, the Pendletonians were

---

[135]Thus, Keynes wrote: " 'To dig holes in the ground,' paid for out of savings will increase, not only employment, but the real national dividend of useful goods and services." John Maynard Keynes, *The General Theory of Employment Interest and Money* (New York: Harcourt, Brace, 1936), p. 220. On pyramid-building, see ibid., pp. 220 and 131.

[136]Unger, *Greenback Era*), pp. 45–48.

[137]Ibid., p. 222.

[138]The federal government had contracted to redeem the *interest* on the wartime public debt in gold, but nothing was contracted about the repayment of the principal.

motivated by a sense of poetic justice, of paying inflated debts in inflated paper, but in doing so they lost sight of the broader hard money goal.[139] This program confused the party struggles of the post-Civil War period, but ultimately it is safe to say that the Democrats had a far greater proportion of congressmen devoted to hard money and to resumption than did the Republicans. Thus, Secretary of the Treasury Hugh McCulloch's "Loan Bill" of March 1866, which provided for contraction of greenbacks in preparation for resumption of specie payments, was passed in the House by a Republican vote of 56-52, and a Democratic vote of 27-1. And in April 1874, the "Inflation Bill," admittedly vetoed later by President Grant, which provided for expansion of greenbacks and of national bank notes, was passed in the House by a Republican vote of 105 to 64, while the Democrats voted against by the narrow margin of 35 to 37.[140]

In the meantime, despite repeated resolutions for resumption of specie payments in 1865 and 1869, the dominant Republican Party continued to do nothing for actual resumption. The Pendleton Plan was adopted by the Democrats in their 1868 platform, and the Republican victory in the presidential race that year was generally taken as a conclusive defeat for that idea. Finally, however, the Democratic sweep in the congressional elections of 1874 forced the Republicans into a semblance of unity on monetary matters, and, in the lame-duck congressional session led by Sen. John Sherman, they came up with the Resumption Act of January 1875.

Despite the fact that the Resumption Act ultimately resulted in specie resumption, it was not considered a hard-money victory by contemporaries. Sherman had forged a compromise between hard and soft money forces. It is true that the U.S. government was supposed to buy gold with government bonds to prepare for resumption on January 1, 1879. But this resumption was four years off, and Congress had expressed intent to resume several times before. And in the meantime, the soft-money men were appeased by the fact that the bill immediately eliminated the $300 million limit on national bank notes, in a provision known as "free banking." The only hard-money compensation was an 80 percent pro-rata contraction of greenbacks to partially offset any new

[139]Similar motivations had impelled many hard-money anti-Federalists during the 1780s to advocate the issue of state paper money for the *sole* purpose of redeeming swollen wartime public debts.

[140]On the McCulloch Loan Bill, see Sharkey, *Money, Class, and Party*, p. 75; on the Inflation Bill, see Unger, *Greenback Era*, p. 410.

national bank notes.[141] The bulk of the opposition to the Resumption Act was by hard-money congressmen, who, in addition to pointing out its biased ambiguities, charged that the contracted greenbacks could be reissued instead of retired. Hard-money forces throughout the country had an equally scornful view of the Resumption Act. In a few years, however, they rallied as resumption drew near.

That the Republicans were generally less than enthusiastic about specie resumption was revealed by the Grant administration's reaction to the Supreme Court's decision in the first legal tender case. After the end of the war, the question of the constitutionality of legal tender came before the courts (we have seen that the California and Oregon courts decided irredeemable paper to be unconstitutional). In the large number of state court decisions on greenbacks before 1870, every Republican judge but one upheld their constitutionality, whereas every Democratic judge but two declared them unconstitutional.[142]

The greenback question reached the U.S. Supreme Court in 1867, and was decided in February 1870, in the case of *Hepburn* v. *Griswold*. The Court held, by a vote of 5 to 3, with all the Democratic judges voting with the majority and the Republicans in the minority. Chief Justice Salmon P. Chase, who delivered the decision denouncing his own action as Secretary of the Treasury as unnecessary and unconstitutional, had swung back to the Democratic Party and had actually been a candidate for the presidential nomination at the 1868 convention.

The Grant administration was upset by *Hepburn* v. *Griswold*, as were the railroads, who had accumulated a heavy long-term debt, which would now be payable in more valuable gold. As luck would have it, however, there were two vacancies on the Court, one of which was created by the retirement of one of the majority judges. Grant appointed not only two Republican judges, but two railroad lawyers whose views on the subject were already known.[143] The new 5-4 majority dutifully

[141]This political and compromise interpretation of the Resumption Act successfully revises the previous hard-money view of this measure. See Unger, *Greenback Era*, pp. 249–263.

[142]See Charles Fairman, "Mr. Justice Bradley's Appointment to the Supreme Court and the Legal Tender Cases," *Harvard Law Review* (May 1941), p. 1131; cited in Unger, *Greenback Era*, p. 174.

[143]The first new justice, William Strong of Pennsylvania, had been a top attorney for the Philadelphia and Reading Railroad, and a director of the Lebanon Valley Railroad. The second jurist, Joseph P. Bradley, was a director of the Camden and Amboy Railroad and of the Morris and Essex Railroad, in New Jersey. On the railroad ties of Strong and Bradley, see Philip H. Burch, Jr., *Elites in American History, Vol. II, The Civil War to the New*

and quickly reconsidered the question, and, in May 1871, reversed the previous Court in the fateful decision of *Knox* v. *Lee*. From then on, paper money would be held consonant with the U.S. Constitution.

The National Banking System was ensconced after the Civil War. The number of banks, national bank notes, and deposits all pyramided upward, and after 1870 state banks began to boom as deposit-creating institutions. With lower requirements and fewer restrictions than the national banks, they could pyramid on top of national banks. The number of national banks increased from 1,294 in 1865 to 1,968 in 1873, while the number of state banks rose from 349 to 1,330 in the same period. Total state and national bank notes and deposits rose from $835 million in 1865 to $1.964 billion in 1873, an increase of 135.2 percent or an increase of 16.9 percent per year. The following year, the supply of bank money leveled off as the Panic of 1873 struck and caused numerous bankruptcies.

As a general overview of the national banking period, we can agree with Klein that "The financial panics of 1873, 1884, 1893, and 1907 were in large part an outgrowth of. . .reserve pyramiding and excessive deposit creation by reserve city and central reserve city banks. These panics were triggered by the currency drains that took place in periods of relative prosperity when banks were loaned up."[144] And yet it must be pointed out that the total money supply, even merely the supply of bank money, did not decrease after the Panic, but merely leveled off.

Orthodox economic historians have long complained about the "Great Depression" that is supposed to have struck the United States in the Panic of 1873 and lasted for an unprecedented six years in 1879. Much of this stagnation is supposed to have been caused by a monetary contraction leading to the resumption of specie payments in 1879. Yet what sort of "depression" is it which saw an extraordinarily large expansion of industry, of railroads, of physical output, of net national product, or real per capita income? As Friedman and Schwartz admit, the decade 1869 to 1879 saw a 3.0 percent per annum increase in money national product, an outstanding real national product growth of 6.8 percent per year in this period, and a phenomenal rise of 4.5 percent per year in real product per capita. Even the alleged "monetary con-

---

Deal (New York: Holmes & Meier, 1981), pp. 44–45. On the reaction of the Grant administration, see Unger, *Greenback Era*, pp. 172–178. For a legal analysis of the decisions, see Hepburn, *History of Currency*, pp. 254–264; and Henry Mark Holzer, ed., *Government's Money Monopoly* (New York: Books in Focus, 1981), pp. 99–168.

[144]Klein, *Money and the Economy*, pp. 145–146.

traction" never took place, the money supply increasing by 2.7 percent per year in this period. From 1873–1878, before another spurt of monetary expansion, the total supply of bank money *rose* from $1.964 billion to $2.221 billion—a rise of 13.1 percent or 2.6 percent per year. In short, a modest but definite rise, and scarcely a *contraction.*

It should be clear, then, that the Great Depression of the 1870s is merely a myth—a myth brought about by the misinterpretation of the fact that prices in general fell sharply during the entire period. Indeed they fell from the end of the Civil War until 1879. Friedman and Schwartz estimated that prices in general fell from 1869 to 1879 by 3.8 percent per annum. Unfortunately, most historians and economists are conditioned to believe that steadily and sharply falling prices *must* result in depression: hence their amazement at the obvious prosperity and economic growth during this era. For they have overlooked the fact that in the natural course of events, when government and the banking system do not increase the money supply very rapidly, free-market capitalism will result in an increase of production and economic growth so great as to swamp the increase of money supply. Prices will fall, and the consequences will be not depression or stagnation, but prosperity (since costs are falling, too) economic growth, and the spread of the increased living standard to all the consumers.[145]

Indeed, recent research has discovered that the analogous "Great Depression" in England in this period was also a myth, and due to a confusion between a contraction of prices and its alleged inevitable effect on a depression of prices and its alleged inevitable effect on a depression of business activity.[146]

It might well be that the major effect of the Panic of 1873 was, not to initiate a Great Depression, but to cause bankruptcies in overinflated banks and in railroads riding on the tide of vast government subsidy and bank speculation. In particular, we may note Jay Cooke, one of the creators of the National Banking System and paladin of the public debt. In 1866, he favored contraction of the greenbacks and early resumption because he feared that inflation would destroy the value of government bonds. By the late 1860s, however, the House of Cooke was expanding everywhere, and in particular, had gotten control of

[145]For the bemusement of Friedman and Schwartz, see Milton Friedman and Anna Jacobson Schwartz, *A Monetary History of the United States, 1867–1960* (New York: National Bureau of Economic Research, 1963), pp. 33–44. On totals of bank money, see *Historical Statistics,* pp. 624–625.

[146]S.B. Saul, *The Myth of the Great Depression, 1873–1896* (London: Macmillan, 1969).

the new Northern Pacific Railroad. Northern Pacific had been the recipient of the biggest federal largesse to railroads during the 1860s: a land grant of no less than 47 million acres.

Cooke sold Northern Pacific bonds as he had learned to sell government securities: hiring pamphleteers to write propaganda about the alleged Mediterranean climate of the Northwest. Many leading government officials and politicians were on the Cooke/Northern Pacific payroll, including President Grant's private secretary, Gen. Horace Porter.

In 1869, Cooke expressed his monetary philosophy in keeping with his enlarged sphere of activity: "Why," he asked, "should this Grand and Glorious Country be stunted and dwarfed—its activities chilled and its very life blood curdled by these miserable 'hard coin' theories—the musty theories of a bygone age—These men who are urging on premature resumption know nothing of the great and growing west which would grow twice as fast if it was not cramped for the means necessary to build railroads and improve farms and convey the produce to market." But in 1873, a remarkable example of poetic justice struck Jay Cooke. The overbuilt Northern Pacific was crumbling, and a Cooke government bond operation provided a failure. So the mighty House of Cooke—"stunted and dwarfed" by the market economy—crashed and went bankrupt, touching off the Panic of 1873.[147]

After passing the Resumption Act in 1875, the Republicans finally stumbled their way into resumption in 1879, fully 14 years after the end of the Civil War. The money supply did not contract in the late 1870s because the Republicans did not have the will to contract in order to pave the way for resumption. Resumption was finally achieved after substantial sales of U.S. bonds for gold in Europe by Secretary of the Treasury Sherman.

Return to the gold standard in 1879 was almost blocked, in the last three years before resumption, by the emergence of a tremendous agitation, heavily in the West but also throughout the country, for the free coinage of silver. The United States mint ratios had been undervaluing silver since 1834, and in 1853 de facto gold monometallism was established because silver was so far undervalued as to drive fractional silver coins out of the country. Since 1853, the United States, while de jure on a bimetallic standard at 16:1, with the silver dollar still technically in circulation though nonexistent, was actually on a gold mono-

[147]Unger, *Greenback Era*, pp. 46–47, 221.

metallic standard with lightweight subsidiary silver coins for fractional use.

In 1872, it became apparent to a few knowledgeable men at the U.S. Treasury that silver, which had held at about 15.5 to 1 since the early 1860s, was about to suffer a huge decline in value. The major reason was the realization that European nations were shifting from a silver to a gold standard, thereby decreasing their demand for silver. A subsidiary reason was the discovery of silver mines in Nevada and other states in the West. Working rapidly, these Treasury men, along with Sen. Sherman, slipped through Congress in February 1873 a seemingly innocuous bill which in effect discontinued the minting of any further silver dollars. This was followed by an act of June 1874, which completed the demonetization of silver by ending the legal tender quality of all silver dollars above the sum of $5. The timing was perfect, since it was in 1874 that the market value of silver fell to greater than 16:1 to gold for the first time. From then on, the market price of silver fell steadily, declining to nearly 18:1 in 1876, over 18:1 in 1879, and reaching the phenomenal level of 32:1 in 1894.

In short, after 1874 silver was no longer undervalued but overvalued, and increasingly so, in terms of gold, at 16:1. Except for the acts of 1873 and 1874, labeled by the pro-silver forces as "The Crime of 1873," silver would have flowed into the United States, and the country would have been once again on a de facto monometallic silver standard. The champions of greenbacks, the champions of inflation, saw a "hard-money" way to increase greatly the amount of American currency: the remonetization of a flood of new overvalued silver. The agitation was to remonetize silver by "the free and unlimited coinage of silver at 16 to 1."

It should be recognized that the silverites had a case. The demonetization of silver was a "crime" in the sense that it was done shiftily, deceptively, by men who knew that they wanted to demonetize silver before it was too late and have silver replace gold. The case for gold over silver was a strong one, particularly in an era of rapidly falling value of silver, but it should have been made openly and honestly. The furtive method of demonetizing silver, the "crime against silver," was in part responsible for the vehemence of the silver agitation for the remainder of the century.[148]

[148]For the best discussion of the crime against silver, see Allen Weinstein, *Prelude to Populism: Origins of the Silver Issue, 1867–1878* (New Haven: Yale University Press, 1970), pp. 8–32. Also see Paul M. O'Leary, "The Scene of the Crime of 1873 Revisited: A Note," *Journal of Political Economy* 68 (1960): 388–392.

Ultimately, the administration was able to secure the resumption of payments in gold, but at the expense of submitting to the Bland-Allison Act of 1878, which mandated that the Treasury purchase $2-$4 million of silver per month from then on.

It should be noted that this first silver agitation of the late 1870s, at least, cannot be considered an "agrarian" or a particularly Southern and Western movement. The silver agitation was broadly based throughout the nation, except in New England, and was, moreover, an urban movement. As Weinstein points out:

> Silver began as an urban movement, furthermore, not an agrarian crusade. Its original strongholds were the large towns and cities of the Midwest and middle Atlantic states, not the country's farming communities. The first batch of bimetallist leaders were a loosely knit collection of hard money newspaper editors, businessmen, academic reformers, bankers, and commercial groups.[149]

With the passage of the Silver Purchase Act of 1878, silver agitation died out in America, to spring out again in the 1890s.

The Gold Standard Era with the National Banking System, 1879-1913

The record of 1879-1896 is very similar to the first stage of the alleged Great Depression from 1873 to 1879. Once again, we have a phenomenal expansion of American industry, production, and real output per head. Real reproducible, tangible wealth per capita rose at the decadel peak in American history in the 1880s, at 3.8 percent per annum. Real net national product rose at the rate of 3.7 percent per year from 1879 to 1897, while per capita net national product increased by 1.5 percent per year.

Once again, orthodox economic historians are bewildered, for there should have been a Great Depression, since prices fell at a rate of over 1 percent per year in this period. Just as in the previous period, the money supply grew, but not fast enough to overcome the great increase in productivity and the supply of products. The major difference in the two periods is that money supply rose more rapidly from 1879-1897, by 6 percent per year, compared with the 2.7 percent per year in the earlier era. As a result, prices fell by less, by over 1 percent per annum as contrasted to 3.8 percent. Total bank money, notes and deposits, rose from $2.45 billion to $6.06 billion in this period, a rise of 10.45

---

[149]Weinstein, *Prelude to Populism*, p. 356.

percent per annum—surely enough to satisfy all but the most ardent inflationists.[150]

For those who persist in associating a gold standard with deflation, it should be pointed out that price deflation in the gold standard 1879-1897 period was considerably less than price deflation from 1873 to 1879, when the United States was still on a fiat greenback standard.

After specie resumption occurred successfully in 1879, the gold premium to greenbacks fell to par and the appreciated greenback promoted confidence in the gold-backed dollar. More foreigners willing to hold dollars meant an inflow of gold into the United States and greater American exports. Some historians have attributed the boom of 1879-1882, culminating in a financial crisis in the latter year, to the inflow of gold coin in the U.S., which rose from $110.5 million in 1879 to $358.3 million in 1882.[151] In a sense this is true, but the boom would never have taken on considerable proportions without the pyramiding of the national banking system, the deposits of which increased from $2.149 billion in 1879 to $2.777 billion in 1882, a rise of 29.2 percent, or 9.7 percent per annum. Wholesale prices were driven up from 90 in 1879 to 108 three years later, a 22.5 percent increase, before resuming their long-run downward path.

A financial panic in 1884, coming during a mild contraction after 1882, lowered the supply of bank money in 1884. Total bank notes and deposits dropped slightly, from $3.19 billion in 1883 to $3.15 billion the following year. The panic was triggered by an overflow of gold abroad, as foreigners began to lose confidence in the willingness of the United States to remain on the gold standard. This understandable loss of confidence resulted from the inflationary sop to the pro-silver forces in the Bland-Allison Silver Purchase Act of 1878. The shift in Treasury balances from gold to silver struck a disquieting note in foreign financial circles.[152]

Before examining the critical decade of the 1890s, it is well to point out in some detail the excellent record of the first decade after the return to gold, 1879-1889.

America went off the gold standard in 1861 and remained off after the war's end. Arguments between hard-money advocates who wanted to eliminate unbacked greenbacks and soft-money men who wanted

[150]Friedman and Schwartz, *Monetary History*, pp. 91–93; *Historical Statistics*, p. 625.

[151]Friedman and Schwartz, *Monetary History*, pp. 98–99.

[152]See Rendigs Fels, *American Business Cycle, 1865–1897* (Chapel Hill, N.C.: University of North Carolina Press, 1959), pp. 130–131.

to increase them raged through the 1870s until the Grant administration decided in 1875 to resume redemption of paper dollars into gold at pre-war value on the first day of 1879. At the time (1875) greenbacks were trading at a discount of roughly 17 percent against the pre-war gold dollar. A combination of outright paper-money deflation and increase in official gold holdings enabled a return to gold four years later, which set the scene for a decade of tremendous economic growth.

Economic recordkeeping a century ago was not nearly as well developed as today, but a clear picture comes through nonetheless. The *Encyclopedia of American Economic History* calls the period under review "one of the most expansive in American history. Capital investment was high;. . .there was little unemployment; and the real costs of production declined rapidly."

Prices, Wages, and Real Wages

This is shown most graphically with a look at wages and prices during the decade before and after convertibility. While prices fell during the 1870s and 1880s, wages fell only during the greenback period, and rose from 1879 to 1889.

Wholesale Price Index

(1910-1914 = 100)

Year	Index	% change
1869	151	——
1879	90	−40.4%
1889	81	−10.0%

Consumer Price Index

1869	138	——
1879	97	−28.8%
1889	93	− 4.2%

Wages

(1900-1914 = 100)

	Urban Labor	Farm Labor	Combined
1869	77	96	87
1879	61	61	61
1889	72	78	75

These figures tell a remarkable story. Both consumer prices and nominal wages fell about 30 percent during the last decade of greenbacks. But from 1879-1889, while prices kept falling, wages rose 23 percent. So real wages, after taking inflation—or the lack of it—into effect, soared.

No decade before or since produced such a sustainable rise in real wages. Two possible exceptions are the period from 1909-1919 (when the index rose from 99 to 140) and 1929-1939 (134-194). But during the first decade real wages plummeted the next year—to 129 in 1920, and did not reach 1919's level until 1934. And during the 1930s real wages also soared, for those fortunate enough to have jobs.

In any event, the contrast to this past decade is astonishing. And while there are many reasons why real wages increase, three necessary conditions must be present. Foremost, an absence of sustained inflation. This contributes to the second condition, a rise in savings and capital formation.

People will not save if they believe their money will be worth less in the future. Finally, technological advancement is obviously important. But it is not enough. The 1970s saw this third factor present, but the absence of the first two caused real wages to fall.

Interest Rates

Sidney Homer writes in his monumental *History of Interest Rates, 2000 B.C. to the Present* that "during the last two decades of the nineteenth century (1880-1900), long-term bond yields in the United States declined almost steadily. The nation entered its first period of low long-term interest rates" finally experiencing the 3-3½ long-term rates which had characterized Holland in the 17th century and Britain in the 18th and 19th: in short, the economic giants of their day.

To gauge long-term rates of the day, it is best not to use the long-term government bonds we would use today as a measure. The National Banking Acts of 1863-1864 stipulated that these bonds had to be used to secure bank notes. This created such a demand for them that, as Homer says, "by the mid 1870's [it] put government bond prices up to levels where their yields were far below acceptable rates of long-term interest." But the Commerce Department tracks the unadjusted index of yields of American railroad bonds. We list the yields for 1878, the year before gold, 1879, and 1889.

Railroad Bond Yields	
1878	6.45%
1879	5.98%
1889	4.43%

We stress that with consumer prices about 7 percent lower in 1889 than they had been the decade before, the *real* rate of return by decade's end was well into double-digit range, a bonanza for savers and lenders.

Short-term rates during the last century were considerably more skittish than long-term rates. But even here the decennial averages of annual averages of both three-to six-month commercial paper rates and (overnight) call money during the 1880s declined from what it had been the previous decades:

	Commercial Paper	Call Money
1870-1879	6.46%	5.73%
1880-1889	5.14%	3.98%

A Burst in Productivity

By some measures the 1880s was the most productive decade in our history. In their *A Monetary History of the United States, 1867-1960,* Professors Friedman and Schwartz quote R.W. Goldsmith on the subject: "'The highest decadal rate [of growth of real reproducible, tangible wealth per head from 1805 to 1950] for periods of about ten years was apparently reached in the eighties with approximately 3.8%.' " The statistics give proof to this outpouring of new wealth.

Gross National Product		
(1958 prices)		
	Total (billions of dollars)	Per capita (in dollars)
Decade average 1869-78	$23.1	$531
" 1879-88	$42.4	$774
" 1889-98	$49.1	$795

This dollar growth was occuring, remember, in the face of general price declines.

Gross Domestic Product	
(1929 prices in billions of dollars)	
1869-1878	$11.6 (average per year)
1879-1888	$21.2 (average per year)

Gross domestic product almost doubled from the decade before, a far larger percentage jump decade-on-decade than any time since.

Labor Productivity	
Manufacturing Output Per Man-Hour	
(1958 = 100)	
1869	14.7
1879	16.2
1889	20.5

The 26.5 percent increase here ranks among the best in our history. Labor productivity reflects increased capital investment.

Capital Formation

From 1869 to 1879 the total number of business establishments barely rose, but the next decade saw a 39.4 percent increase. Nor surprisingly, a decade of falling prices, rising real income, and lucrative interest returns made for tremendous capital investment, insuring future gains in productivity.

Purchase of Structures and Equipment	
(total, in 1958 prices, in billions of dollars)	
1870	$ .4
1880	$ .4
1890	$2.0

This massive 500 percent decade-on-decade increase has never since been even closely rivalled. It stands in particular contrast to the virtual stagnation witnessed by the 1970s.

Private and Public Capital Formation		
(total gross, in billions, 1929 prices)		
Average	1872-1876	$2.6
''	1877-1881	$3.7
''	1882-1886	$4.5
''	1887-1891	$5.9

These five-year averages are not as "clean" as some other figures, but still show a rough doubling of total capital formation from the '70s to the '80s.

It has repeatedly been alleged that the late 19th century, the "golden age of the gold standard" in the United States, was a period especially harmful to farmers. The facts, however, tell a different story. While manufacturing in the 1880s grew more rapidly than did agriculture ("The Census of 1890," report Friedman and Schwartz, "was the first in which the net value added by manufacturing exceeded the value of agricultural output"), farmers had an excellent decade.

Number of Farms	
(in thousands)	
1880	4,009
1890	4,565

Farm Land	
(in millions of acres)	
1880	536,182
1890	623,219

Farm Productivity	
(persons supplied by farm worker)	
1880	5.1
1890	5.6

Value of Farm Gross Output and Product	
(1910-1914 dollars, in millions)	
1880	$4,129
1890	$4,990

So farms, farmland, productivity, and production all increased in the 1880s, even while commodities prices were falling. And as we see below, farm wage rates, even in nominal terms, rose during this time.

Farm Wage Rates	
(per month, with board and room, in 1879, 1889 dollars)	
1879 or 1880	$11.50
1889 or 1890	$13.50

This phenomenal economic growth during the decade immediately after the return to gold convertibility cannot be attributed solely to the gold standard. Indeed all during this time there was never a completely free-market monetary system. The National Banking Acts of 1863-1864 had semicartellized the banking system.

Only certain banks could issue money, but all other banks had to have accounts at these. The financial panics throughout the late 19th century were a result of the arbitrary credit-creation powers of the banking system. While not as harmful as today's inflation mechanism, it was still a storm in an otherwise fairly healthy economic climate.

The fateful decade of the 1890s saw the return of the agitation for free silver, which had lain dormant for a decade. The Republican Party intensified its longtime flirtation with inflation, by passing the Sherman Silver Purchase Act of 1890, which roughly doubled the Treasury purchase requirement of silver. The Treasury was not mandated to buy 4.5 million ounces of silver per month. Furthermore, payment was to be made in a new issue of redeemable greenback currency, Treasury Notes of 1890, which were to be a full legal tender, redeemable in either gold or silver at the discretion of the Treasury. Not only was this an increased commitment to silver, it was a significant step on the road to bimetallism which—at the depreciated market rates—would mean inflationary silver monometallism. In the same year, the Republicans passed the high McKinley Tariff Act of 1890, which reaffirmed their commitment to high tariffs and soft money.

Another unsettling inflationary move made in the same year was that the New York Subtreasury altered its longstanding practice of settling its clearing house balances in gold coin. Instead, in August 1890, it began using the old greenbacks and the new Treasury notes of 1890. As a result, these paper currencies largely replaced gold paid in customs receipts in New York.[153]

Uneasiness about the shift from gold to silver and the continuing free-silver agitation caused foreigners to lose further confidence in the U.S. gold standard, and to cause a drop in capital imports and severe gold outflows from the country. This loss of confidence exerted contractionist pressure on the American economy and reduced potential economic growth during the early 1890s.

Fears about the American gold standard were intensified in March 1891, when the Treasury suddenly imposed a stiff fee on the export of gold bars taken from its vaults so that most gold exported from then on was American gold coin rather than bars. A shock went through the financial community, in the U.S. and abroad, when the United States Senate passed a free-silver coinage bill in July 1892; the fact that the bill went no further was not enough to restore confidence in the gold standard. Banks began to insert clauses in loans and mortgages

[153]See Friedman and Schwartz, *Monetary History*, pp. 106, 106n.

requiring payment in gold coin; clearly the dollar was no longer trusted. Gold exports intensified in 1892, the Treasury's gold reserve declined, and a run ensued on the U.S. Treasury. In February 1893, the Treasury persuaded New York banks, which had drawn down $6 million on gold from the Treasury by presenting treasury notes for redemption, to return the gold and re-acquire the paper. This act of desperation was scarcely calculated to restore confidence in the paper dollar. The Treasury was paying the price for specie resumption without bothering to contract the paper notes in circulation. The gold standard was therefore inherently shaky, resting only on public confidence, and that was giving way under the silver agitation and under desperate acts by the Treasury.

Poor Grover Cleveland, a hard-money Democrat, assumed the Presidency in the middle of this monetary crisis. Two months later, the stock market collapsed, and a month afterwards, in June 1893, distrust of the fractional-reserve banks led to massive bank runs and bank failures throughout the country. Once again, however, many banks, national and state, especially in the West and South, were allowed to suspend specie payments. The Panic of 1893 was on. In a few months, Eastern bank suspension occurred, beginning with New York City. The total money supply—gold coin, treasury paper, national bank notes, and national and state bank deposits—fell by 6.3 percent in one year, from June 1892 to June 1893. Suspension of specie payments resulted in deposits—which were no longer immediately redeemable in cash—going to a discount in relation to currency during the month of August. As a result, deposits became less useful, and the public tried its best to intensify its exchange of deposits for currency.

By the end of 1893, the panic was over as foreign confidence rose with the Cleveland administration's successful repeal of the Sherman Silver Purchase Act in November of that year. Further silver agitation of 1895 endangered the Treasury's gold reserve, but heroic acts of the Treasury, including buying gold from a syndicate of bankers headed by J. P. Morgan and August Belmont, restored confidence in the continuance of the gold standard.[154] The victory of the free-silver Bryanite forces at the 1896 Democratic convention caused further problems for gold, but the victory of the pro-gold Republicans put an end to the problem of domestic and foreign confidence in the gold standard.

---

[154]On silver agitation, the gold reserves, and the Panic of 1893, see Friedman and Schwartz, *Monetary History*, pp. 104–133, 705.

1896: The Transformation of the American Party System

Orthodox economic historians attribute the triumph of William Jennings Bryan in the Democratic Convention of 1896, and his later renominations for President, as a righteous rising up of the "people" demanding inflation over the "interests" holding out for gold. Friedman and Schwartz attribute the rise of Bryanism to the price contraction of the last three decades of the 19th century, and the triumph of gold and disappearance of the "money" issue to the price rise after 1896.[155]

This conventional analysis overlooks several problems. First, if Bryan represented the "people" versus the "interests," why did Bryan lose and lose soundly, not once but three times? Why did gold triumph long before any price inflation became obvious, in fact at the depths of price contraction in 1896?

But the main neglect of the conventional analysis is the disregard of the highly illuminating insights provided in the past 15 years by the "new political history" of 19th-century American politics and its political culture. The new political history began by going beyond national political issues (largely economic) and investigating state and local political contests.[156] It also dug into the actual voting records of individual parishes, wards, and counties, and discovered how people voted and why they voted the way they did. The work of the new political history is truly interdisciplinary, for its methods range from sophisticated techniques for voting analysis to illuminating insights into American ethnic religious history.

In the following pages, we shall present a summary of the findings of the new political history on the American party structure of the late 19th century and after, and on the transformation of 1896 in particular.

First, the history of American political parties is one of successive "party systems." Each "party system" lasts several decades, with each

---

[155]Friedman and Schwartz, *Monetary History*, pp. 113–119.

[156]The *locus classicus* of the new political history in late 19th-century politics is Paul Kleppner, *The Cross of Culture: A Social Analysis of Midwestern Politics, 1850–1900* (New York: The Free Press, 1970). Also see other writings of the prolific Kleppner, especially his magnum opus, *The Third Electoral System, 1853–1892: Parties, Voters, and Political Cultures* (Chapel Hill, N.C.: University of North Carolina, 1979). On the late 19th century, see also Richard J. Jensen, *The Winning of the Midwest: Social and Political Conflict, 1888–1896* (Chicago: University of Chicago Press, 1971). On the Civil War period and earlier, see the works of Ronald Formisano, Joel Sibley, and William Shade. For Eastern confirmation on the Kleppner and Jensen findings on the Middle West, see Samuel T. McSeveney, *The Politics of Depression: Political Behavior in the Northeast, 1893–1896* (Oxford: Oxford University Press, 1972).

particular party having a certain central character; in many cases, the name of the party can remain the same but its essential character can drastically change—in the so-called "critical elections." In the 19th century the second party system (Whigs v. Democrats), lasting from about 1832 to 1854, was succeeded by the third party system (Republicans v. Democrats), lasting from 1854 to 1896.

Characteristic of both party systems was that each party was committed to a distinctive ideology clashing with the other, and these conflicting worldviews made for fierce and close contests. Elections were particularly hard fought. Interest was high since the parties offered a "choice not an echo," and so the turnout rate was remarkably high, often reaching 80 to 90 percent of eligible voters. More remarkably, candidates did not, as we are used to in the 20th century, fuzz their ideology during campaigns in order to appeal to a floating, ideologically indifferent, "independent voter." There were very few independent voters. The way to win elections, therefore, was to bring out your vote, and the way to do that was to intensify and strengthen your ideology during campaigns. Any fuzzing over would lead the Republican or Democratic constituents to stay home in disgust, and the election would be lost. Very rarely would there be a crossover to the other, hated party.

One problem that strikes anyone interested in 19th-century political history is: How come the average person exhibited such great and intense interest in such arcane economic topics as banking, gold and silver, and tariffs? Thousands of half-literate people wrote embattled tracts on these topics, and voters were intensely interested. Attributing the answer to inflation or depression, to seemingly evident economic interests, as do Marxists and other economic determinists, simply won't do. The far greater depressions and inflations of the 20th century have not educed nearly as much mass interest in economics as did the milder economic crises of the past century.

Only the findings of the new political historians have cleared up this puzzle. It turns out that the mass of the public was not necessarily interested in what the elites, or national politicians, were talking about. The most intense and direct interest of the voters was applied to local and state issues, and on these local levels the two parties waged an intense and furious political struggle that lasted from the 1830s to the 1890s.

The beginning of this century-long struggle began with the profound transformation of American Protestantism in the 1830s. This transformation swept like wildfire across the Northern states, particularly Yankee territory, during the 1830s, leaving the South virtually untouched.

The transformation found particular root among Yankee culture, with its aggressive and domineering spirit.[157]

This new Protestantism—called "pietist"—was born in the fires of Charles Finney and the great revival movement of the 1830s. Its credo was roughly as follows: Each individual is responsible for his own salvation, and it must come in an emotional moment of being "born again." Each person can achieve salvation; each person must do his best to save everyone else. This compulsion to save others was more than simple missionary work; it meant that one would go to hell unless he did his best to save others. But since each person is alone and facing the temptation to sin, this role can only be done by the use of the State. The role of the State is to stamp out sin and create a new Jerusalem on Earth.[158,159]

The pietists defined sin very broadly. In particular, the most important politically was "Demon rum," which clouded men's minds and therefore robbed them of their theological free will. In the 1830s, the evangelical pietists launched a determined and indefatigable prohibitionist crusade on the state and local level which lasted a century. Second was any activity on Sunday except going to church, which led to a drive for Sabbatarian blue laws. Drinking on Sunday was of course a double sin, and hence particularly heinous. Another vital thrust of the new Yankee pietism was to try to extirpate Roman Catholicism, which robs communicants of their theological free will by subjecting them to the dictates of priests who are agents of the Vatican. If Roman Catholics could not be prohibited *per se,* their immigration could be slowed down or stopped. And since their adults were irrevocably steeped in sin, it became vital for crusading pietists to try to establish public schools as compulsory forces for Protestantizing society or, as the pietists liked to put it, to "Christianize the Catholics." If the adults

[157]"Yankees" originated in rural New England and then emigrated westward in the early 19th century, settling in upstate (particularly western) New York, northern Ohio, northern Indiana, and northern Illinois.

[158]These pietists have been called "evangelical pietists" to contrast them with the new Southern pietists, called "salvational pietists," who did not include the compulsion to save everyone else in their doctrine.

[159]These pietists are distinguished from contemporary "fundamentalists" because the former were "post-millenialists" who believe that the world must be shaped up and Christianized for a millenium before Jesus will return. In contrast, contemporary fundamentalists are "pre-millenials" who believe that the Second Coming of Jesus will usher in the millenium. Obviously, if everyone must be shaped up before Jesus can return, there is a much greater incentive to wield State power to stamp out sin.

are hopeless, the children must be saved by the public school and compulsory attendance laws.

Such was the political program of Yankee pietism. Not all immigrants were scorned. British, Norwegian, or other immigrants who belonged to pietist churches (whether nominally Calvinist or Lutheran or not) were welcomed as "true Americans." The Northern pietists found their home, almost to a man, first in the Whig Party, and then in the Republican Party. And they did so, too, among the Greenback and Populist parties, as we shall see further below.

There came to this country during the century an increasing number of Catholic and Lutheran immigrants, especially from Ireland and Germany. The Catholics and High Lutherans, who have been called "ritualists" or "liturgicals," had a very different kind of religious culture. Each person is not responsible for his own salvation directly; if he is to be saved, he joins the church and obeys its liturgy and sacraments. In a profound sense, then, the church is responsible for one's salvation, and there is no need for the State to stamp out temptation. These churches, then, especially the Lutheran, had a laissez-faire attitude toward the State and morality. Furthermore, their definitions of "sin" were not nearly as broad as the pietists. Liquor is fine in moderation; drinking beer with the family in beer parlors on Sunday after church was a cherished German (Catholic and Lutheran) tradition; and parochial schools were vital in transmitting religious values to their children in a country where they were in a minority.

Virtually to a man, Catholics and High Lutherans[160] found their home during the 19th century in the Democratic Party. It is no wonder that the Republicans gloried in calling themselves throughout this period "the party of great moral ideas," while the Democrats declared themselves to be "the party of personal liberty." For nearly a century, the bemused liturgical Democrats fought a defensive struggle against people whom they considered "pietist-fanatics" constantly swooping down trying to outlaw their liquor, their Sunday beer parlors, and their parochial schools.

How did all this relate to the economic issues of the day? Simply that the leaders of each party went to their voting constituents and "raised their consciousness" to get them vitally interested in national economic

---

[160]Lutherans, then as now, were split into many different synods, some highly liturgical, others highly pietist, and still others in between. Paul Kleppner has shown a one-to-one correlation between the degree of liturgicalness and the percentage of Democratic Party votes among the different synods.

questions. Thus, the Republican leaders would go to their rank-and-file and say: "Just as we need Big Paternalistic Government on the local and state level to stamp out sin and compel morality, so we need Big Government on the national level to increase everyone's purchasing power through inflation, keeping out cheap foreign goods (tariffs), or keeping out cheap foreign labor (immigration restrictions)."

And for their part, the Democratic leaders would go to their constituents and say: "Just as the Republican fanatics are trying to take away your liquor, your beer parlors, and your parochial schools, so the same people are trying to keep out cheap foreign goods (tariffs), and trying to destroy the value of your savings through inflation. Paternalistic government on the federal level is just as evil as it is at home."

So statism and libertarianism were expanded to other issues and other levels. Each side infused its economic issues with a moral fervor and passion stemming from their deeply held religious values. The mystery of the passionate interest of Americans in economic issues in the epoch is solved.

Both in the second party and third party systems, however, the Whigs and then the Republicans had a grave problem. Partly because of demographics—greater immigration and higher birth rates—the Democratic/liturgicals were slowly but surely becoming the majority party in the country. The Democrats were split asunder by the slavery question in the 1840s and '50s. But now, by 1890, the Republicans saw the handwriting on the wall. The Democratic victory in the congressional races in 1890, followed by the unprecedented landslide victory of Grover Cleveland carrying *both* houses of Congress in 1892, indicated to the Republicans that they were becoming doomed to be a permanent minority.

To remedy the problem, the Republicans, in the early 1890s, led by Ohio Republicans William McKinley and Marc Hanna, launched a shrewd campaign of reconstruction. In particular, in state after state, they ditched the prohibitionists, who were becoming an embarrassment and losing the Republicans large numbers of German Lutheran votes. Also, they modified their hostility to immigration. By the mid-1890s, the Republicans had moved rapidly toward the center, toward fuzzing over their political pietism.

In the meanwhile, an upheaval was beginning to occur in the Democratic Party. The South, by now a one-party Democratic region, was having its own pietism transformed by the 1890s. Quiet pietists were now becoming evangelical, and Southern Protestant organizations began to call for prohibition. Then the new, sparsely settled Mountain states, many of them with silver mines, were also largely pietist. Moreover, a power vacuum, which would ordinarily have been temporary, had been created in the national Democratic Party. Poor Grover Cleveland, a hard-money laissez-faire Democrat, was blamed for the Panic of 1893, and many leading Cleveland Democrats lost their gubernatorial and senatorial posts in the 1894 elections. The Cleveland Democrats were temporarily weak, and the Southern-Mountain coalition was ready to hand. Seizing his opportunity, William Jennings Bryan and his pietist coalition seized control of the Democratic Party at the momentous convention of 1896. The Democratic Party was never to be the same again.[161]

The Catholics, Lutherans, and the laissez-faire Cleveland Democrats were in mortal shock. The "party of our fathers" was lost. The Republicans, who had been moderating their stance anyway, saw the opportunity of a lifetime. At the Republican convention, Rep. Henry Cabot Lodge, representing the Morgans and the pro-gold standard Boston financial interests, told McKinley and Hanna: Pledge yourself to the gold standard—the basic Cleveland economic issue—and drop your silverite and greenback tendencies, and we will all back you. Refuse, and we will support Bryan or a third party. McKinley struck the deal, and from then on, the Republicans, in 19th-century terms, were a centrist party. Their principles were now high tariffs and the gold standard, and prohibition was quietly forgotten.

What would the poor liturgicals do? Many of them stayed home in droves, and indeed the election of 1896 marks the beginning of the great slide downward in voter turnout rates that continues to the present day. Some of them, in anguish at the pietist, inflationist, and prohibitionist Bryanites, actually conquered their anguish and voted Republican for the first time in their lives. The Republicans, after all, had dropped the hated prohibitionists and adopted gold.

The election of 1896 inaugurated the fourth party system in America. From a third party system of closely fought, seesawing races between a pietist/statist Republican vs. a liturgical/libertarian Democratic Party, the fourth party system consisted of a majority centrist Republican party as against a minority pietist Democratic party. After a few years, the Democrats lost their pietist nature, and they too became a centrist, though usually minority party, with a moderately statist ideology scarcely

---

[161]Grover Cleveland himself, of course, was neither a Roman Catholic nor a Lutheran. But he was a Calvinist Presbyterian who detested the takeover of the Presbyterian Church by the pietists.

distinguishable from the Republicans. So the fourth party system went until 1932.

A charming anecdote, told us by Richard Jensen, sums up much of the 1896 election. The heavily German city of Milwaukee had been mainly Democratic for years. The German Lutherans and Catholics in America were devoted, in particular, to the gold standard and were bitter enemies of inflation. The Democratic nomination for Congress in Milwaukee had been obtained by a Populist-Democrat, Richard Schilling. Sounding for all the world like modern monetarists or Keynesians, Schilling tried to explain to the assembled Germans of Milwaukee in a campaign speech that it didn't really matter what commodity was chosen as money, that "gold, silver, copper, paper, sauerkraut or sausages" would do equally well as money. At that point, the German masses of Milwaukee laughed Schilling off the stage, and the shrewdly opportunistic Republicans adopted as their campaign slogan "Schilling and Sauerkraut" and swept Milwaukee.[162]

The Greenbackers and later the pro-silver, inflationist, Bryanite Populist Party were not "agrarian parties"; they were collections of pietists aiming to stamp out personal and political sin. Thus, as Kleppner points out, "The Greenback Party was less an amalgamation of economic pressure groups than an ad hoc coalition of 'True Believers,' 'ideologues,' who launched their party as a 'quasi-religious' movement that bore the indelible hallmark of 'a transfiguring faith.'" The Greenbackers perceived their movement as the "religion of the Master in motion among men." And the Populists described their 1890 free-silver contest in Kansas not as a "political campaign," but as "a religious revival, a crusade, a pentecost of politics in which a tongue of flame sat upon every man, and each spake as the spirit gave him utterance. . . ." The people had "heard the word and could preach the gospel of Populism." It was no accident, we see now, that the Greenbackers almost invariably endorsed prohibition, compulsory public schooling, and crushing of parochial schools. Or that Populists in many states "declared unequivocally for prohibition" or entered various forms of fusion with the Prohibition Party.[163]

The Transformation of 1896 and the death of the third party system meant the end of America's great laissez-faire, hard-money libertarian

---

[162]So intense was the German-American devotion to gold and hard money that even German communist-anarchist Johann Most, leader of a movement that sought the abolition of money itself, actually came out for the gold standard during the 1896 campaign! See Jensen, *Winning of the Midwest*, pp. 293–295.

[163]Kleppner, *Third Electoral System*, pp. 291–296.

party. The Democratic Party was no longer the party of Jefferson, Jackson, and Cleveland. With no further political embodiment for laissez-faire in existence, and with both parties offering an echo not a choice, public interest in politics steadily declined. A power vacuum was left in American politics for the new corporate statist ideology of progressivism, which swept both parties (and created a short-lived Progressive Party) in America after 1900. The Progressive Era of 1900–1918 fastened a welfare-warfare state on America which has set the mold for the rest of the 20th century. Statism arrived after 1900 not because of inflation or deflation, but because a unique set of conditions had destroyed the Democrats as a laissez-faire party and left a power vacuum for the triumph of the new ideology of compulsory cartellization through a partnership of big government, business, unions, technocrats, and intellectuals.

III. Money and Banking in the United States in the 20th Century

After 1896 and 1900, then, America entered a progressive and predominantly Republican era. Compulsory cartellization in the name of "progressivism" began to invade every aspect of American economic life. The railroads had begun the parade with the formation of the ICC in the 1880s, but now field after field was being centralized and cartellized in the name of "efficiency," "stability," "progress," and the general welfare. Theodore Roosevelt, Taft, and Wilson were each in his way progressives, and each advanced the cause of cartellization, with the process culminating in the Presidency of Woodrow Wilson. In particular, various big business groups, led by the J. P. Morgan interests often gathered in the National Civic Federation and other think tanks and pressure organizations, saw that the voluntary cartels and the industrial merger movements of the late 1890s had failed to achieve monopoly prices in industry. Therefore, they decided to turn to governments, state and federal, to curb the winds of competition and to establish forms of compulsory cartels, in the name, of course, of "curbing big business monopoly" and advancing the general welfare.[1]

America's bankers had long chafed to cartellize the banking industry still further. The National Banking System was a long step forward, from their point of view, but it was still only quasi-centralized. Bank credit and money pyramided on top of New York (and after 1887, also Chicago and St. Louis) banks. But this system was, to use a universally adopted term, "inelastic"—that is, it could not assure the pumping in of more money during contractions or runs on banks. "Inelastic" was a code word for not enough assured inflation of the money supply.[2] The growing consensus, then, was to redirect the banking system by establishing, at long last, a central bank. The central bank would have

---

[1]See in particular, Gabriel Kolko, *The Triumph of Conservatism: A Reinterpretation of American History*, 1900–1916 (Glencoe, Ill.: The Free Press, 1963.) While in less harsh a form, variants of this interpretation have now swept the field in Progressive Era historiography. Thus, see the works of Samuel Hays, James Weinstein, Arthur Ekrich, Louis Galambos, William Graebner, Jordan Schwarz, Ellis Hawley, Joan Hoff Wilson, and many others.

[2]National banks also had a particular form of "inelasticity." Their issue of notes was limited by their deposit of government bonds at the Treasury. Yet government bonds were generally 40 percent over par, which imposed a penalty on further issue. See Robert Craig West, *Banking Reform and the Federal Reserve, 1863–1923.* (Ithaca: Cornell University Press, 1977).

an absolute monopoly of the note issue, and reserve requirements would then ensure a multilayered pyramiding on top of these central bank notes, which could bail out banks in trouble, and, moreover, could inflate the currency in a smooth, controlled, and uniform manner throughout the nation.

In addition to this chronic problem, the large banks, particularly on Wall Street, saw financial control slipping away from them. The state banks and other non-national banks began to grow instead and outstrip the nationals. Thus, while in the 1870s and the 1880s, most banks were national, by 1896 non-national banks comprised 61 percent of the total number of banks, and by 1913, 71 percent. By 1896, these non-national banks had 54 percent of the total banking resources of the country, and 57 percent in 1913. The inclusion of Chicago and St. Louis as central reserve city banks after 1887 diluted Wall Street's power. With Wall Street no longer able to cope, it was time to turn to the United States government to do the centralizing, cartellizing, and controlling instead.[3]

It often takes a crisis to focus one's mind, and it takes a financial crisis or notable event to move men to institutional reform. The Civil War was the previous occasion for overhaul of the nation's money and banking system. The Panic of 1907 provided the spark for a return to central banking.

The Republicans fulfilled their promise, and, in March 1900, finally placed the United States officially on a monometallic gold standard. All paper was to be redeemable in gold, and silver continued as a subsidiary metal.

An unusual increase in gold production from discoveries in South Africa and Alaska doubled the world's gold stock from 1890 to 1914, causing a rise of U.S. prices of nearly 50 percent from 1897 to 1914, or two and one-half percent per year. Until after World War II, this was the largest sustained rise in prices in peacetime, but still the rise only returned to approximately 1882 levels. In the United States, the gold supply rose at a rate of seven and one-half percent per year in this period. But despite this impact, the bulk of the increase in the supply of money in the period came from bank deposits pyramiding on top of the increase in gold. Thus, from June 1896 to June 1914, total bank deposits rose from $3.43 billion to $14.32 billion, or an increase of 317.5 percent or an annual rise of 17.6 percent—a substantially greater percentage than the seven and one-half percent per year increase of the gold stock. Once again, fractional reserve banking under the National

[3]See Kolko, *Triumph*, p. 140.

Banking System was far more to blame for price rises than international movements in gold.

There were several mini-panics, averted or stopped by infusions of Treasury money, after 1900; but the Panic of 1907 frightened the banks into calling for a new central banking system. Wall Street and the Morgans could not save the New York banks themselves. There was general speculation of specie payment throughout the country, and premiums of currency over deposits. Again, the Treasury was called upon to intervene. The Wall Street banks now knew that they could not cope, and federal government cartellization and support for fractional reserve banking would be necessary.[4]

All banks, and both parties, now agreed on some form of central banking, and the rest of the story is jockeying for minor advantage. The Wilson administration finally established central banking with the creation of the Federal Reserve System in 1913—the symbolic end of the Jacksonian hard-money heritage in the Democratic Party. From 1913 until 1933, the United States would be formally under a gold standard, but actually governed by a Federal Reserve System designed to inflate uniformly and bail out banks in trouble. The banking systems would now be pyramiding on the U.S. issue of paper money.

By establishing the Federal Reserve System, the federal government changed the base of the banking pyramid to the Federal Reserve Banks. Only the Federal Reserve could now print cash, and all member banks could now multiply their deposits on top of Federal Reserve deposits. All national banks were required to join the Federal Reserve, and their gold and other lawful money reserves had to be transferred to the Federal Reserve. The Federal Reserve, in turn, could pyramid its deposits by three-to-one on top of gold. This centralization created an enormous potential for inflationary expansion of bank deposits. Not only that, reserve requirements for the nation's banks were deliberately cut in half in the course of establishing the Federal Reserve System, thereby inviting the rapid doubling of the money supply. Average reserve requirements for all banks prior to the Federal Reserve Act is estimated to be 21 percent. In the original Act of 1913, these were cut to 11.6 percent and three years later to 9.8 percent. It is clear then that the Federal Reserve was designed from the very beginning to be an instrument for a uniform and coordinated inflation of bank money.[5]

[4]See Kolko, *Triumph*, pp. 153–158; Friedman and Schwartz, *Monetary History*, pp. 156ff.
[5]See the illuminating discussion in C. A. Phillips, T. F. McManus, and R. W. Nelson, *Banking and the Business Cycle* (New York: Macmillan, 1937), pp. 23–29.

Indeed, total bank deposits were $14.0 billion at the beginning of the Federal Reserve System in January 1914; after six years, in January 1920, total bank deposits had reached $29.4 billion, an enormous increase of 110 percent or 18.3 percent per year. The creation of the Federal Reserve had made that expansion possible.

The Gold-Exchange Standard

Faced with a global inflation of unprecedented volume and destruction both during World War I and immediately after it, the world attempted to restore monetary stability. But while most officials wanted gold to re-appear as the monetary anchor, they also wanted to be able to keep inflating. Put another way, they wanted to have their cake and eat it too.

Preeminent victims of this delusion were the British; with a burgeoning welfare state in the early 1920s, and especially with rigid wage rates, it was difficult politically to end inflation. Further, Britain wanted to return to gold, but for reasons of national "prestige" she wanted to go back at the pre-war, pre-inflation rate of $4.86 per pound. In effect, she wanted to pretend that the inflation had never happened. There was only one way Britain could get away with enthroning an artificially overvalued pound: by making other countries play along. Other nations had to be persuaded (or forced) into either likewise returning to gold at an unrealistic rate or inflating their monies so as not to cripple Britain's exports (also priced artificially high).

Britain accomplished this at the Genoa Conference of 1922. Emerging from that first post-war economic meeting was not a gold standard, but a more slippery "gold-exchange" standard. Here's how it worked: Only the United States stayed on the old gold-coin standard, where anyone could present notes totalling $20.67 to the Treasury and receive an ounce of gold in return. But Britain began redeeming pounds not just in gold, but in Federal Reserve notes or dollars. Further, the other nations began predominantly using British pounds as their backing. And importantly, when they did pay gold they only paid in large bullion bars, not coins, so the average citizen was not able to redeem his currency. The Genoa Accord made the pound as well as the dollar as good as gold, even though sterling was not in fact a sound currency. Britain now printed its "gold" with American support—the U.S. agreed to inflate enough to keep Britain's reserves of dollars or gold from flowing to America.

This inflationary charade was played to buttress Britain's fading dreams as an imperialist world power. But also involved was the rise of the new doctrines of John Maynard Keynes, who by the early 1920s had become a foe of the "barbarous relic" gold and extolled instead the alleged virtues of a politically managed paper currency. That these ideas became so influential so fast in London banking circles was due in no small part to the catastrophic loss suffered during World War I of truly the finest minds of a generation. These would have normally become leaders during the 1920s. This left a gap which affected Britain as it did few other countries. For at the risk of broad-brush painting, the British are a people that have always put more stock in practical knowledge than the more philosophical French or Germans. But pragmatism depends less on book knowledge than on skills handed down orally. The annihilation of a generation thus created a gap in the continuity of knowledge those more bookish nations escaped. So as one contemporary observer of London financial circles perceptively explained, by the mid-1920s, there would be few remaining grandfathers who remembered the virtues of sound money. And there would be their grandsons "miseducated by Keynes." Between them was a gap, which created such "a barrier in ideas that it was not easy for tradition and practical knowledge to pass."[6]

American Inflation 1922–28

With the "discovery" of open-market operations around 1922, the Federal Reserve thought it had found a way to smooth out business cycles. In practice, it caused a substantial six-year bank credit inflation by buying securities on the open market and printing the money to pay for them. This money—bank reserves—was pyramided several-fold by means of the fractional reserve banking system. This policy of stabilizing the price level was deliberately engineered by the leader of the Federal Reserve System, Benjamin Strong, to follow the proto-monetarist theory of Yale economist Irving Fisher.

The 1920s are not often seen as an inflationary period because prices did not rise. But the money supply can rise even without prices rising in absolute terms. The 1920s saw such a burst of American technological advancement and cheaper ways of producing things that the natural tendency was for prices to *fall* (i.e., more goods chasing the same number of dollars). But the inflation caused prices to rise *relative* to

[6]Benjamin Anderson, *Economics and the Public Welfare* (Indianapolis: Liberty Press, 1979), p. 174.

what they would have done. So a "stable" price level was masking the fact that inflation was going on and creating distortions throughout the economy.

Between mid-1922 and April 1928, bank credit expanded by over twice as much as it did to help finance World War I. As with all inflations, this caused speculative excess; in this case, new money poured into the stock market and real estate. The cooling of this speculative fever in 1928 by officials who tightened the money supply because they were finally afraid of the overheated economy led to the Depression, which in turn led to the world's abandonment of the gold standard. We would do well to examine this period closer.

Bailing Out Britain

Britain during this time used her power to treat the pound like gold, as one might expect, keeping interest rates artificially low and inflating recklessly, thus piling up billions of pounds at the Bank of France, which finally began asking for gold. Panicked, the Bank of England in mid-1927 induced the New York Federal Reserve Bank to lower its interest rates and step up open-market purchases of securities, thus fueling inflation further. (This move to make unnecessary the payment of British gold obligations to France and to keep England inflating by causing America to inflate was disguised as "helping the farmer." It was the Kansas City Federal Reserve Bank which first lowered its discount rate, the others following.)

A major reason for the inflationary pro-British policies of the 1920s was the close personal connection formed between Benjamin Strong, the dominant leader of the Federal Reserve System, and Montagu Norman, head of the Bank of England. In several secret conferences with Norman, unknown to the rest of the Federal Reserve or the American government, Strong agreed to inflate money and credit in order to bail out England. The ties between Norman and Strong were not only personal; both were intimately allied with the House of Morgan. Before he became the first leader of the Federal Reserve, Strong was head of the Morgan-created Bankers Trust Company in New York. He was urged to accept the post by his two closest personal friends, Henry P. Davison and Dwight Morrow, both partners at the Morgan Bank. The Morgan connection with Britain was very close; J. P. Morgan and Company was the fiscal agent for the Bank of England and underwrote the massive sale of British bonds in the United States during World War I. Montagu Norman himself had close personal connections with the United States investment banks and had worked in the offices of Brown Brothers in New York. Only the death of Strong in 1928 ended the inflationary Federal Reserve policy designed to help Britain.

By April of 1928, the new Governors of both the Federal Reserve Board and the New York Federal Reserve Bank, made an effort to hold down bank credit expansion. But those efforts were stymied by following two conflicting goals. Federal Reserve officials wanted both to reduce credit going into stock market speculation yet at the same time not to tighten money either at home or abroad (this latter for fear of pulling gold out of Britain).

And while the anti-inflationist policy predominated, it is not easy to reduce inflation in an economy grown accustomed to it, which by 1928 America had. Further, 1928 was a presidential election year, with great pressure to inflate. It therefore took about a year before the money supply was under control. But as the tables below show, the long money-supply inflation was over by the end of 1928. At mid-1929 money-supply growth was creeping at an annual rate of only 0.7 percent, a marked deceleration from previous years. The depression caused by years of inflation was about to begin, and with it would come the end of the American gold standard.

Total Money Supply of the United States, 1921–29

(in billions of dollars)

Date	Total Money Supply	Percent Annual Change From Previous
1921—June 30	45.30	. . . .
1922—June 30	47.16	4.1
1923—June 30	51.79	9.8
1923—Dec. 31	53.06	4.9
1924—June 30	54.67	6.1
1924—Dec. 31	57.85	11.6
1925—June 30	59.86	7.1
1925—Dec. 31	62.59	9.2
1926—June 30	63.62	3.3
1926—Dec. 31	64.96	4.2
1927—June 30	66.91	6.0
1927—Dec. 31	69.61	8.1
1928—June 30	71.12	4.4
1928—Dec. 31	73.00	5.2
1929—June 30	73.26	0.7

Federal Reserve Bank Credit, 1914–1934
($ millions)

End of Year	Total loans and securities	Reserve bank credit outstanding Through purchase of bills and securities
1914	11	0
1915	84	40
1916	222	184
1917	1060	395
1918	2291	526
1919	3090	874
1920	3235	547
1921	1524	379
1922	1326	708
1923	1211	489
1924	1249	927
1925	1395	749
1926	1335	696
1927	1591	1009
1928	1783	717
1929	1548	903
1930	1352	1093
1931	1825	1156
1932	2128	1888
1933	2670	2570
1934	2457	2436

Source: U.S. Department of Commerce, *Historical Statistics of the United States, Colonial Times to 1957*, series X 245–254 (1961), p. 642.

The International Crisis: 1931

The stock market collapse in late 1929 was only a harbinger of things to come. It was not until 1931 that international bank collapses caused abandonment of gold. The first to go was Austria.

Kredit-Anstalt, Austria's largest bank, supported by the Austrian government, had for years been making bad loans on a meager reserve base. Austria had been part of the "sterling bloc," buttressed by Britain—a development resented by France, heavy with gold claims on

Britain. The formation of an Austrian customs union with Germany in late March 1931 was feared by France, who saw it as a step to political union. The French central bank now insisted upon immediate repayment of her short-term debts from Austria and Germany. Austrian banks clearly could not meet their liabilities, and in late May, Kredit-Anstalt went bankrupt, taking Austria off the gold standard. A run on German banks now started. That country had been quickly affected by the tightened American credit conditions in mid-1928 and was quite vulnerable. Runs continued, and even though President Hoover declared on June 20 a moratorium on German debt, France was not immediately inclined to go along. She delayed too long; and on July 15 Germany declared national bankruptcy by going off the gold standard.

It must be said that both these nations fought desperately to maintain gold redemption, and when the end came, each regarded the act with shame. Not so with Britain. The country that had caused the others to inflate for her and did more than any other to bring on the crisis went off the gold standard without a fight.

As runs on British gold increased through the summer, Britain refused to defend the pound by raising interest rates. Instead, as gold flowed out of the banks, the Bank of England created new money to replenish the banks' reserves. The Bank of France cooperated loyally and didn't present many claims. The French bank held sterling claims worth fully seven times its capital, and thus feared for a Britain off the gold standard. Indeed, France joined America in offering massive loans to Britain. But the Bank of England didn't even take full advantage of these credit lines, and two days after assuring the Netherlands Bank (with all its capital in sterling) that England would not go off the gold standard, that is exactly what happened. The announcement was made on September 20, 1931, thus capping 17 years of gradual monetary disintegration.

Britain had for centuries been the world's premier financial power, so that announcement left the world stunned. Moreover, other governments had been deliberately deceived. The capital of the central banks of France and Holland had been made worthless in one day. Governments could no longer trust each other's financial promises, and the stage was set for perhaps the most treacherous decade in international economic relations, a decade from which we have not yet recovered. As Chase economist and contemporary eyewitness Benjamin Anderson recalled, "An immense world asset was destroyed when the Bank of England and the British government broke faith with the world. Years later after we in the United States had also broken faith with the world, the head of the national bank of one of the Scandinavian countries said, 'I have lost money in sterling. I have lost money in dollars. I have never lost money by holding gold.'"[7]

America Breaks Faith

If sterling was not good, the world asked itself, what was? It looked nervously at America, and had presented claims for $728 million of our gold by the end of October 1931. But Americans thought any such fears were silly. After all, we had continued to pay gold to foreigners even in the crisis of 1895, with a low point of only $41 million of gold in the Treasury. Alone among belligerents, we had not gone off gold in World War I, although we had stopped the export of gold. Certainly few Americans cashed in notes for gold in late 1931. They may have doubted the solvency of some banks, but few if any doubted the good faith of the American government's promise to redeem notes for gold. The platforms of both parties in 1932 contained vows that the gold standard would be maintained. The Democratic platform was largely written by Sen. Carter Glass of Virginia and Cordell Hull, later secretary of state. As events proved, both these men were sincere.

The first sign of shakiness in the American position was a foolish and false statement by President Hoover one month before the November election. He charged that the Federal Reserve had been within two weeks of going off the gold standard earlier that year. The statement was soon proved untrue, but it aroused doubts for the first time in people's minds.

These grew into rumors beginning in late December that President-elect Roosevelt was going to take the country off the gold standard. Roosevelt would not deny them, and American hoarding of gold started for the first time on a grand scale.

The feelings of disquietude were made worse by a paralyzed government. The new President was not to take office until March 4 (the old Inauguration date) and a lame-duck Congress had many members due to retire. In the cabinet departments, anyone whose job was not protected by civil-service rules was preparing to find a new job in the midst of a terrible depression.

Runs on banks by depositors anxious to get cash, and runs on the Federal Reserve Banks by cash holders eager to turn their paper into gold, accelerated. It should not have come as a surprise when on February 14 Michigan became the first state to declare a bank "holiday,"

[7]Anderson, *Economics and the Public Welfare*, p. 254.

i.e., to close the banks to depositors. Michigan had been the home of some of the more reckless lending by banks during the boom. Nine days later Indiana followed, and then a score of states in a cluster. Late on the night of March 3, the big New York banks reluctantly agreed to close; though they were not in trouble, smaller upstate banks were. Roosevelt became President the next day with almost every bank in America closed. He kept them all closed until March 13, when the Federal Reserve banks opened, with others a day or two later. The public, assuaged by FDR's promise that the reopened banks would be good, poured both gold and cash back into the banks. But on March 9 Congress passed, at Roosevelt's request, a bill "to provide relief in the existing national emergency in banking, and other purposes." It gave him the power to do all he pleased regarding money and banking, including authority to seize the American people's gold coins, bullion, and gold certificates.

America Off the Gold Standard

Within a month this power was used. On April 5, it became illegal to own or hold any form of monetary gold, either coins, bullion, or certificates. (Industrial users of gold were not affected.) The banking crisis had been brought on by past inflation. But that crisis, ironically, was made the excuse to abandon the gold standard.

At first, it was stressed that these measures were temporary, only to be used as long as the crisis lasted. But on May 12 a law was passed (the Thomas Amendment to the Agriculture Adjustment Act) which gave the President the ability to increase vastly the money supply and to reduce by up to half the weight of gold dollar. Democratic Senator Glass called it "dishonor. . . . This great government, strong in gold, is breaking its promises to pay gold to widows and orphans to whom it has sold government bonds with a pledge to pay gold coin of the present standard value. It is breaking its promise to redeem its paper money in gold coin of the present standard of value. It's dishonor, sir."[8] Another Democratic Senator, Thomas Gore of Oklahoma, was asked by the President for his opinion about another law (signed on June 5) abolishing the gold clause in all past debt obligations: "Why, that's just plain stealing, isn't it, Mr. President?" Later in Senate debate, Gore also added that "Henry VIII approached total depravity but the vilest thing he ever did was to debase the coin of the realm."[9]

[8]Ibid., p. 315.
[9]Ibid., p. 317.

One final step remained. Using the Gold Reserve Act of January 30, 1934, President Roosevelt arbitrarily reduced the weight of gold that would define each dollar. The "old" dollar had been defined as 25.8 grains of gold, nine-tenths fine. The new devalued dollar would only be worth 15⁵⁄₂₁ grains, nine-tenths fine. So even the act of abandoning gold was done with the implicit admission that the dollar was still defined in terms of it.

The London Conference

Just as he had taken America off gold, Roosevelt took steps to ensure that there would be no international return to gold. The Gold Bloc of remaining gold standard nations, France, Belgium, Switzerland, Holland, and Italy, had called the London Conference for June 1933 to persuade Great Britain and the United States that "gold should be reestablished as the international measure of exchange value"—and that non-gold countries should agree that their ultimate objective was to restore the gold standard. Even the official American delegation, which included Secretary of State Cordell Hull, approved this declaration, and all were shocked when Roosevelt's reply rejected the proposals. Said he, "The sound internal economic system of a nation is a greater factor in its prosperity than the price of its currency in changing terms of other nations." He thus missed the point of a gold standard, which defines all currencies as an unchanging weight of gold. Incredibly, the President stated that the new order would mean currency stability: "Let me be frank in saying that the United States seeks the kind of dollar which a generation hence will have the same purchasing and debt-paying power as the dollar value we hope to maintain in the near future." Seven months later, the dollar was devalued by 40.9 percent. And we of "a generation hence" know what has happened to the purchase power of the dollar.

Gold Remains the World's Money

Finding no support, all the remaining Gold Block countries stopped redeeming their paper for gold, Holland and Switzerland being the last in 1936. But gold was far from banished. The deteriorating European political situation after 1936 caused everyone from homeless Jews to central bankers to trust gold over any paper currency and to transfer gold to the United States, the safest haven. Further, the stabilization funds set up by governments to stabilize now floating currencies settled their differences in gold. Remembering British and American actions to change arbitrarily the value of their currencies, no one would trust anything else.

Nor was there reason to. Beggar-thy-neighbor policies were the order of the day. International economic peace was shattered during the 1930s by economic nationalism, competitive devaluation, high tariffs, and exchange controls. Moreover, this poisoned atmosphere played its part in causing World War II.

The Coming of Bretton Woods

Try as they might, countries just before World War II were unable to carry on unsound currency and fiscal policies without seeing their currencies depreciate in terms of gold, their capital flee, or their credit markets crippled. The only pre-war exception was Nazi Germany, which achieved those goals at the cost of a complete and unprecedented economic regimentation. With the coming of war, other nations as well achieved far-reaching control over internal and foreign exchange. The end of war found government officials wishing they could retain those controls, which allowed them to inflate and run budget deficits as they pleased while still having access to easy credit, stable foreign exchange rates, and an absence of international "flight capital."

This was the root idea behind the international monetary conference in mid-1944 at Bretton Woods, New Hampshire, which set up the monetary order that would break down 25 years later. For while the new Bretton Woods system was supposed to restore the currency stability of the gold standard, it was designed to do so without gold. The system placed its trust, not in the workings of the marketplace, but in the judicious restraint of the American government. It therefore contained within itself the seeds of its own destruction.

The Rules of the Game

While the dollar would be convertible into gold at $35 an ounce, it would be so only to foreigners, and after 1962 only to foreign governments. All other currencies were defined in terms of the dollar, which itself was defined as $\frac{1}{35}$ of an ounce of gold. But the upshot of the arrangement gave America the power to have the dollar treated as gold. The Bretton Woods rules called for stable currency values: No currency was allowed to either rise or fall more than one percent. The Swiss franc, for example, was, at the time of the agreement (1944), fixed at 22.9 cents; it could go no lower than 22.7 cents and no higher than 23.1 cents. If the franc threatened to break these limits, the Swiss central bank was obliged to enter the exchange market and either buy or sell francs to hold its currency within the narrow margin. As the franc was usually bumping against the upper limits of this margin, Swiss authorities were usually selling francs and buying dollars. Most other governments were doing the same, especially those whose currencies were not inflating as much as the dollar was. But all of these nations were soothed with the promise that the dollar was indeed "as good as gold," and that any foreign holder of dollars, individual or government, could present American currency to the U.S. Treasury at any time to collect one ounce of gold for 35 of their paper dollars. Many, of course, took advantage of this opportunity. The U.S. government continued inflating the dollar, and our gold supply plummeted from a peak of 701 million ounces in 1949 to 296 million ounces in March 1968.

No government in history had held the kind of power handed to the United States in 1944: having its paper money treated like gold. But this action overlooked the stark reality that paper is not gold, that gold cannot be printed wildly, as paper can. Another effect of the Bretton Woods regime was to subsidize American consumers at the expense of foreigners. For a long time, America prospered at the expense of her trading partners. For years, the dollar's value was artificially high, and therefor actually bought more than it should have been able to buy. This meant that foreign products were available to Americans at bargain prices. This left foreign consumers less to enjoy. Moreover, the foreigners had to pay more for their own goods, thanks to American "exporting" of inflation by, in effect, forcing foreign central banks to print more of their own currency to absorb the unwanted, overvalued dollars they accepted.

Predictably, those nations who had managed their own monetary affairs most conservatively were the ones hardest hit by the American action. Switzerland, that paragon of monetary restraint, now madly printed francs to pay for all dollars shunned by Swiss commercial banks. Switzerland's money supply soared 22 percent in 1971 alone. (Ironically, Switzerland had never signed the Bretton Woods agreement, but chose nevertheless to continue to adhere to the strictures— to its own great detriment—long after the system's founder and chief beneficiary, the United States, had broken its commitment.) Switzerland could not be expected to continue this suicidal policy forever; as we will see later, it was Swiss action which finally brought the injustice of the post-war system to an abrupt end.

The London Gold Pool

Dollars flooded the world through the 1950s, and few worried about the gold reserves leaving the U.S. Treasury. But sometime in the early 1960s the market price of gold threatened to rise above the official $35 per ounce figure. For many years, the $35 figure was above the market price, making holding dollars attractive. In response to this rise in gold's price, the West's major central banks in 1961 established the London Gold Pool. With the U.S. in the lead, the banks agreed to sell gold whenever the price threatened to rise above $35. But this was successful only as long as world inflation fears abated. However, by the late 1960s the world had paused to assess the effects of a massive dollar inflation to pay for both the Great Society programs and the Vietnam War. The U.S. dollar had now clearly become overvalued, gold's price under-valued.

Britain was the first major nation to violate the fixed-exchange regime by devaluing in November of 1967. This caused a massive flight into gold, the first of the post-war era. Billions of dollars were spent by central banks in the next four months trying to force the market gold price down. Finally in March, governments threw in the towel and gave up suppressing the market's wishes.

The Approaching Crisis

From March 1968 to August 1971, during the period of the "two-tier" gold market, the political world pretended that the dollar was still convertible, and for most of that time, the monetary scene was placid. This was due in part to the moderate lessening of American inflation during the recession of 1969–1970. But after that brief respite, the printing presses again went into high gear. The results were predictable. By early 1971, astute financial observers began to sense the imminent collapse of the dollar. One of the signs they saw was the lowering of American interest rates compared with European ones. When any nation inflates, money usually becomes cheaper, if only in the beginning, and therefore easier to borrow. The interest rate charged by banks to borrowers of money declines, and the interest rate paid by banks to depositors of money also declines. Money then flows out of those low-interest rate countries into countries where it can enjoy higher returns. During the beginning months of 1971, the outflow of funds from New York to European money markets accelerated. This forced most European currencies hard against their upper ceiling. Because Germany in particular had maintained a very tight credit stance—a low inflation rate—the mark was besieged with an unprecedented flood of buyers. Events now began to move swiftly.

In early May, on the heels of a joint report by major German economic institutes that the mark should be inflated or revalued upward, massive speculation hit that currency. Dollars poured into Germany and the Bundesbank was forced to buy them in mounting volume—more than $1 billion on May 3–4 and a further $1 billion during the first 40 minutes of trading on May 5. At that point, the German central bank gave up the struggle, withdrew from the market, and let the mark float. Neighboring countries, afraid of seeing now-homeless dollars careen across their own borders, were quick to join Germany.

The following weekend the central banks of the Netherlands, Switzerland, Belgium, and Austria likewise ceased support operations and set their currencies afloat. In the cases of Austria and Switzerland, revaluations of 5 to 7 percent were also realized. Not surprisingly, the newly-floated currencies continued appreciating, most of them rather sharply. There were rumblings inside the Nixon administration—especially in the Treasury Department—that the gold "window" ought to be slammed unequivocally shut.

It is important to realize that while other governments theoretically could redeem their dollars for gold, most handled the U.S. Treasury with kid gloves: Only a golden trickle left Washington. Some nations, such as Germany, did this because they were obliquely threatened with U.S. troop pullbacks, but there were others who sincerely believed that their sacrifices were going toward the maintenance of the world monetary order.

As in any unnatural economic imbalance, speculators had jumped into the fray and began betting against the dollar. The reasons for their position were justified by every piece of economic news emerging from the United States by mid-1971. Each monthly figure was worse than its predecessor; the nation had slipped into severe trade and payments deficits. But the allies were patient; only a relatively paltry $300 million in gold left the U.S. from January to early August 1971. Rumors spread among foreign central banks that the gold window was about to be shut. Rumblings from the Bank of England suggested that they were preparing to turn in dollars for gold in huge amounts. As Treasury Secretary Connally said (privately) at the time, "We're completely exposed. Anybody can topple us anytime they want to."

On August 6, a congressional subcommittee report concluded that the dollar had become overvalued and called outright for an exchange rate realignment. That same day more than $1 billion in gold or other reserve assets were drained from the Treasury, and over that next week almost $4 billion fled the country.

During the week ending Friday, August 13, the U.S. Treasury borrowed almost $3 billion in foreign currency to try to halt the dollar's decline (by buying dollars with that currency). But it soon became obvious that the anti-dollar forces had too much strength.

President Nixon responded by declaring international bankruptcy. In a televised address on Sunday, August 15, 1971, he announced that no more gold would be given in exchange for dollars. There were now absolutely no checks on the ability of the United States to inflate.

Nixon's speech to the world that night was a cunning attempt to lay the burden of guilt for this assault upon the shoulders of America's trading partners, who had maintained, Nixon astonishingly asserted, "unfair exchange rates." The cause of the problem had indeed been inequitable exchange rates, but not in the way that Nixon meant. The injustice of this statement is unsettling even 10 years after it was made.

"Unfair" Japan

It is interesting to trace the immediate reactions of one of those "unfair" partners, Japan. Unlike Western Europe, whose exchanges were closed when news of the announcement came, it was Monday morning in the Far East. Trading was already underway when Nixon stepped before the cameras. Paralyzed by the news, the Japanese nevertheless kept their foreign exchange market open—not only for the rest of the day, but for two weeks afterward. As the European markets had sensibly remained closed, Tokyo became the dumping ground for anyone who wanted to get rid of dollars. During those two weeks the Bank of Japan absorbed $4.5 billion. Finally, on August 28, they threw in the towel and joined the other currencies in floating.

The European markets had remained closed, stunned and confused by the president's action. But they could not remain shut forever, and after efforts to decide upon a common course of action failed, they opened on August 23 on an uncoordinated basis. Even though they all continued to adhere officially to their pre-August 15 parities with the dollar, virtually all of them stopped defending the upper limits of their exchange rates.

In the months that followed, the spotlight turned on the United States as other nations waited for an American move. Their view was the understandable one that since the United States had thrown the monetary system out of kilter, it was up to America to make the first move.

American officials finally revealed a plan whereby most other currencies would be revalued upward against the dollar; no mention at all was made of the United States devaluing its dollar by raising the official price of gold. This overture naturally struck America's trading partners as still one more affront. When the director of the IMF, Pierre-Paul Scheitzer, suggested that the United States might share in this realignment by a minor increase in the gold price, he was immediately moved onto the "most wanted" column of the Nixon administration's enemy list. But the Europeans were intransigent; the American plan made no headway.

The "Greatest Agreement"

Massive runs continued on the dollar, belying Nixon's August 15 claim that a dollar cut from gold would "never again be subject to international speculation." By mid-December—four months later—the dollar had declined by 12.5 percent against the mark, 12.3 percent against the yen, and had even lost ground to the lire and the pound, falling by 5.4 percent and 4.1 percent respectively. The world monetary situation not only continued in disarray, it seemed to be getting worse.

On December 18, 1971, the Smithsonian agreement was announced. For the first time in the post-war era, the dollar was devalued by raising the official gold price from $35 to $38 an ounce (8.6 percent). But gold convertibility was not restored, so the devaluation meant little.

Nixon's aim was to recreate an international order with fixed exchange rates—but without gold. He referred to this as "the greatest monetary agreement in the history of the world," but it was clear that no system would break down faster than a system of fixed rates fixed to nothing, neither to gold nor to anything else.

Nixon's "greatest monetary agreement" was smashed on the shoals of economic reality barely 14 months later, because the dollar and pound sterling continued to be drastically overvalued in terms of the other industrialized nations' currencies and, most importantly, in terms of gold. The lack of confidence in the dollar sent gold prices soaring to $90 an ounce, almost tripling the formerly sacred $35 figure. There continued to be periodic flights from the dollar.

Finally, on January 24, 1973, the Swiss government stopped supporting the dollar. Other governments quickly followed: They had all had enough. One month later, the entire fixed-rate order collapsed. The actual story of how it happened would be a dreary repetition of the tales recounted about billions of unwanted dollars reluctantly bought; another frantic but fundamentally ineffective dollar devaluation in an unsuccessful attempt to restore tranquility and, ultimately, a closure of the world exchange markets. When those markets reopened, they did so without fixed rates. And the absence of fixed rates meant, logically, de facto floating rates. Floating rates had not really been adopted; rather, fixed rates had been abandoned.

Floating and Sinking

Since 1973 we haven't had the former condition of "public crises" where inflationist governments would be forced to spend millions in the foreign exchange markets defending their currencies until finally giving up and devaluing their currencies. For all its messiness, that system at least called people's attention to the fact that offending governments were in effect publicly confessing their sins. What we have had since is rather a quiet but constant withering away of values of those currencies, which are inflated more than others, and a large drop in the value of all currencies in terms of gold. While the dollar—and even the Swiss franc—is not today what it was in 1973, an ounce of gold remains an ounce of gold.

Even under the flawed Bretton Woods fixed rates, there were limits to how far governments could inflate. Granted, it took a quarter-century, but the United States eventually inflated to such a degree it lost too much gold.

The floating rate system has given, however, complete control of the value of each currency to the respective governments. They need not worry about gold flowing into other central banks. There are thus no institutional limits to inflate, and it should come as no surprise that the past decade has seen a marked jumped in average annual world inflation.

The only effect of internal inflation now is a drop in the currency exchange rate, a currency falling in value. But in each country there are special interests who desire just that. These include domestic businessmen who can't compete with the better-made or lower-cost products of other lands. If these inefficient firms' goods are priced in a currency becoming cheaper, consumers of stronger-currency countries can more easily buy those goods. But the reverse of this is that goods from those stronger currency countries, priced as they are in currencies rising in value, become more expensive for the consumers of the nation whose currency is falling. Their living standards thus fall as they are in effect forced to subsidize inefficient domestic producers. Also, gainers in a depreciating currency country are *all* export firms, inefficient or otherwise. They can exert powerful pressure in favor of international inflation.

But as one can guess, this system does not exactly promote international harmony. Temptations are great for the "competitive" devaluations which so upset world economic peace in the 1930s. As we enter the 1980s, unpleasant rumblings in favor of protectionism and high tariff barriers are being heard on a grand scale for the first time in half a century. The world economy is being pulled apart. It is no coincidence that world trade wars are threatened more now than at any time since the *last* regime of floating exchange rates, during the depression-ridden 1930s.

Islands of Calm in a Churning Sea

There have been attempts to operate localized fixed rate systems amidst the generalized floating. Foremost among these attempts have been the two efforts of that most cohesive and interdependent group of countries, the European Common Market.

Being linked by culture, geography, and the need for trade, they realize more than America does what havoc floating rates have wreaked, and it is a hopeful sign that these nations are more and more including gold in their dealings.

The first of these stabilizing attempts was the Common Market "snake," so-called because all the currencies moving up or down within predetermined limits called to mind the undulations of a moving snake. Begun in 1972, it was over by 1976 simply because several different governments, each with its own inflation rate, from the start moved away from each other, flinging accusations of bad faith at each other while they did.

Having more flexible limits, Western Europe tried again and in March 1979 inaugurated the European Monetary System (EMS). While the EMS enables countries to revalue more easily, each time a member does, it strains the very cohesion the system was meant to foster. It was nonetheless successful during its first two and a half years of operation. Traditionally strong currencies like the German mark weakened while perpetually weak ones like the French franc and Italian lira were strong.

There was therefore only one major realignment until October 1981. Since then, though, there have been two (the most recent on February 21, 1982) and signs point to European currencies falling back into their usual patterns. But while EMS is likely in for a hard time, in the background of this latest attempt at monetary union has been a gradual but clear remonetization of gold, the only stable unifying force among currencies.

Even before EMS's 1979 birth, both Italy and Portugal borrowed billions of dollars from other European nations and used as collateral part of their gold holdings. But in those cases in the mid-'70s, the gold was valued at around 20 percent below the prevailing free-market price.

With EMS's founding, things took a turn. In exchange for member gold deposits, nations received a new currency called the European Currency Unit (ECU). The hope is that one day ECU will be the European currency. This currency not only represents deposits in gold, but the gold is valued at the free-market rate. Further, under EMS rules, gold can act as a means of settlement between members. So gold now fulfills in the EMS two of three functions of money: It is both a reserve instrument and an instrument of payment. Gold only lacks the final prerequisite for money, a standard of value. This is so because current IMF rules (effective April 1, 1978) forbid all reference to gold in defining currency values. This has led to the absurd situation where currency A is defined in terms of B, C, and D; B in terms of A, C, and D, and so on. Each currency is thus defined in terms of others which themselves depend for definition upon it.

The market has not been fooled by any of this. It knows how to value currencies—in terms of gold. And that valuation has been since 1971 embarrassing for every currency. One-tenth of an ounce of gold will today buy as many dollars as one ounce did 10 years ago.

The market has delivered its verdict on the battle between gold and the dollar waged throughout the 1970s by the American government; first the 1971 suspension of any remaining convertibility, and then two devaluations in rapid succession. At the Jamaica Conference of 1976, the IMF approved the U.S. wish to demonetize gold by abolishing the official price and selling over 600 tons, one-sixth of all IMF holdings (returning another one-sixth to member nations). The U.S. Treasury itself announced in January 1978 that it would sell gold beginning that May. But all during the time of the sales (which totalled about 500 tons) gold's price rose. Finally realizing it was throwing away a precious resource, Treasury ceased its gold sales after November 1979. The Treasury thus implicitly backed up the enhanced roles which Europeans had given gold earlier that year.

Indeed, as pointed out by Yves Laulan, chief economist of Société Génerale (one of France's largest banks), the U.S. Treasury, in an attempt to demonetize gold, authorized its sale to end circulation among individual Americans. Paradoxically, that act caused people to value it even more.

This subjective revaluation of gold has since spread to the Treasury, which now realizes that it holds far more gold reserves than any other country. Those who wish to reestablish American dominance in the world are not blind to the fact that gold is a powerful weapon. It is thus unlikely that Washington will wage last decade's war on gold again.

Conclusion

Our historical experience illustrates the overwhelmingly superior case for the gold standard as against any form of paper standard. There has never, in peacetime American history, been any sustained rate of inflation to match the inflation since 1941. The same, in fact, is true of wartime, which at least has never lasted more than a few years. And it is not an accident that the highest, most accelerated rate of inflation has taken place since 1971, when the United States went off the international aspects of the gold standard and went over completely to fiat paper.

The same conclusion is true if we consider price stability. Even deflation has been more acute under the fiat standard than under gold, as happened in the fiat standard war of 1873–79 as contrasted to the gold standard period from 1879–1896.

Bimetallism doesn't work either, as America learned painfully from a century's experience. Gresham's Law, driving out undervalued moneys, works there as it does whenever the government overvalues one money and undervalues another. The dollar must be defined once again as a fixed weight of gold, with coinage and paper dollars always redeemable one into another at that weight. Ideally, full-bodied silver would fluctuate freely alongside the gold dollar; short of that, fractional, subsidiary silver, as well as other metals such as copper, would circulate in minor capacity along with gold.

The dollar must be redefined as a unit of weight of gold again, and gold coins should be encouraged to actually circulate among the public, to be used not simply as long-range investment but as a medium of exchange functioning as money. As Mises' "regression theorem" showed in 1912, new currency units cannot be imposed *de novo* from above, by politicians or economists.[10] They must emerge out of the experience and the valuations of the public on the market. The public is now long

[10]See Ludwig Mises, *The Theory of Money and Credit* (Irvington-on-Hudson, New York: The Foundation for Economic Education, 1971).

used to the "dollar" as the money unit, and therefore the "gold gram" or "gold ounce" cannot be simply adopted by the public as a money out of the clear blue sky. The eventual adoption of a gold gram or gold ounce is basically a two-phase process: First, the "dollar," now of course the common currency unit, must be firmly and permanently tied to gold at a fixed weight; the public must become accustomed to this concept; and then finally, the currency unit can *become* that fixed weight directly.

What weight we choose to define the dollar is a matter of convenience, since any *initial* definition is arbitrary, and we can pick the most useful one. This is no more "fixing the price of gold" and violating the free market than defining that two nickels as equal to one dime "fixes the prices" of these two entities, or any more than defining that one pound as equal to 16 ounces "fixes the price" of ounces and pounds. *What* the definition should be depends on the preferred use and what the remainder of the monetary and banking system will look like.

Eventually, too, we must abolish the central government's monopoly of the minting business. Surely the idea that the sovereignty of the king must be expressed through stamping his face on a coin can now be discarded as a relic of a bygone age. There is no reason why private firms cannot mint coins as well, or better, than the national mint. Free competition should come, at long last, to the minting business. The cost would be far cheaper and the quality of the coins much improved.

From our historical analysis, it becomes clear that the problems of money and the business cycle under the gold standard, of inflation and contraction in the 1818–36 era, of World War I inflation, of the boom of the 1920s and the disasters of the Great Depression of 1929–33, stemmed not from the gold standard but from the inflationary fractional-reserve banking system within it. This inflationary banking system was made possible by the government's imposition of a central bank: the Federal Reserve, the Bank of the United States, or by the quasi-centralized system of the national banking era after the Civil War. These booms and busts would not have occurred under "free banking," i.e., the system in which banks are decentralized, able to issue either notes or deposits, cannot be bailed out by a leader of last resort, and are forced to close their doors permanently if they fail to redeem their liabilities in specie. The quasi-free banking period from the 1830s to the Civil War was far sounder and more stable than any period before or since in American history—as historians are now coming to recognize. It would have been far better but for the periodic suspensions of specie payment that governments continued to permit. The legalization of branch banking would have made it far easier to call upon banks for redemption.

Once again, it was the intervention of government that caused the difficulty, not the market. Laissez faire has not been consistently applied to banking. The historical evidence shows that monetary freedom does not fail, intervention by the government does.

IV. The Case For Monetary Freedom

America's First Free Market Gold Coins

Most people assume that governments must be the only parties allowed to mint money. Private minters, the argument goes, will put out coins of uncertain quality and take advantage of people. But not only have privately minted coins flourished; in at least one instance admitted by the U.S. Treasury's mintmaster, the private minter had the edge over the government.

The first coiners of American copper and silver money were private citizens. Copper coins were minted by one John Higley of Granby, Connecticut. From 1737 to 1739 he issued coins that first were marked with a three pence value. But as he minted more of them, and used them mostly to buy drinks at the neighborhood bar, objections were raised to valuing them at his "high" rate. So he "lowered" his price, and the legend was changed to read "VALUE ME AS YOU PLEASE—I AM GOOD COPPER."[1] Actually, after he stopped minting them, they came to be valued by the market at two shillings, six pence—or 30 pence.

The first American silver was coined after the Revolution in 1783 by I. Chalmers, an Annapolis goldsmith. There had been a shortage of silver, with Spanish silver circulating by being cut into "pieces of eight," that is into eight "eights." But unscrupulous cutters were cutting the coin into nine or ten "eights," and Chalmers' idea of minting American shillings and pence was well-received. Unfortunately, Chalmers succumbed to the same temptation that has afflicted national money issuers: He started putting in less silver for the same face value.

Coin shortages plagued early America, with all the minor inconveniences associated with that condition. People responded by making their own money. As William Wooldridge wrote, in his fine chapter on private coinage in *Uncle Sam the Monopoly Man*, people made money "in whatever quantity suited the need or the impulse of the moment, out of whatever medium they found most convenient, and emblazoned it with whatever device, portrait or motto they fancied. They passed it on to whoever would take it and then made some more. Not only did the United States have a private coinage, it had dozens, at one point hundreds, of private coinages simultaneously."

[1]Sylvester S. Crosby, *Early Coins of America and the Laws Governing Their Issue* (New York: Burt Franklin Publishing Co., 1970 [1875]).

Many of these have survived. One particularly affecting copper coin has on its obverse a kneeling slave woman in chains with the legend, "AM I NOT A WOMAN AND A SISTER[?]." On the reverse is "UNITED STATES OF AMERICA," and "LIBERTY/1838" within an olive wreath. Some copper coins cleverly skirted the counterfeit laws, rarely enforced in times of shortage. One penny-size coin says "NOT ONE CENT, BUT JUST AS GOOD." At least some of these coins, minted before 1840, were still found in circulation as late as 1879.

Gold Coins

By their nature, gold coins don't usually serve as small change. Therefore, we find private gold much less frequently than silver and copper. And their issuance was local, only in places where the U.S. Mint had not provided adequate assaying or coining facilities. Further, because gold is much more valuable, any private mintmaster would have to build up his reputation for integrity over many years. This also limited the number of minters.

There were some private gold coins, however. The first were minted by Templeton Reid in Lumpkin County, Georgia. He produced $10, $5, and $2.50 gold pieces roughly the same in weight and fineness as "official coins" of like value. Although all his coins are dated 1830, he minted after that, but no one knows for how long. It is known that he was doing business in California in 1849.

The brightest name in American private gold coinage is Christopher Bechtler, a German immigrant who arrived in Rutherfordton, in western North Carolina in 1830, then the premier gold-producing area in America. He began minting coins one year later and continued until he died in 1842. There was a crying need: The nearest federal mint was in Philadelphia, too far to provide much circulating gold or to enable miners to travel there easily and have their gold coined.

Bechtler minted, along with $2.50 and $5 coins, the first American gold one dollar, 18 years before the United States did. By 1840 he had minted $2,241,840.50 worth of gold—roughly one-fourth of the total North Carolina coin values from the first mint record in 1804 through 1839. He coined for a profit of two and one-half percent of the bullion he handled. But he never accumulated great wealth, and his integrity became legendary. A book published in London in 1847 by G. W. Featherstonebaugh (*A Canoe Voyage Up the Minnay Sotor*) related how impressed people were with his honesty in making his coins the same value as official U.S. coins.

Both Bechtler's coins and his reputation were known far and wide. The emigrations of the 1850s brought many of his coins out west. And in Massachusetts constitutional lawyer Lysander Spooner argued that if Bechtler was allowed to coin money constitutionally then surely Spooner's private American Letter Mail Company (which made him a folk hero for carrying mail faster and cheaper than the post office) should be allowed to carry mail privately.

In fact, only a legislative oversight long since changed kept Bechtler out of jail. While private coinage of copper was considered counterfeiting, there was at that time no similar prohibition on silver and gold coinage.

So highly regarded was the Bechtler dollar that even when the United States Mint opened an office in Charlotte, North Carolina in 1838, Bechtler successfully competed with it. His equipment is now in museums: his dies at the North Carolina Hall of History at Raleigh, and his press at the American Numismatic Society in New York. They act as proof that someone once successfully competed with the government in money, the service which "everyone knows" only the government can provide.

Other Gold Coins

During the California gold rush government minting offices were sometimes slow in appearing and private firms filled the breach. By 1852, 14 companies had sprung up. While the absolute amount coined by these firms ($4,240,000) was larger than by Bechtler, they handled a much smaller percentage share of the roughly $260,000,000 worth of gold coined by 1854.

But though the general appearance of these $5, $10, $20, and $50 coins resembled each other, their value was not uniform, and some of the firms were not completely honest in their minting. In any case, in 1854 the San Francisco mint was established, and private coinage was discouraged. But at least $2 million worth of these coins circulated for years to come.

Other Western states were host to private gold coinage. The Orange Exchange Company in Oregon City, Oregon, issued $5 and $10 coins in 1842. The Mormons struck $2.50, $5, $10, and $20 coins in 1849 and 1860. They bore the legend "HOLINESS TO THE LORD" on one side, and the letters "G.S.L.C.P.G." (Great Salt Lake City Pure Gold) on the other. In discussing one assay of these coins, *Bankers' Magazine* (vol. 4, 1849–50, p. 669) opined, "If this assay at the mint be a fair test of the value of the whole of the Great Salt Lake manufacture of coin—the

Mormons seem to know what they are about, and to be determined to make the best of their gold mines."

Three Colorado companies minted $2.50, $5, and $10 coins in 1860–61. They made quite a bit of the coins, which had circulation all over the West. They were larger than "official" gold coins, but had more of a silver alloy in them, making them paler in color than other gold coins. Of the three minters, only those coins of Clark, Gruber and Company tested out well against government coins. The others presumably traded at discount. The desire for these coins continued until the Denver mint was established in 1863. Finally, a Leavenworth, Kansas, mint issued in 1871 a half-dollar gold piece (which must have been very small). But it tested out at only 17 cents, and its creators were prosecuted—not for fraud, as they should have been, but for counterfeit. The state of Kansas had passed in June 1864 the first act prohibiting private gold coinage.

Altogether, then, we find private gold coins minted in seven states and territories. In 1851, when the Philadelphia mint assayed 27 different kinds of gold coins, no less than 15 private mints were represented. That was the peak of private gold activity because with the Civil War the nation went off the gold standard, though in the West gold continued to circulate. And by 1879, when gold redemption was restored, non-governmental minting of gold coins was generally illegal.

Granted, the short history of private gold contains instances of dishonest minters. Gold Rush California in particular was the site of fly-by-night operations. And yet the example of Bechtler hints to us that if the government would have gotten out of the way, and private minters given more time to establish their reputations, a sturdy system of private coins of sound repute and wide circulation would have arisen. They could have done so either by weight or stamped-dollar value. Without a doubt, not all of them would have kept honest. The temptation to debase coins has always been strong. And yet the firms doing so would have lost business to the Bechtlers of the trade. In a system of competing private money, when one goes bad, consumers can always turn to another. But today, when only Washington has the monopoly on money, what protects us when the government debases its currency?

Free Banking in Scotland (1714–1844)[2]

Not only does economic freedom work with regard to coinage, it has had spectacular results when applied to banking. As shown in chapter

[2]We are indebted to Lawrence J. White of New York University for the work he has done on this subject.

two, one of the prime causes of economic instability in the 19th century was the special privilege conferred on banks by either the state or federal governments. These privileges, which protected the banks from their creditors and allowed them to pyramid money supplies, caused the banking panics of the last century. But if one were to eliminate those privileges, the resulting instability would also disappear.

There once was a country with a stable banking system the envy of the rest of the world. While there's nothing so extraordinary in that, it was a system with aspects almost everyone would call—were it proposed to them—unworkable. Not only was there no central bank, there were no legal tender laws, no political banking regulations, no monetary policy, and no restrictions on the right of anyone to form a bank and issue his own money. The country was Scotland from 1714–1844. When English law put an effective end to this "free banking" regime, there were 19 different banks issuing their own notes.

The Bank of England, the first central bank, was founded in 1694. A year later, a Bank of Scotland was founded by the Scottish Parliament. (They were still technically two different countries.) The Bank was given a monopoly of issuing paper money for 21 years. This expired in 1716, and no effort was made to renew it. All apparently thought that there would never be any other note issuers.

It's important to realize that despite its official-sounding name, the Bank of Scotland was a completely private institution, with no governmental connection. Indeed, the act creating the Bank prohibited it from lending to the Scottish government. But after 1707, there was no more sovereign Scottish government, as the two parliaments merged into one, in London. This was in the reign of Queen Anne, a (Scottish) Stuart. When she died a few years later, the German Hanovers acceded to the throne, and their descendants still sit upon it. But this did not sit well with many Scots, who longed for a Stuart king. Their men were called Jacobites, and England would wage war upon them until "Bonnie Prince Charlie" was finally defeated in 1745.

All this is important to our story. In 1727, the Bank of Scotland's first real rival in note issuance was formed, the Royal Bank of Scotland. The Bank of Scotland petitioned the English king for monopoly status, but the English ignored the request, aware of the Bank's Jacobite sympathies.

There now began something unprecedented: a "note duel" whereby each bank would send large quantities of the other's bank notes back to it and demand specie redemption. The old Bank, having less silver, lost the duel and for several months in 1728 suspended silver payments.

It intended to reopen, though, and it did. All the while it paid a 5 percent interest rate to its note holders to keep demand from collapsing. The Bank's notes traded at par all this time. The Royal Bank soon began paying interest rates on deposits; this, long before English banks did. It was an obvious benefit of competition in banking.

The two banks remained the only rivals until 1750. Each were Edinburgh banks and each sponsored a Glasgow bank to act as its note "salesman" in that city. To the surprise of each, both banks soon began issuing their own money. Neither note-dueling nor a cartellization attempt to divide the nation into two "districts" worked, and a proliferation of "banks of issue" occurred. There were a few who issued far more paper than they had silver to back it, and they soon went bankrupt. But most were successful. One of these newcomers, the British Linen Company (later Bank), became the world's first innovator in branch banking, having 12 branches by 1793.

During this time, there were sporadic attempts by the first two or three banks to obtain a money-issuing monopoly for themselves, but these failed. What laws did pass left the system largely intact. The Act of 1765 outlawed notes in smaller denominations than one pound and insured that all notes were to be redeemable in gold on demand. The total number of Scottish banks (issuing money or otherwise) climbed from five in 1740 to 32 in 1769. In that year the Ayr Bank was founded on the inflationist schemes which the Scotsman John Law had tried unsuccessfully to get the Bank of Scotland to adopt in 1705. (He later got the French government to listen to him and caused the first nationwide paper money inflation.) Law's idea was for a bank to issue notes not backed by gold or silver, but on the reputation of the issuer and "backed" by land.

In a mere three years, the Ayr Bank managed to create a tremendous amount of unbacked paper, and when it finally collapsed in 1772 losses amounted to two-thirds of a million pounds, a staggering amount for those days.

But the intriguing thing is that the Ayr Bank's collapse had limited repercussions. It took with it only eight small private banks in Edinburgh. This is largely because of a well-developed clearinghouse mechanism that the large Scottish banks employed. They accepted each others' notes and returned those notes to the issuing bank. Suspicious of the Ayr Bank's issue, other banks made a practice of quickly returning Ayr's notes to it. When the collapse came, they were not affected.

Nevertheless, to insure public confidence (and get their own notes into wider circulation) the two largest banks, the Royal Bank and the

Bank of Scotland, announced that they would accept the bankrupt bank's notes. This was not as mad as it may appear. The collapse had few rippling effects because of Scotland's extraordinary practice of unlimited liability on the part of the bank's shareholders. So Ayr's loss was borne completely by the 241 shareholders, who paid all creditors in full.

Scottish banking grew apace, and around 1810 a new development occurred. This was the founding of the Commercial Bank of Scotland on joint-stock principles. Joint-stock banks, unlike private banks, raise their capital by selling shares of stock. This development grew and with it branch banking. By 1845, there were 19 banks of issue with a total of 363 branches across Scotland, or one branch for every 6,600 Scots. This compares with one for every 9,405 Englishmen and one for every 16,000 Americans at that time.

This was the heyday of Scottish free banking. The arrangement approached the ideal: many competing banks with none disproportionately large; their notes circulating throughout the country (and even in northern England) being exchanged effectively by the banks themselves through a clearinghouse; and competition keeping profits down, with small spreads between the interest they paid depositors and the interest they charged borrowers.

These banks were the envy of thoughtful Englishmen. Scottish banks consistently proved themselves more stable than their English counterparts. While English provincial, or "country," banks were able to issue their own notes until 1845, there were many differences. The Bank of England (a state institution) limited their size and refused to accept their notes. Further, the Bank did not branch out of London until an 1826 law encouraged it to do so. So for years, England was bedevilled with small, unstable country banks and an uncompetitive Bank of England (which unlike Scottish banks paid no interest not only on demand deposits, but even on six-month certificates).

During the financial panics of 1793, 1797, 1815, 1825–26, and 1837, English country banks collapsed right and left, while the record for Scotland was always far better. When in trouble, Scottish banks could always turn to each other for help, which the stronger banks would give for reasons of self-interest as we saw in the extreme case of the Ayr Bank. English country banks had no one to turn to.

From 1797 to 1821, England suspended gold payments. Scotland went along not because it had to but because it realized that its gold would be drained if it didn't. And there is evidence that Scottish banks quietly continued gold payments to their best customers.

English and Scottish Bank Failures, 1809–1830

Year	English bankruptcies/1,000	Scottish bankruptcies/1,000
1809	5.7	0
1810	25.6	0
1811	5.1	0
1812	20.6	0
1813	8.7	14.3
1814	28.7	0
1815	27.3	9
1816	44.5	14.1
1817	4.0	0
1818	3.9	0
1819	16.5	0
1820	5.2	13.2
1821	12.8	0
1822	11.6	13.0
1823	11.6	0
1824	12.8	0
1825	46.4	12.0
1826	53.1	11.0
1827	11.9	0
1828	4.5	0
1829	4.4	11.4
1830	20.9	0
Avg/ yr.	18.1	4.0

In computing the Scottish bank failure rate, up to three branches of a bank were similarly included in the computation, while non-issuing banks were excluded. The number of branches was estimated by interpolation where figures for a particular year were not available. No more than one Scottish bank failed during any year in the sample.

This difference between the two nations is graphically illustrated by a cartoon published in the *Northern Looking Glass* in 1825, a year of severe panic in Britain. (This is reproduced in Checkland's *Scottish Banking, A History: 1695–1973* (Collins, 1975), p. 407.) Entitled "State of the Money Market," it shows two scenes: "England" with a fat banker in the midst of banks and paper crashing down around him and "Scotland," where two tartaned Scots are happily dealing in coin, with bags more of it visible across the banker's desk. While 60 English banks collapsed in 1825–26, none in Scotland did, although some partners sustained severe losses.

As an interesting aside, counterfeiting was never a problem for Scottish banks, a situation unlike the Bank of England, especially during the latter's suspension of gold payments. Perhaps this is due to the much shorter average life of Scottish notes. Turnover was heavy and the issuing bank quick to catch on. Even so, Scotch banks would honor counterfeits if turned in by innocent parties. To do anyting else would have been bad business in a truly businesslike atmosphere.

The first editor of the London *Economist*, James Wilson, wrote in 1847 that "we have only to look at Scotland to see what has been the effect of a long career of perfect freedom and competition upon the character and credit of the banking establishment of that country." Yet two years before those words were written, legal action finally brought the "career of perfect freedom" to an end. Peel's Act of 1844 and the Scottish Banking Act of 1845 abolished freedom of entry into banking and the right of those remaining banks of freedom of note issue. However, Bank of England notes were not forced upon Scotland as legal tender; only gold was so established.

Abolition of free entry caused a gradual reduction in banks issuing notes, and Scottish pound notes today have long since become like those of any other part of Great Britain. That is, with one exception. If you go to Scotland today, you will see pound notes issued by the three remaining banks of issue in business before 1845: the Bank of Scotland, the Royal Bank of Scotland, and Clydesdale Bank. These are actually as good—or as bad—as the Bank of England's notes circulating throughout the rest of the United Kingdom because everything else about them is dictated by the Bank of England. But they provide daily proof that once there was a free market in money issuance with no legal tender laws and that the system worked very well.

V. Real Money: The Case For the Gold Standard

In chapters two and three, it was made clear that the economic shortcomings of the past were due to abuse of the gold standard, not to the standard itself. Men and governments have failed in the past; gold has not. The rule of law has been challenged by the rule of men throughout history, and this will continue. But the rule of law and the sovereignty of the people are much more likely to prevail with gold than with paper. For many economic reasons it is critical that the rule of law and gold win the great debate on monetary policy.

Low Interest Rates

The most pressing problem today for consumers and businessmen is high interest rates. Even those who do not understand the process of inflation easily recognize the great harm brought to an economy through high interest rates. The real interest rate, usually three percent to 5 percent, the cost of using another's capital, remains relatively stable. The inflationary premium charged in an age of inflation changes inversely to the confidence the market places in the monetary authorities and the spending habits of Congress. Contrary to popular belief, this premium is not equivalent to the current rate of price increases. This is certainly a factor, but only one of many in determining the anticipation of the future purchasing power of the currency. If prices are accelerating at an annual rate of 10 percent, the inflation premium can still be 15 percent if the market anticipates a more rapid rate of currency depreciation in the future. The further a nation is down the road of inflationary policies the more difficult it is to reverse the expectations of more inflation by the people. In the early stages of inflation, more people are deceived and interest rates are actually lower than one would project if only computer analysis were used. In the later stages the rates, some claim, "are higher than they should be." This is what we are hearing today.

The inflationary premium is completely removed if a true gold standard exists. There would be no need to anticipate a depreciation of the currency, for the record is clear that gold maintains or increases its purchasing power. This ought not to be confused with sharp fluctuations in dollar-denominated prices of gold in a period of dollar speculation. The problem under those circumstances is the inflationary policies of the government, not the natural variation in the purchasing power of gold. Dr. Roy Jastram, in his book *The Golden Constant*, has demonstrated quite clearly that gold maintains its value over both long and short periods of time.

With the classical gold standard, long-term interest rates were in the range of three to four percent. There is no reason to believe that these same rates or lower rates would not occur with a modern gold standard. The economic benefit of low rates of interest is obvious to every American citizen. Accelerated real economic growth would result from such interest rates, and it cannot be achieved apart from these low rates.

Increased Savings

When a currency sustains steady and prolonged depreciation, as the dollar has for decades, the incentive to save is logically decreased. Savings by American citizens have been one of the lowest in the world. If the dollar were guaranteed not to lose any value, and three percent interest were paid on savings, as under a gold standard, a high savings rate would be quickly achieved. Getting $1.03 of purchasing power after one year for every dollar saved is much better than getting 94 cents, as happens if $1 is saved in a conventional savings account today. A nine-percent differential provides a real incentive to save under a gold standard and a strong disincentive under an irredeemable paper standard. The benefits of a gold standard for savings—the source of capital in a growing economy—should be obvious to all doubters. One reason it is hard to accept is that the marketplace—the people and voluntary exchange—is compatible with the gold standard, while government management and coercion are relied on with a paper standard. We as a nation have grown to mistrust and misunderstand a free system and have become dependent upon and misled by the money managers and central planners found in all interventionistic economies.

Revival of Long-Term Financing

Under the gold standard, bonds were sold for 100 years at four to five percent interest. Today the long-term bond market is moribund. Mortgages for houses are so costly that few Americans can qualify. With lower interest rates, increased savings, and trust that the money will maintain its value, the long-term financial markets will be revitalized—all without government subsidies or temporary government programs. Reviving the economy without restoring a sound currency is a dream. Only with a currency that is guaranteed not to depreciate will we ever be able to have once again low long-term rates of interest.

Debt Held in Check

During the time we were on a gold standard federal deficits were very small or nonexistent. Money that the government did not have, it could not spend nor could it create. Taxing the people the full amount for extravagant expenditures would prove too unpopular and a liability in the next election.

Justifiably, the people would rebel against such an outrage. Under the gold standard, inflation for the purpose of monetizing debt is prohibited, thus holding government size and power in check and preventing significant deficits from occurring. The gold standard is the enemy of big government. In time of war, in particular those wars unpopular with the people, governments suspend the beneficial restraints placed on the politicians in order to inflate the currency to finance the deficit. Strict adherence to the gold standard would prompt a balanced budget, yet it would still allow for "legitimate" borrowing when the people were willing to loan to the government for popular struggles. This would be a good test of the wisdom of the government's policy.

Finally, the inflationary climate has encouraged huge deficits to be run up by governments at all levels, as well as by consumers and corporations. The unbelievably large federal contingent liabilities of over $11 trillion are a result of inflationary policies, pervasive government planning, and unwise tax policies.

Full Employment

In a growing economy, labor is in demand. In a recession or depression, unemployment apparently beyond everyone's control plagues the nation. The unemployment is caused by the correction that the market must make for the misdirection of investment brought on by government inflation and artificial wage levels mandated by "full employment" policies. Full employment occurs when maximum economic growth is achieved with a sound monetary system and wages are allowed to be determined by the marketplace.

Some would suggest that at times those rates are too low and must be raised by law. This can be done only at the expense of someone else losing a job to pay another a higher wage than deserved. The forced increases in wage benefits increase corporate debt and contribute to their need for more inflationary credit to help keep them afloat. Although only government can literally inflate, higher-than-market wages in certain businesses prompt the accommodation of monetary policy to keep these companies going, Chrysler Corporation being a prime example. High wages contributed to Chrysler's financial plight and government-guaranteed loans (inflation) were used to "solve" the problem. It's well to remember that working for $8 an hour is superior to having a wage of $16 an hour but no job. For awhile the artificially high wage seems to be beneficial, but the unemployment and the recession that eventually come make the program a dangerous one. For years it was believed that "inflation" stimulated the economy and lowered unemployment rates. But in the later stages of inflation its ill effects are felt, and unemployment increases while real wages fall. More inflation and wage controls to keep wages high will make the problem significantly worse and only raise the unemployment rates. Only a sound currency and a market determination of wages can solve this most explosive social problem of ever-increasing unemployment.

Economic Growth Enhanced

The record for real economic growth while we were on a gold standard surpasses the growth we have experienced during the past 10 years. Current economic statistics show the conditions worsening with no end to the crisis in sight. Only with a gold standard will we see revitalization of a productive economic activity.

The "Austrian" economists, and in particular Ludwig von Mises, have demonstrated clearly that the business cycle is a result of unwise monetary policy (frequently compounded by other unwise government policies such as wage controls and protectionist legislation). The business boom results from periods of monetary growth; the recession results from the restraints that are eventually placed on this money growth, either by the government or the market. As government increases the money supply, false signals are sent to the market, causing lower than market interest rates, easy access to investment funds and, therefore, a misdirection of investment. This misdirection must later be corrected by market forces. This whole process is aggravated by massive disruption in the market direction of investment by government guaranteeing hundreds of billions of dollars of loans, which prompts more monetary growth. Government becomes a direct participant in credit allocation in an inflationary economy. Although during all stages and in isolated cases "benefits" are demonstrated, the overall economic harm done by inflation and malinvestment is overwhelming. We are seeing those results all around us today.

Money Growth Not Necessary

Advocates of discretionary and monetarist monetary policies claim that money growth is needed to "accommodate" economic growth.

Economic growth is *not* dependent on money growth. Economic growth comes from productive efforts which are encouraged by savings, low interest rates, reliable currency, and minimal taxes. Attempting to control and stimulate economic growth with monetary growth does the opposite; it destroys the environment required for real growth to occur.

With the gold standard and the free market, investments are strictly made by enterprising individuals eager to make a profit. Those done carefully and prudently are encouraged. Successful investments bring rewards, and mistakes bring penalties to the investors. In contrast, a government-directed economy, backed up by unlimited supplies of paper money and fabricated credit, prompts the bailing out of unsuccessful enterprises and promotes investments for political, not economic, reasons. It is inevitable that the system of inflation and government-directed investment will fail.

With a gold standard the money supply would probably increase on an average of two percent per year. If the growth is smaller or larger, prices will adjust, posing no limitation on economic growth due to a "shortage" of capital. With the gold standard, confidence in the monetary unit would exist, and credit extended from one business to another, to consumers and purchasers, would be greatly encouraged. Information on the credit needs of the market would be available immediately, in contrast to the late information the Federal Reserve always receives. (The Federal Reserve never planned to increase the money supply at a rate of 19 percent in January 1982—it was only able to react to it after the fact.) Under a real gold standard, "controlling" the money supply is irrelevant as long as the market—an absolutely free pricing mechanism—is allowed to adjust the perceived value of gold, with no wage or price controls of any sort instituted.

Price "Stability"

Prices are never rigid in a free market. A gold standard permits price adjustments to accommodate the flow of gold into and out of a country as well as to regulate new production of gold. In contrast to popular belief, the goal of stable—that is, rigid—price levels as proclaimed by paper money managers is not the goal of the gold standard. The irony, however, is that the goal of rigid prices set by the paper money managers is completely elusive, but a gold standard, in which the goal is honesty and freedom and flexibility of prices, achieves significant price "stability."

Economic Calculation

A precisely defined unit of account by weight, an ounce of gold for instance, provides a needed objective measurement to allow reasonable economic calculations. Under socialism, economic calculation is impossible. Without a gold standard, economic calculation is extremely difficult. Without a precise unit of account, sound economic planning becomes practically impossible, resulting in only speculative ventures and barter. Having a unit of account that has no definition or one that changes continually produces a situation equivalent to a carpenter using a yardstick that on an hourly basis changes the number of inches it contains. It is easy to see how foolish it would be to have any other unit of measurement changing in definition on a constant basis, yet many believe that a whole nation's economy can operate with a monetary system in which the "dollar" has no definition and its measurement and value depend on politicians and bureaucrats.

Trade is enhanced domestically and internationally when a precise unit of account is used. The failure of the Confederation was due principally to the absence of a unit of account that all the colonies could use to facilitate exchange. This problem was solved when the Constitutional Convention precisely defined the dollar. The chaotic conditions that are developing today will only be solved when we once again accept a sound monetary system.

Internationally, all payments with the gold standard could be made by the actual transferring of gold. Such a policy would limit the ability of nations to export their inflation. The decrease in the gold supply of an importing nation would prompt prices to drop, allowing for more competitive prices and more competition in world markets. The key to Third World economic success is not their gold supply (or imported inflation in terms of Eurodollars) but whether or not they can work and produce a product that is exportable. This is dependent on the degree of economic freedom that the people have and their right to own property. The policy that guarantees a continuation of Third-World starvation and poverty is the present policy of continued worldwide inflation and centrally controlled economies.

Economic Limitations of Gold

The economic advantages of the gold standard are many and compelling. However, it is important that one does not expect from the gold standard something that cannot be achieved. The errors of a government-planned economy cannot be cancelled out by instituting a gold standard alone. Abusive tax policies must be changed to allow an economy to thrive. And although sound money goes a long way toward protecting a worker's real income, it will not overcome bad labor laws.

Gold is used as money in a free market because the people throughout history have chosen gold. Although historically a free market means a gold standard, a gold standard by itself will not ensure a free market. When a market economy is in place, a gold standard holds in check the ability of the government officials to expand their power.

Some claim that a gold standard cannot be put into place until big government is brought under control and the budget is balanced; they further claim that it *then* becomes unnecessary. It is necessary to balance the budget and institute a gold standard together. The discipline and determination required for one mandates the other. If government is to be limited in size, the budget balanced and the market free, gold will be a necessary adjunct. It will give assurance that the size and scope of government will be held in check. If government is to continue running the economy and accumulating massive deficits, inflationary monetary policy will persist. A gold standard cannot exist in a vacuum; it must be part of a broader freedom philosophy. When we as a nation reject political control of the economy and the money, the gold standard will return in a modern version—far surpassing all previous attempts at establishing sound money. Until then, as we opt for more and more ad hoc "solutions" to the government-created problems, freedom will be further diminished, the economy will deteriorate further, and inflation will accelerate. Gold must be allowed to perform its vital service in building a healthy economy and restraining the tendency of all governments to become large and oppressive.

Common Objections to Gold

In any debate about the gold standard, certain objections are repeatedly raised by opponents of monetary freedom, even though those objections have been refuted many times before. Some of these objections are:

1) There is not enough gold;
2) The Soviet Union and South Africa, since they are the principal producers of gold, would benefit from our creation of a gold standard;
3) The gold standard causes panics and crashes;
4) The gold standard causes inflation;
5) Gold is subject to undesirable speculative influences.

The first objection, there isn't enough gold, is based upon a misunderstanding of a gold standard. It assumes that the present exchange ratio (or a lower ratio) between a weight of gold and a greenback is the exchange ratio that must prevail in a gold standard. Such obviously is not the case. Doubling the exchange ratio, for example, doubles the money supply. Lower prices under a gold standard eliminate the necessity for such large sums. One can buy a suit that costs 400 paper dollars with 20 gold dollars.

In 1979, there were a total of 35,000 metric tons of gold in central banks and non-Communist government treasuries alone. The United States government, officially holding 264 million ounces (8,227 tons), owns about one-fourth of that total. The best estimate on the total amount of gold in the world is three billion ounces, meaning that about one-third of the world's gold is held by governments and central banks, and two-thirds by private persons. Far from being a dearth of gold, there are enormous amounts in existence. Gold, unlike most commodities, remains in existence. It is not burned or consumed, and the amounts actually lost are insignificant when compared to the amounts now in public and private possession.

The second objection, concerning the Soviet Union and South Africa, is equally groundless. These nations, as the world's largest producers of gold, have profited handsomely from the massive increase in gold prices in the past 10 years. Such increases do not occur under a gold standard.

Recently a newsmagazine reported that "the Soviet Union holds an estimated 60 million ounces of gold and has unmined reserves of perhaps 250 million ounces more. At today's prices that would give the Soviets a $146 billion stranglehold on western economies." But let us put these figures in perspective. Below is a table showing the gold holdings of major central banks.

Official Gold Holdings
September 30, 1979
(tons)

United States	8,227
Canada	657
Austria	657
Belgium	1,063
France	2,546
German Federal Republic	2,961
Italy	2,074

Japan	754
Netherlands	1,367
Portugal	689
South Africa	374
Switzerland	2,590
U.K.	584
OPEC	1,207
Other Asia	607
Other Europe	1,209
Other Middle East	461
Other Western Hemisphere	654
Rest of World	320
Unspecified	113
Total	29,110
IMF	3,217
European Monetary Cooperation Fund	2,664

This table, taken from the *Annual Bullion Review 1980* of Samuel Montagu & Co., is based on IMF statistics.

The Soviet Union's alleged 60 million ounces is less than 1,900 tons, less than one-fourth of the U.S. official gold holdings. Even the alleged 250 million ounces of "unmined reserves" are less than the United States has in Fort Knox and our other bullion depositories.

Consolidated Gold Fields Ltd. of London has estimated the net outflow of gold from the Communist empire:

Year	Net Outflow (tons)
1970	−3
1971	54
1972	213
1973	275
1974	220
1975	149
1976	412
1977	401
1978	410
1979	199
1980	90

In 1976, the Soviets exported 412 tons, 1.2 percent of the governmental holdings of the non-Communist world. Assuming they could export at this rate continuously—a very doubtful assumption—it would take them almost a century just to match current official holdings. If one includes private holdings, the percentage drops to about one-half of one percent, and the time required extends to more than two centuries. The fear of the Soviet Union and South Africa either dumping or withholding gold and thereby wrecking a gold standard by altering significantly the purchasing power of gold is baseless. The only reasons sales by such governments now influence the market is that official holdings are immobilized and the value of the paper dollar fluctuates violently. Were we to institute a gold standard, those holdings would once again enter the market. We should stop giving such windfalls to the Soviets and South Africans as they have enjoyed during the last 10 years. The real fear should be the massive increase in the money supply caused by the Federal Reserve in the last 10 years and the probability of still further massive inflation. The red herring of external shock destroying a gold standard is designed to distract one's attention from the threat of internal shock caused by the Federal Reserve.

The third objection, that the gold standard causes panics and crashes, is also false. The extensive examination of the monetary history of the United States during the 19th century demonstrated that it was not the gold standard, but government intervention in the banking systems, that caused the problems. The legal prohibition of branch and interstate banking prevented the prompt and convenient clearing of notes issued by those banks. Frequent suspensions of specie payments were special privileges extended to the banks by the government. Fractional reserves, wildcat banking, the National Banking System, and the issuance of greenbacks all contributed to the instability experienced during the 19th century.

But even with these interventions, as long as the dollar was defined as a weight of gold, the benevolent influences of the gold standard were felt. Chapter two of the Commission's report indicates that the problems of the 19th century were due to abuses and lapses of the gold standard, not the standard itself. Victor Zarnowitz has found evidence that the so-called recessions of 1845, 1869, 1887, and 1899 were mere pauses in growth.[1] Jeffrey Sachs categorized recessions since 1893 by their severity. He found only one strong and one moderate contraction

---

[1]"Business Cycles and Growth: Some Reflections and Measures," *NBER Working Paper #665*, April 1981.

in the period of 1893–1913. Since the institution of the Federal Reserve, however, we have had three strong contractions and three—now four— moderate contractions.[2]

Economist Alan Reynolds has pointed out:

> Michael Parly found that unemployment rates in the 1930's had been exaggerated by failure to count those on government work programs . . . as employed. When the adjusted unemployment rate is added to the consumer inflation rate to arrive at Art Okun's "discomfort index," the last two administrations experienced the worst combination of inflation and unemployment (16 per cent) of any in this century except for Franklin Roosevelt's first term (15.7 per cent) and President Wilson's second (19.6 per cent). Unemployment *averaged* more than 7 per cent from 1975 to date. From 1899 to 1929, unemployment reached 7 per cent in only two years. We are in no position to be smug about the relative performance of a seemingly old-fashioned monetary standard. The fact is that it worked very well under conditions more difficult than those we face today.[3]

In a report prepared by EMB Ltd. and submitted to the Commission, it was stated that "in the United States there were 12 panics and crises between 1815 and 1914." Dr. Roy Jastram's testimony to the Commission demolished that popular myth:

> This draws upon a book by Willard Thorp, *Business Annals*, published by the National Bureau of Economic Research in 1926. Year-by-year Thorp gleaned his characterization of the year stated from the contemporary press and writers of the day. When I was at the National Bureau we considered Professor Wesley C. Mitchell as the patron saint of objectivity. Mitchell wrote in the *Introduction* to Thorp's book: "'Crisis,' then, is a poor term to use . . . But sad experience shows how much misunderstanding comes from the effort to use familiar words in new technical senses."
>
> Both the Commission Staff and I agree that the true gold standard ran between 1834–1861 and 1879–1914. Even with Professor Mitchell's admonition about the use of the terms, this leaves us with 8 instead of EMB's 12 "crises" or "panics" associated with a real gold standard. A consultation of the original Thorp volume shows that EMB is simply wrong about 1882 and 1890—Thorp does not label either of them as "crisis" or "panic." So the count is reduced to 6. In 4 of these 6, part

[2]"The Changing Cyclical Behavior of Wages and Prices: 1890–1975," *NBER Working Paper #304*, December 1978.

[3]Testimony before the United States Gold Policy Commission, Washington, D.C., November 13, 1981.

of the year is called by Thorp "prosperity." Hence we have only 2 out of the EMB's original 12 that were labeled in the original source as being unmitigated crises or panics during an actual gold standard. This kind of misinformation cannot go unchallenged.

And I might close with a thought of my own: if we were to use today these terms in their archaic sense, every *week* of the past two years could have been labeled a "panic."[4]

The fourth objection, that the gold standard causes inflation, can also easily be disposed of. Dr. Reynolds, in his appearance before the Commission, did so:

When the 1968–1980 period is compared with the "purest" gold standard, 1879–1914, it is not at all clear that even short-term price stability was superior in recent years. Average changes in consumer prices were zero under gold, over 7% under paper; the standard deviation of those prices was 2.2% under gold, 3.1% under paper. Annual variations appear slightly wider under the old wholesale price index for 1879–1914 than under the recent producer price index for finished goods, but that is probably due to the greater importance of volatile farm commodities and crude materials a century ago. As Sachs points out, farm prices were 43% of the wholesale index as late as 1926, but only 21% in 1970.

Perfect short-term price stability has never been achieved anywhere, so the issue is relative stability and predictability. By comparing unusual peak years to recession lows, as Professor Allan Meltzer does, it is possible to show annual rates of inflation or deflation of 2–3% in wholesale prices under the gold standard. Exaggerated as that is, it still doesn't sound too bad for price indexes dominated by farm products. The most persistent inflation under a gold standard was from 1902–07, when Gallman's estimate of the price deflator rose by 2.4% a year.

Long-term interest rates were much lower and more stable under any form of gold standard than in recent years, and annual price changes were typically smaller. James Hoehn of the Federal Reserve Bank of Dallas concludes that, "Short-run monetary stability is no better today than it was in the gold standard period. This result is surprising and difficult to explain in view of the greater present day stability of the banking system."

One indication of the loss of long-term stability was provided by Benjamin Klein, who found that the average maturity of new corporate debt fell from over 37 years in 1900–04 to 20 years in 1968–72.[5]

[4]Ibid.
[5]Ibid.

Now that the market for long-term bonds has been destroyed by 10 years of paper money and the United States has experienced its worst price inflation in its national history, it is difficult to take seriously the charge that the gold standard causes inflation.

Dr. Roy Jastram, in his seminal work *The Golden Constant*, presents the statistical evidence that gold provides protection against inflation and actually results in gently falling prices. Such gentle falls in turn cause increases in the real wages of workers. Below is a table showing the index of whole commodity prices for the United States from 1800–1981. The figures are quite surprising to anyone who has come to regard continual price inflation as a fact of life to which we all must adjust.

The Index of Wholesale Commodity Prices
United States 1800–1981
(1930 = 100.0)

Year	Index	Year	Index	Year	Index
1800	102.2	1841	72.9	1882	85.7
1801	112.6	1842	65.0	1883	80.0
1802	92.8	1843	59.4	1884	73.8
1803	93.5	1844	61.0	1885	67.5
1804	100.0	1845	65.9	1886	65.0
1805	111.9	1846	65.9	1887	67.5
1806	106.3	1847	71.3	1888	68.2
1807	103.1	1848	65.0	1889	64.1
1808	91.3	1849	65.0	1890	65.0
1809	103.1	1850	66.6	1891	64.6
1810	103.8	1851	65.9	1892	60.3
1811	100.0	1852	69.7	1893	61.9
1812	103.8	1853	76.9	1894	55.4
1813	128.5	1854	85.7	1895	56.5
1814	144.4	1855	87.2	1896	53.8
1815	134.8	1856	83.2	1897	53.8
1816	119.7	1857	88.1	1898	56.1
1817	119.7	1858	73.8	1899	60.3
1818	116.6	1859	76.3	1900	64.8
1819	99.1	1860	73.8	1901	63.9
1820	84.1	1861	70.6	1902	68.2
1821	84.1	1862	82.5	1903	69.1
1822	84.1	1863	105.4	1904	69.1
1823	81.6	1864	153.1	1905	69.5

Year	Index	Year	Index	Year	Index
1824	77.8	1865	146.6	1906	71.5
1825	81.6	1866	137.9	1907	75.3
1826	78.5	1867	128.5	1908	72.9
1827	77.8	1868	125.3	1909	78.3
1828	76.9	1869	119.7	1910	81.4
1829	76.2	1870	107.0	1911	75.1
1830	72.2	1871	103.1	1912	80.0
1831	74.4	1872	107.8	1913	80.7
1832	75.3	1873	105.4	1914	78.7
1833	75.3	1874	100.0	1915	80.5
1834	71.3	1875	93.5	1916	98.9
1835	79.4	1876	87.2	1917	135.9
1836	90.4	1877	84.1	1918	152.0
1837	91.3	1878	72.2	1919	160.3
1838	87.2	1879	71.3	1920	178.7
1839	88.8	1880	79.4	1921	113.0
1840	75.3	1881	81.6	1922	111.9
1923	116.4	1943	120.2	1963	211.9
1924	113.5	1944	120.2	1964	212.3
1925	119.7	1945	122.4	1965	216.6
1926	115.7	1946	139.7	1966	223.8
1927	110.5	1947	171.5	1967	224.2
1928	112.1	1948	185.7	1968	229.8
1929	110.1	1949	176.5	1969	238.8
1930	100.0	1950	183.4	1970	247.5
1931	84.3	1951	204.3	1971	255.4
1932	75.3	1952	198.7	1972	267.0
1933	76.2	1953	196.0	1973	302.0
1934	86.5	1954	196.4	1974	359.0
1935	92.6	1955	196.9	1975	392.2
1936	93.5	1956	203.4	1976	410.2
1937	99.8	1957	209.2	1977	435.5
1938	90.8	1958	212.1	1978	469.3
1939	89.2	1959	212.6	1979	528.2
1940	90.8	1960	212.6	1980	602.8
1941	101.1	1961	212.1	1981	657.8
1942	114.1	1962	212.6		

In the 67 years prior to the beginning of the Federal Reserve system in 1913 the consumer price index in this country increased by 10 percent, and in the 67 years subsequent to 1913 the Consumer Price Index increased 625 percent. This growth has accelerated since 1971 when President Nixon cut our last link to gold by closing the gold window.

In 1833, the index of wholesale commodity prices in the U.S. was 75.3. In 1933, just prior to our going off the domestic gold standard, the index of wholesale commodity prices in the U.S. was 76.2: a change in 100 years of nine-tenths of one percent. The index of wholesale commodity prices in 1971 was 255.4. Today, the index is 657.8. For 100 years on the gold standard wholesale prices rose only nine-tenths of one percent. In the last 10 years of paper money they have gone up 259 percent.

The final objection to the gold standard, that gold is subject to speculative influence and therefore too unstable to be used as a standard for anything, is also spurious. During the past decade, gold has become a major hedge against inflation. The run-up in gold prices from $35 to $850 per ounce came as a result of fears about the value of paper currencies and developing international crises. This speculation—actually a seeking of protection from the continual devaluation of paper currencies—has markedly accelerated in recent years. Not only is the decline of the paper dollar causing larger investments in gold coins, but also in real estate, collectibles of all types, and any other good that promises to retain its value. The Commodity Exchange reports that there are now over 100 different futures contracts offered by the nation's 11 exchanges. Since 1975, 42 new futures contracts have been introduced, and 37 proposed contracts are currently pending government approval. This enormous growth in speculation has occurred during the last 10 years. People who object to gold because it is speculative confuse cause and effect. Were we on a gold standard, there would be no speculation in gold at all. Gold is currently an object of "speculation" precisely because we have an irredeemable paper money system and people are trying to protect themselves from it. The real speculation is in the anticipation of the further depreciation of the dollar.

All these objections to gold cannot shake the overwhelming historical and theoretical arguments for a gold standard. But there are other arguments for gold as well. We will now take them up in turn.

Money and the Constitution

In addition to the compelling economic case for the gold standard, a case buttressed by both historical and theoretical arguments, there is a compelling argument based on the Constitution. The present monetary arrangements of the United States are unconstitutional—even anti-constitutional—from top to bottom.

The Constitution actually says very little about what sort of monetary system the United States ought to have, but what it does say is unmistakably clear. Article I, section 8, clause 2 provides: "The Congress shall have power . . . to borrow money on the credit of the United States . . . [clause 5:] to coin money, regulate the value thereof, and of foreign coin, and fix the standards of weights and measures . . . [and clause 6:] to provide for the punishment of counterfeiting the securities and current coin of the United States. . . ." Further, Article I, section 10, clause 1 provides: "No state shall . . . coin money; emit bills of credit; [or] make anything but gold and silver coin a tender in payment of debts. . . ."

When the Founding Fathers wrote the Constitution in the summer of 1787, they had fresh in their minds the debacle of the paper money printed and issued by the Continental Congress during the Revolutionary War. The paper notes, "Continentals" as they were called, eventually fell to virtually zero percent of their original value because they were not redeemed in either silver or gold. They were "greenbacks," and were the first of three major experiments with "greenbacks" that this nation has conducted.[6] The Continental greenback failed miserably, giving rise to the popular phrase "not worth a Continental."

Consequently, when the Constitutional Convention met in 1787, the opposition to paper money was strong. George Mason, a delegate from Virginia, stated that he had a "mortal hatred to paper money." Delegate Oliver Ellsworth from Connecticut thought the Convention "a favorable moment to shut and bar the door against paper money." James Wilson, a delegate from Pennsylvania, argued: "It will have a more salutary influence on the credit of the United States to remove the possibility of paper money." Delegate Pierce Butler from South Carolina pointed out that paper was not a legal tender in any country of Europe and that it ought not be made one in the United States. John Langdon of New Hampshire said that he would rather reject the whole Constitution than allow the federal government the power to issue paper money. On the final vote on the issue, nine states opposed

---

[6]The other two experiments were during the Civil War, 1862–1879, and the present period from 1971. The second experiment had a happy conclusion because the Civil War greenbacks were paid off dollar for dollar in gold. As chapter two shows, the colonies also frequently experimented with paper money.

granting the federal government power to issue paper money, and only two favored granting such power.

The framers of the Constitution made their intention clear by the use of the word "coin" rather than the word "print," or the phrase "emit bills of credit." Thomas M. Cooley's *Principles of Constitutional Law* elaborates on this point: "To coin money is to stamp pieces of metal for use as a medium of exchange in commerce according to fixed standards of value."

Congress was given the exclusive power (as far as governments are concerned) to coin money; the states were explicitly prohibited from doing so. Furthermore, the states were explicitly forbidden from making anything but gold and silver coin a tender in payment of debt, while the federal government was not granted the power of making anything legal tender.

In his explanation of the Constitutional provisions on money, James Madison, in *Federalist* No. 44, referred to the "pestilent effects of paper money on the necessary confidence between man and man, on the necessary confidence in the public councils, on the industry and morals of the people, and on the character of republican government." His intention, and the intention of the other founders, was to avoid precisely the sort of paper money system that has prevailed for the past 10 years.

This intention was well understood throughout the 19th century, and was denied only when the Supreme Court found it expedient to do so. For example, Daniel Webster wrote:

> If we understand, by currency, the legal money of the country, and that which constitutes a lawful tender for debts, and is the statute measure of value, then undoubtedly, nothing is included but gold and silver. Most unquestionably, *there is no legal tender, and there can be no legal tender in this country under the authority of this government or any other, but gold and silver,* either the coinage of our mints or foreign coins at rates regulated by Congress. *This is a constitutional principle, perfectly plain and of the very highest importance.* The states are expressly prohibited from making anything but gold and silver a tender in payment of debts, and although no such expressed prohibition is applied to Congress, yet as Congress has no power granted to it in this respect but to coin money and to regulate the value of foreign coins, *it clearly has no power to substitute paper or anything else for coin* as a tender in payment of debts in a discharge of contracts. . . .
>
> The legal tender, therefore, the constitutional standard of value, is established and cannot be overthrown. *To overthrow it would shake the whole system.* (Emphasis added.)

In 1832, the Select Committee on Coins of the House of Representatives reported to the Congress that "the enlightened founders of our Constitution obviously contemplated that our currency should be composed of gold and silver coin. . . . The obvious intent and meaning of these special grants and restrictions [in the Constitution] was to secure permanently to the people of the United States a gold or silver currency, and to delegate to Congress every necessary authority to accomplish or perpetuate that beneficial institution."

The Select Committee stated its conclusion that "the losses and deprivation inflicted by experiments with paper currency, especially during the Revolution; the knowledge that similar attempts in other countries . . . were equally delusive, unsuccessful, and injurious; had likely produced the conviction [in the minds of the framers of the Constitution] that gold and silver alone could be relied upon as safe and effective money."

Twelve years later, in 1844, the House Committee on Ways and Means concluded:

> The framers of the Constitution intended to avoid the paper money system. Especially did they intend to prevent Government paper from circulating as money, as had been practised during the Revolutionary War. The mischiefs of the various expedients that had been made were fresh in the public mind, and were said to have disgusted the respectable part of America. . . . The framers [of the Constitution] . . . designed to prevent the adoption of the paper system under any pretext or for any purpose whatsoever; and if it had not been supposed that such object was effectively secured, in all probability the rejection of the Constitution might have followed.

Later in the century, Justice Stephen Field presciently wrote in the case *Julliard* v. *Greenman* (1884):

> There have been times within the memory of all of us when the legal tender notes of the United States were not exchangeable for more than half of their nominal value. The possibility of such depreciation will always attend paper money. This inborn infirmity, no mere legislative declaration can cure. If Congress has the power to make the [paper] notes legal tender and to pass as money or its equivalent, why should not a sufficient amount be issued to pay the bonds of the United States as they mature? Why pay interest on the millions of dollars of bonds now due when Congress can in one day make the money to pay the principal; and why should there be any restraint upon unlimited appropriations by the government for all imaginary schemes of public improvement if the printing press can furnish the money that is needed for them?

Justice Field foresaw exactly what would happen in the 20th century when the federal government has used the printing press—and the computer—as the means of financing all sorts of "imaginary schemes of public improvement."

Under the Constitution, Congress has power to coin money, not print money substitutes. Such money is to be gold and silver coin, nothing else. It is significant that this power of coining money is mentioned in the same sentence in the Constitution as the power to "fix the standards of weights and measures," for the framers regarded money as a weight of metal and a measure of value. Roger Sherman, a delegate to the Constitutional Convention, wrote that "if what is used as a medium of exchange is fluctuating in its value, it is no better than unjust weights and measures . . . which are condemned by the Laws of God and man. . . ."

The founders were greatly influenced by both the English common law and biblical law. Sherman's comment about unjust weights and measures and the juxtaposition of the powers to coin money and fix the standards of weights and measures in the Constitution are examples of that influence.

For the framers of the Constitution, money was a weight of precious metal, not a weightless piece of paper with green ink printed on it. The value of the money was its weight and fineness, and its value could be accurately determined.

Today's paper money system, issued by a coercive banking monopoly, has no basis in the Constitution. It is precisely the sort of government institution—one far more clever than the bumbling efforts of Charles I to confiscate wealth—that can forcibly exact financial support from the people without their consent. As such, it is a form of taxation without representation, and a denial of the hard fought and won principle of consent before payment of taxes.

Remarkably enough, the Supreme Court has not decided any cases challenging the constitutionality of the present irredeemable paper money system; in fact such a case has not yet been adjudicated before the Court or at the federal appellate level.

It is to be hoped that this will soon change, and the Court forced to recognize, as was recognized throughout history, that the states may make only "gold and silver coin a tender in payment of debt." Anything else is unconstitutional. As for the Congress, we strongly recommend that the Congress abide by the supreme law of the land by repealing those laws that contravene it.

The Moral Argument for Gold

A monetary standard based on sound moral principles is one in which the monetary unit is precisely defined in something of real value such as a precious metal. Money that obtains its status from government decree alone is arbitrary, undefinable, and is destined to fail, for it will eventually be rejected by the people. Since today's paper money achieves its status by government declaration and not by its value in itself, eventually total power over the economy must be granted to the monopolists who manage the monetary system. Even with men of good will, this power is immoral, for men make mistakes, and mistakes should never have such awesome consequences as they do when made in the management of money. Through the well-intentioned mismanagement of money, inflation and depression are created. Political control of a monetary system is a power bad men should not have and good men would not want.

Inflation, being the increase in the supply of money and credit, can only be brought about in an irredeemable paper system by money managers who create money through fractional reserve banking, computer entries, or the printing press. Inflation bestows no benefits on society, makes no new wealth, and creates great harm; and the instigators, whether acting deliberately or not, perform an immoral act. The general welfare of the nation is not promoted by inflation, and great suffering results.

Gold is honest money because it is impossible for governments to create it. New money can only come about by productive effort and not by political and financial chicanery. Inflation is theft and literally steals wealth from one group for the benefit of another. It is possible to have an increase in the supply of gold, but the historical record is clear that all great inflations occur with paper currency. But an increase in the supply of gold—presuming that it is not accomplished through theft—is quite different from an increase in the supply of irredeemable paper currency. The latter is a creature of politics; the former is a result of productive labor, both mental and physical. Gold is wealth; it is not just exchangeable for wealth. Today's notes are not wealth. They are claims on wealth that the owners of wealth must accept as payment.

No wealth is created by paper money creation; only shifts of wealth occur, and these shifts, although significant and anticipated by some, cannot always be foreseen. They are tantamount to theft in that the assets gained are unearned. The victims of inflation suffer through no fault of their own. The beneficiaries of the inflation are not necessarily the culprits in the transfer of wealth; the policymakers who cause the inflation are.

Legally increasing the money supply is just as immoral as the counterfeiter who illegally prints money. The new paper money has value only because it steals its "value" from the existing stock of paper money. (This is not true of gold, however. New issues of paper money are necessarily parasitic; they depend on their similarity to existing money for their worth. But gold does not. It carries its own credentials.) Inflation of paper money is one way wealth can be taken against another's wishes without an obvious confrontation; it is a form of embezzlement. After a while, the theft will be reflected in the depreciation of money and the higher prices that must be paid. The guilty are difficult to identify due to the cleverness of the theft. They are never punished because of the legality of their actions. Eventually, though, as the paper money becomes more and more worthless, the "legalized counterfeiting" becomes obvious to everyone. Anger and frustration over the theft results and is justified, but it is frequently misdirected and may even lead to a further aggrandizement of governmental power.

Ideally, the role of government in a sound monetary system is minimal. Its purpose should be to guarantee a currency and assure that it cannot be debased. The role would be similar whether it is protecting a government gold standard or private monies. Neither the government nor private issuers of money can be permitted to defraud the people by depreciating the currency. The honesty and integrity of the money should be based on a contract; the government's only role should be to see that violators of the contract are punished. Depreciating the currency by increasing the supply and diluting its value is comparable to the farmer who dilutes his milk with water yet sells it for whole milk. We prosecute the farmer, but not the Federal Reserve Open Market Committee. Those who must pay the high prices from the inflation are like those who must drink the diluted milk and suffer from its "debased" content.

The Coinage Act of 1792 recognized the importance of not debasing the currency and prescribed the death penalty for anyone who would steal by debasing the metal coins. Yet today the Treasury is closing the very office set up to assure honest money, the New York Assay Office. Though largely symbolic since 1933, this office is the most important office of the federal government if we are ever again to commit ourselves to money that cannot be arbitrarily destroyed by the politicians in office.

Throughout history, rulers have used inflation to steal from the people and pursue unpopular policies, welfarism, and foreign military adventurism. Likewise throughout history the authorities who have inflated have resorted to blaming innocent citizens, who try to protect themselves from the government-caused inflation. Such citizens are castigated as "speculators" out of ignorance, as well as from a deliberate desire to escape deserved blame.

Gold money is always rejected by those who advocate significant government intervention in the economy. Gold holds in check the government's tendency to accumulate power over the economy. Paper money is a device by which the unpopular programs of government intervention, whether civilian or military, foreign or domestic, can be financed without the tax increases that would surely precipitate massive resistance by the people. Monetizing massive debt is more complex and therefore more politically acceptable, but it is just as harmful, in fact more harmful, than if the people were taxed directly.

This monetizing of debt is literally a hidden tax. It is unevenly distributed throughout the population, one segment paying much more than another. It is equivalent to a regressive tax, forcing the working poor to suffer more than the speculating rich.

Deliberately debasing the currency for political reasons, that is, paying for programs that the politicians need in order to be reelected, is the most immoral act of government short of deliberate war. The tragedy is that the programs that many believe helpful to the poor usually end up making the poor poorer, destroying the middle class, and enriching the wealthy. Sincere persons vote for programs for the poor not fully understanding the way in which the inflation used to finance the programs brings economic devastation to those intended to be the beneficiaries.

Great power is granted to the politicians and the monetary managers with this authority to create money. Bankers, through fractional reserve banking laws, can create new money. Those who receive the newly created money first benefit the most and have a vested interest in continuing the process of inflation. These are generally the government, large corporations, large banks, and welfare recipients. Paper money is political money with the politician in charge; gold is free-market money with the people in charge.

John Locke argued for the gold standard the same way he argued for the moral right to own property. To him the right to own and exchange gold was a civil liberty equal in importance to the liberty to speak, write, and practice one's own religion. Free people always choose to trade their goods or services for a marketable commodity. Money is the most marketable of all commodities, and gold the best of all money. Gold has become money by a moral commitment to free choice and honest trade, not by government edict. Locke claimed the right to own property was never given to the individual by society, but that government was established to ensure integrity in contracts and honest money, not to be the principal source of broken contracts or the instigators of a depreciating currency. Gold is not money because government says it is: It is money because the people have chosen to use it in a free country.

Eliminating honest money—commodity money defined precisely by weight—is a threat to freedom itself. It sets the stage for serious economic difficulties and interferes with the humanitarian goal of a high standard of living for everyone, a standard which results from a free market and a sound monetary standard. For centuries kings have used the debasement of coins to raise funds for foreign and aggressive wars that otherwise would not have been supported by people voluntarily loaning money to the government or paying taxes. Even recently, inflation has been resorted to in order to finance wars about which the people were less than enthusiastic. Inflation is related to preventable wars in another way. As the economy deteriorates in countries that have inflated and forced to go through recession and depressions, international tensions build. Protectionism (tariffs) and militant nationalism generally develop and contribute to conditions that precipitate armed conflict. The immorality of inflation is closely linked to the immorality of preventable and aggressive wars.

Money, when it is a result of moral commitment to honesty and integrity, will be trusted. Trustworthy money is required in a moral society. This requires *all* paper money and paper certificates to be convertible into something of real worth. Throughout history, money has repeatedly failed to maintain trust due to unwise actions of governments whose responsibility was to protect that trust, not destroy it. Without trust in money gained by a moral commitment to integrity, a productive economy is impossible. Inflation premiums built into the interest rates cannot be significantly altered by minor manipulations in the growth rate of the supply of money, nor by the painful decreases in the demand for money brought on by a weak economy. Only trust in the money can remove the inflation premium from our current financial transactions.

Trust is only restored when every citizen is guaranteed convertibility of money substitutes into tangible money at will. False promises and hopes cannot substitute for a moral commitment of society to honest money—ingrained in the law and not alterable by the whims of any man. The rule of moral law must replace the power of man in order for sound money to circulate once again. Ignoring morality in attempts to stop inflation and restore the country's economic health guarantees failure. A moral commitment to honest money guarantees success.

In the 7th century B.C., the Greeks began the first coinage, striking silver into pieces of uniform weight. Greek mints were located in temples. The Athens mint was either in or adjacent to the temple of Athene. This was done for a purpose, for the temple marks were designed—and accepted—as evidence of the honesty of the coins. In Rome, the coinage began in the temple of Juno Monere, from which we get our word "money."

Biblical law, which informs the common law and has shaped the legal institutions of Western Europe and North America, regards money as a weight, either of silver or gold, and stern commands against dishonest weights and measures were enforced with severe punishments. The prophet Isaiah condemned Israel because "your silver is become your dross, wine mixed with water." Debasement of the money was very severely condemned. In his *Commentary on the Epistle to the Romans,* Martin Luther wrote, "Today we may apply the Apostle's words [Romans 2:2–3] first to those [rulers] who without cogent cause inflict exorbitant taxes upon the people, or by changing and devaluating the currency, rob them, while at the same time they accuse their subjects of being greedy and avaricious."

It is not surprising, then, given this background, that the Congress of 1792 imposed the death penalty on anyone convicted of debasing the coinage. Debasement, depreciation, devaluation, inflation—all stand condemned by the moral law. The present economic crisis we face is a direct consequence of our violations of that law.

VI. The Transition to Monetary Freedom

Our present monetary system is failing. The time is ripe for fundamental monetary reform. Yet there are two distinct and different processes through which this reform may be achieved. We have already discussed the type of monetary system most desirable; yet there are different methods of reaching that goal. For simplicity's sake, we shall refer to these procedures as "descending" reform and "ascending" reform. The first term refers to action taken by the government directly to create the system desired; it is from the top down. The danger of this type of reform is that the government will not create a real gold standard but a pseudo-gold standard. The second term refers to the absence of government action and the subsequent appearance of the reforms despite the government's inaction; it is bottom-up reform. There is a third type of reform which mixes both the ascending and the descending procedures whereby the government clears the obstacles now impeding reform from the bottom up. It is our opinion that this third type of reform would be the least painful for reasons shortly to be made clear.

During the course of a monetary crisis—such as we are experiencing now—there comes a time when descending reform becomes much more difficult. It is our belief that we have not yet reached that point, but that we are rapidly approaching it. There is still time to proceed with the reforms outlined below, but that time is rapidly slipping away. In order to achieve this descending reform, the Congress must quickly repeal certain laws that have created our present crisis: the legal tender laws, the authority of the Federal Reserve to conduct open-market operations, and so forth. Failure to do so will result in a complete collapse of our economic system.

The process of mixed reform is preferable because it can achieve the desired end with a minimum of injury to the people. It can avert an economic calamity if executed in time; but should descending reform not occur in time—and it now appears that it will not, given the unwillingness of the Commission to make more far-reaching recommendations to the Congress—we can hope that ascending reform will still be possible.

Should the Congress not adopt the reforms we advocate, we can expect our economic situation to deteriorate further. First, there will be a continuation of both price increases and high interest rates. Such prices and rates may fluctuate in a cyclical pattern, but they will not secularly decline. The prime rate has already reached 21.5 percent. Perhaps within a year it will move to 25 percent, fall back, and then surge ahead to 30 percent. The exact figures are not as important as realizing that the present irredeemable paper money system is just that: irredeemable. Such systems have not worked and cannot work for any significant period of time.

Further cyclical price and interest rate increases will, in turn, trigger many more bankruptcies, both commercial and personal. Bank runs, panics, and holidays will occur as the people lose confidence in the financial institutions. Such collapses will, in turn, trigger higher unemployment—reaching levels not seen since the 1930s—larger federal deficits, and further inflation. The paper economy is a circle of dominoes; once they start to fall, they bring others down with them. Real wage rates will slide; applications for welfare will accelerate.

These economic events will have social and political consequences; inflations always do. The inflation of the 1920s led to the rise of Hitler in Germany, and that of the 1940s to the victory of Mao Tse-tung in China. The increase in the size and scope of government is a significant effect of such crises, yet it is the effect that threatens to choke off any possibility of ascending reform. Such reform, when it comes, will have to emerge from the marketplace, either through the legalization of competing currencies, or through development in the underground (illegal) economy. Economists already believe that there may be an underground economy in the U.S. one-fifth the size of the official economy. With the collapse of the official money and the official economy, the underground economy might be able to shift to using silver and gold coins, and thus some ascending reforms might be possible.

However, simply waiting for the present system to collapse is neither responsible nor moral. As members of the Gold Commission, we must urge Congress to act upon our specific suggestions for reform as speedily as possible. We do not believe that we overestimate the gravity of the present situation, and we think it is better by far to be two years too early than two days too late.

Specific Reforms Required

The growth of the American government in the late 19th and 20th centuries is reflected in its increasing presence and finally monopolization of the monetary system. Any attempt at restoring monetary freedom must be part of a comprehensive plan to roll back government and once again confine it within the limits of the Constitution. That comprehensive plan may be divided into four sections: monetary legislation, the budget, taxation, and regulation. We shall begin with monetary reforms, and conclude with a word about international cooperation and agreement.

Monetary Legislation

Legal Tender Laws

As we have seen, the Constitution forbids the states to make anything but gold and silver coin a tender in payment of debt, nor does it permit the federal government to make *anything* a legal tender. One of the most important pieces of legislation that could be enacted would be the repeal of all federal legal tender laws. Such laws, which have the effect of forcing creditors to accept something in payment for the debts due them that they do not wish to accept, are one of the most tyrannical devices of the present monetary authorities.

Not only does the Federal Reserve have a coercive monopoly in issuing "money," but every American is forced to accept it. Each Federal Reserve note bears the words, "This note is legal tender for all debts, public and private." The freedom to conduct business in something else—such as gold and silver coin—cannot exist so long as the government forces everyone to accept its paper notes. Monetary freedom ends where legal tender laws begin.

The United States had no such laws until 1862, when the Congress—in violation of the Constitution—enacted them in order to ensure the acceptance of the Lincoln greenbacks, the paper notes printed by the U.S. Treasury during the wartime emergency. That "emergency" has now lasted for 120 years; it is time that this unconstitutional action by the Congress be repealed. Freedom of contract—and the right to have such contracts enforced, not abrogated, by the government—is one of the fundamental pillars of a free society.

Defining the Dollar

A second major reform needed is a legal definition of the term "dollar." The Constitution uses the word "dollar" at least twice, and it is quite clear that by it the framers meant the Spanish-milled dollar of 371¼ grains of silver. Since 1968, however, there has been no domestic definition of "dollar," for in that year redemption of silver certificates and delivery of silver in exchange for the notes ended, and silver coins were removed from circulation.

In 1971, the international definition of the "dollar" as ¼₂ of an ounce of gold was also dropped. The Treasury and Federal Reserve still value gold at $42.22 per ounce, but that is a mere accounting device. In addition, IMF rules now prohibit any member country from externally defining its currency in terms of gold. The word "dollar," quite literally, is legally meaningless, and it has been meaningless for the past decade. Federal Reserve notes are not "dollars"; they are notes denominated in "dollars." But what a "dollar" is, no one knows.

This absurdity at the basis of our monetary system must be corrected. It is of secondary importance whether we define a "dollar" as a weight of gold or as a weight of silver. What is important is that it be defined. The current situation permits the Federal Reserve—and the Internal Revenue Service for that matter—to use the word any way they please, just like the Red Queen in *Alice in Wonderland*.

No rational economic activity can be conducted when the unit of account is undefined. The use of the meaningless term "dollar" has all but wrecked the capital markets of this country. If the "dollar" changes in meaning from day-to-day, even hour-to-hour, long-term contracts denominated in "dollars" become traps that all wish to avoid. The breakdown of long-term financing and planning in the past decade is a result of the absurd nature of the "dollar." There is very little long-term planning occuring at the present. The only way to restore rationality to the system is to restore a definition for the term "dollar." We suggest defining a "dollar" as a weight of gold of a certain fineness, .999 fine. Such a fixed definition is the only way to restore confidence in the markets and in the "dollar." Capitalism cannot survive the type of irrationality that lies at the basis of our present monetary arrangements.

A New Coinage

We are extremely pleased that the Gold Commission has recommended to the Congress a new gold coinage. It has been almost 50 years since the last United States gold coins were struck, and renewing this constitutional function would indeed be a cause for celebration and jubilee.

We believe that the coins should be struck in one ounce, one-half ounce, one-quarter ounce, and one-tenth ounce weights, using the most beautiful of coin designs, that designed by Augustus Saint Gaudens in 1907. A coinage in such weights would allow Americans to exchange their greenbacks for genuine American coins; there would no longer be any need for purchasing Canadian, Mexican, South African, or other foreign coins. Combined with the removal of capital gains taxation on the coins and the elimination of all transaction taxes, such as excise and sales taxes, the new American coinage could quickly become an alternative monetary system to our present paper monopoly.

In addition to the new official coinage, private mints should also be permitted to issue their own coins under their own trademarks. Such trademarks should be protected by law, just as other trademarks are. Furthermore, private citizens should once again enjoy the right to bring gold bullion to the Treasury and exchange it for coins of the United States for a nominal minting fee.

In the last six years, Nobel laureate Friedrich Hayek has called attention once again to the economic advantages of a system of competing currencies. In two books, *Choice in Currency* and *Denationalization of Money*, Professor Hayek proposes that all legal obstacles be removed and that the people be allowed to choose freely what they wish to use in transactions. Those competing monies might be foreign currencies, private coins, government coins, private bank notes, and so on. Such unrestricted freedom of choice would result in the most reliable currencies or coins winning public acceptance and displacing less reliable competitors. Good money—in the absence of government coercion— drives out bad. The new coinage that the Gold Commission has recommended and which we strongly endorse is a first step in the direction of allowing currencies to compete freely.

The Failure of Central Banking

By a strict interpretation of the Constitution, one of the most unconstitutional (if there are degrees of unconstitutionality) of federal agencies is the Federal Reserve. The Constitution grants no power to the Congress to set up such an institution, and the Fed is the major cause of our present monetary problems. The alleged constitutional authority stems from a loose and imaginative interpretation of the implied powers clause.

Functioning as the central bank of the United States, the Federal Reserve is an anachronism. It was created at a time when faith in control of the economy by Washington was growing, but since it started operations in 1914, it has caused the greatest depressions (1929–1939), recessions (too numerous to mention), inflations, and unemployment levels in our nation's history. The only useful function it performs, the clearing of checks between banks, could be much better handled through private clearinghouses or eliminated entirely by electronic funds transfer. Given its record, there simply is no good reason for allowing the Federal Reserve a monopoly over the nation's money and banking system. Eliminating the power to conduct market operations must be achieved if we expect to stop inflation and restore monetary freedom.

Such a step may alarm some, however. They might be concerned about what will happen to all the Federal Reserve notes now in circulation and what they will be replaced with. First, the present Federal Reserve notes would be retired and replaced by notes redeemable in gold or silver or some other commodity. Such notes would be similar to travelers checks now in use which are, at the present time, redeemable only in paper notes. Like travelers checks, such notes would not be legal tender and no one would be forced to accept them in payment. And since they would be promises to pay, any institution that issued them and then failed to redeem them as promised would be subject to both civil and criminal prosecution, unlike the Federal Reserve, which is subject to neither.

As for the present circulating Federal Reserve notes, they could be made redeemable for gold once a "dollar" is defined as a weight of gold. Anyone who wishes to redeem them could simply do so by exchanging them for gold coins at his bank.

It is important to note that should we institute a gold standard before the Federal Reserve System is ended, that system must function along classical gold standard lines. As Friedman and Schwartz pointed out, it was the failure of the Federal Reserve to abide by the classical gold standard rules that caused the panic of 1929 and the subsequent depression.

In chapters two and three, we demonstrated the disruptive effects fractional reserve banking has caused in the United States. Since we still suffer with that system, it is imperative that a fundamental reform of it be made. That reform is simply that all promises to pay on demand, whether made in the form of notes or deposits, be backed 100 percent by whatever is promised, be it silver, gold, or watermelons. If there is any failure to carry 100 percent reserves or to make delivery when demanded, such persons or institutions would be subject to severe penalties. The fractional reserve system has created the business cycle, and if that is to be eliminated, its cause must be also.

Audit, Inventory, Assay, and Confiscation

One of the areas in which we believe a majority of the Gold Commission erred is in not requiring a thorough and complete assay, inventory, and audit of the gold reserves of the United States on a regular basis. Perhaps there is less of an argument for such a procedure when the gold reserves are essentially stable, but when there is any significant change in them—as will happen when a new coinage is issued—careful scrutiny of the government's gold supplies is necessary.

There have been cases of employee thefts at government bullion depositories, unrecorded shipments of gold from one depository to another, and numerous press reports about millions of dollars worth of gold missing. It seems elementary that the government ought to ascertain accurately its reserves of this precious metal, and that the present 10-year "audit" of the gold inventory is totally inadequate for this purpose. We are quite sure that the Federal Reserve has a much better idea of how many Federal Reserve notes are printed and circulating than the Treasury does of the weight and fineness of its gold assets. This irrational treatment of paper and gold must be corrected immediately.

Finally, there are laws on the books empowering the President to compel delivery, that is, to confiscate privately owned gold bullion, gold coins, and gold certificates in time of war. There can be no monetary freedom when the possibility of such a confiscation exists.

The Budget

One of the standard objections raised against a gold standard is that while it may have worked in the 19th century, it would not work today, for government has grown much larger in the past 100 years.

There is an element of truth in such an argument, for the gold standard is not compatible with a government that continually incurs deficits and lives beyond its means. Growing governments have always sought to be rid of the discipline of gold; historically they have abandoned gold during wars in order to finance them with paper dollars, and during other periods of massive government growth—the New Deal, for example.

Because gold is honest money, it is disliked by dishonest men. Politicians, prevented from buying votes with their own money, have learned how to buy votes with the people's money. They promise to vote for all sorts of programs, if elected, and they expect to pay for those programs through deficits and through the creation of money out of thin air, not higher taxes. Under a gold standard, such irresponsibility would immediately result in high interest rates (as the government borrowed money) and subsequent unemployment. But through the magic of the Federal Reserve, these effects can be postponed for awhile, allowing the politicians sufficient time to blame everyone else for the economic problems they have caused. The result is, as John

Maynard Keynes said many years ago, that not one man in a million understands who is to blame for inflation.

Because the gold standard would be incompatible with deficit financing, a major reform needed would be a balanced budget. Such a balance could easily be achieved by cutting spending—surprising as it may be, no cuts have been made yet—to the level of revenue received by the government.

But beyond that, there should be massive cuts in both spending and taxes, something on the order of what President Truman did following World War II, when 75 percent of the federal budget was eliminated over a period of three years. Honest money and limited government are equally necessary in order to end our present economic crisis.

As part of this budget reform, the government should eventually be required to make all its payments in gold or in gold denominated accounts. No longer would it be able to spend "money" created out of thin air by the Federal Reserve.

Taxation

In order to make such gold payments, the government should begin accepting gold as payment for all taxes, duties, and dues. As a tax collector, the government must specify in what form taxes may be paid (or must be paid), and it should specify that taxes must be paid in either gold or silver coins or certificates. Such an action should occur, of course, as one of the last actions in moving toward a sound monetary system. All of the other reforms discussed here should be accomplished first. Such a requirement to pay taxes in gold or silver would yield the necessary flow to put the government on the gold standard and allow it to make all payments in gold.

But long before this is achieved, since gold is money, there should be no taxation of any sort on either gold coins or bullion. The Commission has judged rightly in recommending that capital gains and sales taxes be eliminated from the new American coinage. We would go further, in the interest of monetary freedom, and urge that all taxation of whatever sort be eliminated on all gold and silver coins and bullion. That would mean the elimination of not only capital gains and sales taxes, but also the discriminatory treatment of gold coins in Individual Retirement Accounts, for example. Persons saving for their retirement should be free to keep their savings in gold coins without incurring a penalty. One reform that might be accomplished immediately would be to direct the Internal Revenue Service to accept all U.S. money at face value for both the assessment and collection of taxes. At the present time, the IRS accepts pre-1965 silver coins at face value in the collection of taxes, but at market value in the assessment of taxes. This policy is grossly unfair, has no basis in law, and should be corrected immediately.

Regulations

Together with monetary, tax, and budget reforms, a comprehensive plan for a gold standard and monetary freedom requires several improvements in our present regulatory structure.

For example, mining regulations, which make it difficult and expensive to open or operate gold and silver mines, would have to be eliminated. All regulations on the export, import, melting, minting, and hoarding of gold coins would also have to be repealed.

But the major reforms needed are in our banking laws. Under present law, there is no free entry into the banking industry; it is largely cartelized by the Federal Reserve and other federal and state regulatory agencies. Deregulation of banking, including free entry by simply filing the legal documents with the proper government clerk, is a must for monetary freedom. All discretion on the part of the regulators must be ended.

At the same time, there would need to be stricter enforcement of the constitutional prohibition against *states* "emitting bills of credit." It must be clearly recognized that the states, neither directly nor indirectly through their creatures, state chartered banks, may get into the paper money business.

A Constitutional Amendment

Although we believe that there is actually nothing in the Constitution that legitimizes our present banking and monetary arrangements, the present system has been with us for so long that a constitutional amendment is probably needed to reaffirm what the Constitution says.

We propose that the following language become Article 27 to the Constitution:

> Neither Congress nor any state shall make anything a tender in payment of private debts, nor shall they charter any bank or note-issuing institution, and states shall make only gold and silver coins as tender in payment of public taxes, duties, and dues.

An International Agreement

While the achievement of monetary freedom can be accomplished without any international conferences or agreements, there is no need to spurn such conferences should they be requested by other nations, or should they be thought advisable simply as a way of informing other nations of our plans. Were we to adopt the proposals outlined in this Report, the dollar would once again become as good as gold, and paper currencies would fall in value against it on the international exchanges. In that case, one would expect other nations to define their currencies also as weights of gold, simply out of self-defense. Were that to happen, we would see the end of the worldwide inflation that has plagued us since 1971. Fixed exchange rates—though not fixed by any international agreement—would also result, simply because currencies would be defined as weights of gold.

Thus, the wholly domestic reforms suggested here would have worldwide repercussions, international effects that would solve one of our most troubling problems: worldwide inflation and the breakdown of world trade.

The Transition to Gold

The transition from the present monetary system to a sound system will probably not be painless, as some have suggested. Whenever the increase in the supply of money slows, there are always recessions. They are the inevitable consequences of the previous inflationary boom. The present system, relying as it does on the political creation of new purchasing power rather than the economic creation of such power, has distorted and disrupted the pattern of economic activity that would result were the markets for goods and money allowed to function freely. In any transition to a sound monetary system there will, of necessity, have to be readjustments made in various sectors of the economy. Such readjustments will temporarily hurt certain individuals and enterprises. The alternative, of course, is to continue with our present system and destroy the entire economy with the evils of hyperinflation and depression. It is our conclusion that the temporary economic hazards of the transition to a gold standard are far less significant than those posed by a continued attempt to make the paper system work.

We have a precedent for a return to gold in the 19th century. During the Civil War, the Union had issued United States notes that were not redeemable in gold. In that respect, they were somewhat similar to the Federal Reserve notes that circulate today. A major difference between the experience following the Civil War and our situation today is, of course, that the U.S. gold coinage continued to circulate during and after the war. Today, such coins have been removed from circulation by law, and they must be restored to circulation by law. That is essentially the recommendation of the Commission, a recommendation that we fully support. Such an action will facilitate the transition to a full gold coin standard. Once it is achieved, the transition to a full gold standard could be done as simply as during the 19th century, with the economic consequences roughly the same.

We must now discuss the transition effect—not the long-term effects—of monetary reform on various sectors of the economy. We have selected six sectors for brevity's sake: real estate, agriculture, heavy industry, small business, exports, and banking. Let us begin with real estate.

Transition Effects on the Real Estate Sector

The concern of many people with monetary reform is that it will affect them or their businesses adversely. They would prefer to continue with the present system, hoping that it will not collapse, rather than seeking to correct it through fundamental change. In this attitude, they are similar to the patient with an abdominal pain who refuses to be examined by a doctor, hoping that the discomfort will cease or at least not worsen. When his appendix bursts, however, the patient realizes that he would have been much better off to have the needed examination and surgery in time. At least the surgery—the timely correction of the problem—would not have threatened his life.

How will a transition to gold affect the real estate market? It is important to realize that there is no single real estate market, but several. The commercial market is quite different from the residential, for example. Within the residential, the single-family housing market is quite different from the rental housing market. While there may be factors that affect all markets, it is necessary to realize that the various markets will be affected differently by the same factors, and also by different factors.

During the last 10 years of paper inflation, real estate of all sorts has become both an inflation hedge and a haven against exorbitant taxation. In a transition to gold, there will be falling inflationary expectations, and, if our recommendations are pursued, lower taxes. Both these effects will gradually eliminate the desire to use real estate as a shield against inflation and taxation. The result generally will be falling prices for real estate of all kinds, as people shift from protecting their capital in real estate to more productive enterprises. It is likely the paper values of both residential and commercial properties will fall during the transition to a sound money system.

This in turn would have several effects. First, as residential prices fall, more young couples who cannot afford a house at the present time would be able to purchase. More houses—but at lower prices—would be sold during each year of the transition to gold. For state and local governments this would mean an expanding property tax base, but it would also offer some relief to the badgered homeowners who have seen their property taxes skyrocket because of inflated housing prices. The passage of Proposition 13 in California in 1978 was a result of this property tax rise. With a transition to gold, homeowners across the whole nation, not just California, would be afforded some tax relief.

Lower home prices will eventually translate into a booming market for both single-family and rental units, spurring new construction. Lower prices would also affect all forms of commercial property, allowing more economical expansion of the business use of property.

Along with lower prices, there will be lower interest rates. Market interest rates are ordinarily divided into three components by economists: originary interest, the risk premium, and the inflation premium. As the transition toward gold is accomplished, the inflation premium would gradually disappear, as the people's confidence in money was restored. It is also probable that both the risk and originary components would decrease, although not nearly so much as the inflation component, for people will once again begin to plan for longer than 12 months into the future. And as the size of government shrinks, the risk premium will also shrink. One great area of risk and uncertainty—actions by federal bureaucrats and regulators—will be eliminated.

Falling interest rates would also encourage greater activity in all real estate markets. The result would be greater access by first-time owners—younger couples and small businessmen.

Transition Effect on Agriculture

Closely related to real estate is agriculture. Speculation in real estate in the past 10 years—speculation resulting from inflation and taxation by the government—has caused the price of prime farmland to be bid up to levels higher than prevailed 10 years ago. One serious consequence of this has been the almost total inability of new, small farmers to buy farms, and of older small farmers to retain farms. High land values, while giving many farmers paper wealth, have raised property taxes exorbitantly, and have forced more and more small farmers to sell out to larger competitors. The result has been the growth of agribusiness and euthanasia of the family farmer.

During the transition to a gold system, interest rates and land values would both fall, the former primarily because of lower inflation expectations, the latter primarily because there would be far less demand for land as an inflation hedge.

A parallel may be found in the 19th century. From 1880 to 1890, immediately after the return to the gold standard, the number of farms in the U.S. increased by over 500,000, the number of acres on these farms by almost 90 million, farm productivity by 10 percent, and the value of farm output by over $800 million.

During this time, however, farm commodity prices were falling, an effect of the transition to gold that many fear. But wholesale prices for the goods farmers used were falling as well, faster than were prices for the goods they produced. The real income of farmers—and of all workers—was actually rising during this period, unlike, for example, the past 10 years. The transition to a sound monetary system, while it may adversely affect a few farmers and real estate holders, will enormously benefit most, and will allow more entry into farming.

Transition Effects on Heavy Industry

One of the prime benefits of sound money and small government is the low long-term interest rates that prevail in such an environment. During the 19th century it was common for 100-year bonds to be offered and sold at 4 percent and 5 percent, and even for bonds in perpetuity to be sold at those rates. Today, after a decade of paper money, long-term means three years, and the prime rate is 16½ percent. Transition to a gold system will include a fall in interest rates from their present historically unprecedented levels to levels approximating those of the late 19th and early 20th centuries. For the decade 1880–1889, three-to-six-month commercial paper averaged 5.14 percent. Call money averaged 3.98 percent. Railroad bond yields averaged 4.43 percent in 1889.

Such rates will once again allow heavy industry to expand, perhaps even matching the unsurpassed real growth for the economy in the decade 1879–1889. The recent concern about the revitalization of America, or the "reindustrialization of America" is a genuine and legitimate concern. What is important to realize, however, is that it is the paper money, high tax, and regulatory policies of the government that have impeded long-term planning and capital investment. Anyone who expresses concern about the industrial strength of America and advocates a continuation of the policies that have caused the present recession/depression has not yet learned elementary economics.

Some heavy industries that have been "protected" by government action may suffer some setbacks when that "protection" is removed. However, if regulatory burdens and subsidies are eliminated in an evenhanded fashion during the transition, those industries, as well as others, should quickly enjoy rapid growth.

Further, there will be a desire of investors, now concerned about sheltering their capital in the unproductive areas of real estate, collectibles, and gold coins, to invest in productive enterprises. There would be a market shift of investment from such "speculative" areas to industry.

Transition Effects on Small Business

The shift of capital investment from the more "speculative" areas to the more productive will directly affect small business. The stock market would come to life, perhaps even making up for the horrendous losses in constant dollars it has suffered since 1965. Business investment would skyrocket, and a great deal of this investment would flow to smaller businesses. As with real estate and farming, it would be the newcomer—the young couple buying a house, the young farmer, and the small businessman—who would benefit most during the transition to economic and monetary freedom.

Small businesses would no longer be crushed by large corporations and bloated government absorbing all the capital in the capital markets. Funds would flow to establish new enterprises rather than being invested in Treasury securities at 14 percent or 15 percent. A gold system would see the gradual elimination of "hot money"—a phenomenon that did not exist before the formation of the Federal Reserve in 1914—racing from investment to investment as interest rates fluctuated.

The growth in small business would, of course, mean the creation of new jobs. The unemployment that is an inevitable product of a paper money system—after all, John Maynard Keynes liked the system because it was a device to cheat the workers—would be eliminated and fall to the frictional rate, perhaps two percent or three percent.

The transition to freedom would also mean the gradual elimination of the "underground economy," since the reasons for its existence, high taxes and inflation, would disappear. Such illegal economic activities would once again become part of the official economy. The elaborate bartering systems that have evolved in the past 10 years would be ended. It is ironic that opponents of gold deride transactions made in gold as a form of barter, for it is precisely the high-tax, paper-money system that encourages barter as a way to avoid both taxation and inflation.

Transition Effects on Exports

To understand the effects of the reforms we recommend on export industries, it is necessary to keep two more fundamental effects of the transition in mind: No more general price increases will occur, and interest rates will actually fall by at least 50 percent. Price stability in all products, including those for export, will open up greater overseas markets for U.S. goods. On the other hand, the present complicated system of export subsidies—such as guaranteed loans and direct loans—will come to an end during the transition to freedom, and those companies (and banks) that benefitted from such sweetheart deals with the government will have to make it on their own or fail.

The government's policies for the past 10 years and longer have diverted a great deal of capital, that should and would have been invested in the U.S., to foreign nations. This misdirected investment would be corrected during transition, as foreign aid programs were phased out, the Export-Import Bank eliminated, and the various other government programs that have put us in a very precarious position are terminated.

In the long run, of course, exports are not a worry. No one worries about the balance of trade or the balance of payments between Texas and California or New Jersey and New York. With the end of a paper system, with its chaotic exchange rates, some semblance of order will return to the world economy. The exporting of inflation will be gradually eliminated, and rather than moving toward protectionism and isolationism, the international economy will gradually open up to further investment and trade.

Export industries may be the most affected of all industries during a transition to a sound money system, but that is only because they have been so heavily subsidized by a government that has had to print the paper to subsidize them. In the long run, such industries also will benefit from a return to freedom.

Transition Effects on Banking

The last of the six sectors is perhaps the one that will be most adversely (in the short run) affected by the reforms we propose. To understand why this is so, one must understand the cartellization of the financial industries in the 1930s, accomplished primarily by the McFadden Act and the Glass-Steagall Act. The breakdown of this cartel has already begun, as a result of the high interest rates now prevailing, and it will proceed whether the reforms here suggested are adopted or not. The only question is whether a new cartel or whether freedom will be allowed to flourish.

The McFadden Act, among other things, forbade interstate branching. Chase Manhattan could open a branch in Moscow, for example, but not in Minneapolis. This resulted in a great deal of interest in overseas loans, with a tremendous diversion of capital from domestic to foreign investment. The Glass-Steagall Act, among other things, erected a wall of separation between banking and commercial enterprises, a wall that now more resembles a Swiss cheese. But such a separation, combined with other restrictions on free entry, enhanced the privilege and profitability of banks.

The reforms we advocate include free entry into banking. Anyone would be permitted to open a bank and issue 100 percent redeemable notes simply upon filing the legal documents with the county (or state or federal) clerk. Such free entry will result in greater competition in the banking industry, and lower margins of profit. Not only would the competition benefit consumers financially, more and more services would also be offered. Thus if Anytown Savings and Loan wished to give away toasters for new deposits, the Depository Institutions Deregulation Committee could not stop them from doing so. And if their neighbors, Anytown Credit Union, wished to offer electronic funds transfer and free travelers checks, no regulator would prevent that from happening.

But there are further effects that would become apparent during transition to a gold system. As interest rates fell, the current crisis among financial institutions would be alleviated. Unless such a transition begins quickly, we can expect to see the most massive failure of depository institutions in our history. A movement toward sound money, while opening up all financial institutions to the sort of competition they should have faced all along, will, at the same time, relieve some of the pressure on the most critical of these institutions. The alternative, of course, is massive government bailouts costing tens—perhaps hundreds—of billions of dollars.

Conclusion

We have selected these six sectors of the economy as bases for discussing what effects a transition to monetary freedom will have on the economy. While the results have not been uniformly optimistic, it is clear that the major effects of stable prices and falling interest rates will open all sectors up to newcomers: new farmers, new homeowners, new small businessmen, and new bankers. Those companies that have been subsidized by the government will suffer most from a movement toward freedom. Those that have profited from the misdirection of capital investment by the government will also suffer. A "gold standard recession," however, would be quite different from a paper money recession, such as we are now suffering. Were the government to refuse to interfere with the adjustment process, the recession would be over very rapidly, as we saw in the last "free market recession" of 1921.[1] And while the recession would be short, it would also not be sharp. There would undoubtedly be a tremendous outpouring of new savings and investments in response to the new confidence in honest money and the realization that inflation was a thing of the past. The transition to a gold system will bring increasing prosperity, real growth, lower unemployment, higher real wages, and greater capital investment. The transition to freedom, in short, is the only way out of the economic crisis we are now in.

---

[1]See Benjamin M. Anderson, "The Road Back to Full Employment," in P. Homan and F. Machlup, eds., *Financing American Prosperity* (New York: Twentieth Century Fund, 1945), pp.25–28.

VII. The Next 10 Years

The transition to gold, as we have outlined it in chapter six, should be accomplished in no more than three years, with any resulting recession lasting about a year. The following 10 years should be ones of prosperity, high real economic growth, and low levels of unemployment. Inflation and the business cycle would be things of the past, as a genuine free banking system would eliminate the possibility of national inflations and contractions. Interest rates would fall to the "normal" interest rates that prevailed for centuries before our national and international experiment with paper money.

Confidence in the monetary unit—the gold dollar—would elicit enormous savings and investments. Prices could be expected to fall gently, resulting in large real wage increases for all workers. In short, the next 10 years with gold would be similar to the prosperity, full employment, and rapid economic growth this nation experienced in the last third of the 19th century. If anyone would like to know what the next 10 years with a gold standard and monetary freedom would be like, he can get a pretty good idea from studying the American economy in the last portion of the last century.

In their *Monetary History of the United States*, Friedman and Schwartz write:

> Both the earlier [1879–1897] and the later [1897–1914] periods were characterized by rapid economic growth. The two final decades of the nineteenth century saw a growth of population of over 2 percent per year, rapid extension of the railway network, essential completion of continental settlement, and an extraordinary increase both in the acreage of land in farms and the output of farm products. The number of farms rose by nearly 50 percent, and the total value of farm lands and buildings by over 60 percent—despite the price decline. Yet at the same time, manufacturing industries were growing even more rapidly, and the Census of 1890 was the first in which the net value added by manufacturing exceeded the value of agricultural output. A feverish boom in western land swept the country during the eighties. "The highest decadal rate [of growth of real reproducible tangible wealth per head from 1805 to 1950] for periods of about ten years was apparently reached in the eighties with approximately 3.8 percent." . . . [G]enerally declining [at 1 percent per year] or generally rising [at 2 percent per year] prices had little impact on the rate of growth, but the period of great monetary uncertainty in the early nineties produced sharp deviations from the longer-term trend.[1]

[1]Milton Friedman and Anna J. Schwartz, *Monetary History* (Princeton: Princeton University Press, 1963), pp. 92–93.

It was the return of the United States to the gold standard in 1879 that stimulated this real economic growth, and it was the "monetary uncertainty in the early nineties" that slowed and almost stopped that growth. Today it is once again "monetary uncertainty" that has brought us to our present crisis.

The pre-1914 gold standard was invented by no one. More important, it was also managed by no one. Modern economists too often look upon the classical gold standard and attribute its success to the Bank of England's ability to follow the "rules of the game." But in fact the system worked to the extent the authorities let it work. Of course, there had to exist an environment where governments kept their promises to define and redeem their currencies in a specific weight of gold, and would allow gold to be traded freely. But to call their success in doing this *managing* gold is to play with language. Gold can manage itself if governments do not hinder it.

The best of all worlds would be to have Bank and State separated the way Church and State are. That is what we propose. For a gold standard still coupled with government monopoly on note issue would only be as sound as the promise of the government to redeem their notes.

In the classical gold standard before 1914, promises made by governments were kept. Everyone expected that they would be. And not only the promises of governments to their citizens, but to other governments. Those governments who broke faith with other governments were treated as pariahs. Treaties were taken seriously.

If it is too much to expect that governments will always be honest, at least we can improve matters whereby governments are condemned and punished for breaking promises. If the government debases its paper money, there ought to be alternatives that people can use for exchange.

The contrast is stark between a regime of money regulated by the marketplace and our system manipulated by politicians. John Maynard Keynes rhapsodized on the world before 1914 in *The Economic Consequences of the Peace*:

> What an extraordinary episode in the economic progress of man that age was which came to an end in August, 1914! The greater part of the population, it is true, worked hard and lived at a low standard of comfort, yet were, to all appearances, reasonably contented with this lot. But escape was possible, for any man of capacity or character at all exceeding the average, into the middle and upper classes, for whom life offered, at a low cost and with the least trouble, conveniences, comforts, and amenities beyond the compass of the richest and most

powerful monarchs of other ages. The inhabitant of London could order by telephone, sipping his morning tea in bed, the various products of the whole earth, in such quantity as he might see fit, and reasonably expect their early delivery upon his doorstep; he could at the same moment and by the same means adventure his wealth in the natural resources and new enterprises of any quarter of the world, and share, without exertion or even trouble, in their prospective fruits and advantages; or he could decide to couple the security of his fortunes with the good faith of the townspeople of any substantial municipality in any continent that fancy or information might recommend. He could secure forthwith, if he wished it, cheap and comfortable means of transit to any country or climate without passport or other formality, could despatch his servant to the neighboring office of a bank for such supply of the precious metals as might seem convenient, and could then proceed abroad to foreign quarters, without knowledge of their religion, language, or customs, bearing coined wealth upon his person, and would consider himself greatly aggrieved and much surprised at the least interference. But, most important of all, he regarded this state of affairs as normal, certain, and permanent, except in the direction of further improvement, and any deviation from it as aberrant, scandalous, and avoidable. The projects and politics of militarism and imperialism, of racial and cultural rivalries, of monopolies, restrictions, and exclusion, which were to play the serpent to this paradise, were little more than the amusements of his daily newspaper, and appeared to exercise almost no influence at all on the ordinary course of social and economic life, the internationalization of which was nearly complete in practice.[2]

The next 10 years with gold hold great promise. But to realize that promise, Congress must act quickly to clear the legal underbrush and obstacles out of the way of free men. Their failure to do so will result in a totally unnecessary and totally avoidable tragedy.

10 Years without Gold

Since 1971, America's monetary unit has been both undefined and undefinable. The meaning of the term "dollar" has changed from year-to-year, month-to-month, even day-to-day. The economic consequences of this irrationality are clear; there is no need to review them again. The question we must attempt to answer in this concluding section is, quite simply, what will happen if the American people are forced to endure another decade without gold and monetary freedom?

[2]John Maynard Keynes, *The Economic Consequences of the Peace* (New York: St. Martin's Press, 1919), pp. 10–12.

What is likely to occur should Congress fail to act on the recommendations we have made in chapters five and six?

Without a gold standard, and continuing roughly with the present system, we can expect more of the same—except worse. For every year, as inflationary expectations become more and more imbedded, we can expect the central "core" rates of both inflation and unemployment to rise. We should never forget that Richard Nixon imposed price-wage controls in 1971 because the government was panicking at a 4.5 percent per annum rate of inflation. In 1982, we would consider returning to this rate tantamount to reaching the state of nirvana. The prime interest rate in July 1971 was 6 percent. Each year we get accustomed to more and more inflation, so that now any inflation rate below 10 percent ("double digit") is considered a virtual end to inflation. Should Congress not adopt the recommendations outlined above, we can expect core inflation rates to rise over the next decade, and at an accelerated rate—so that 10 years from now we can expect cheering in the media when the inflation rate falls below 50 percent. As inflation deepens and accelerates, inflationary expectations will intensify, and prices will begin to spurt ahead faster than the money supply.

It will be at that point that a fateful decision will be made—the same that was made by Rudolf Havenstein and the German Reichsbank in the early 1920s: whether to stop or greatly slow down the inflation, *or* whether to yield to public outcries of a "shortage of money" and a "liquidity crunch" (as business called it in the mini-recession of 1966).

In the latter case, the central bank will promise business or the public that it will issue enough money supply to "catch up" with prices.[3] When that fateful event occurs, as it did in Germany in the early 1920s, prices and money could spiral upward to infinity and it could cost $10 billion to buy a loaf of bread. America could experience the veritable holocaust of runaway inflation, a cataclysm which would make the Depression of the 1930s—let alone an ordinary recession—seem like a tea party.

That this horror *can* happen here can be seen in the reaction to the first peacetime double-digit inflation (1973–1974) by the former Chairman of the Council of Economic Advisers, Walter Heller. Writing in the Federal Reserve Bank of Philadelphia *Review* in 1974, Heller pointed out that in the past year, prices had risen faster than the money supply, and that *therefore* [sic] an increase in the money supply could not be a

[3]See Fritz K. Ringer, ed. *German Inflation of 1923* (New York: Offshore University Press, 1969), p. 96.

cause of the inflation. On the contrary, opined Dr. Heller, it was the duty of the Federal Reserve to increase the money supply fast enough so that the *real* money stock (M corrected for price changes) would return to pre-1973 highs. In short, while using modern jargon, Heller said exactly the same thing as Rudolf Havenstein had said a half century earlier: that the authorities must increase the money supply fast enough to catch up with the prices. That way lies disaster, and who of us is to say that the United States, at some point in the next 10 years without gold, will not take the very same course?

Heller's claim that the money supply growth did not cause the price inflation is an example of many current economists' befuddlement over money. In a similar way we saw the coining of a new word in the 1974–75 recession: "stagflation," to describe the event of rising prices in a business slump. This appeared mysterious to the conventional economists, yet was predicted by the hard-money, free-market economists. Depreciating a currency through monetary inflation always brings escalating prices with recessions in the latter stages of a currency destruction. In the early stages of a currency destruction, recession may well slow the increase in prices, but that is only because not too many people have caught on to the monetary policies of the government. As the inflation progresses, more and more people catch on.

There now is consternation among orthodox economists over persistently high interest rates in the midst of a severe recession—a very bad monetary and financial signal. Conventional economists remain baffled over the modest price inflation currently associated with record high "real" interest rates, exclaiming they are "higher than they should be." This confusion comes from ignoring the fact that computer calculations of the money supply cannot project interest rates accurately. It fails to address the subject of trust in and the quality of money. Interest rates are set in the market, taking into consideration money's quality, anticipated future government monetary policy, and trust in the officials, in addition to immediate short-term changes in the supply and demand for money and credit.

Precise price correlation (to money supply increases), stagflation, and high interest rates are all understood and anticipated by the advocates of sound money who emphasize the importance of the quality of money as well as its quantity.

In short, if we continue to stay on the course of fiat money, facing America at the end of the road is the stark horror—the holocaust—of runaway inflation. Such an inflation would wipe out savings, pensions, thrift instruments of all kinds; it would eliminate economic calculation;

and it would destroy the middle and poorer classes. In America, hyper-inflation will not be the relatively "moderate," steady 100 percent per year or so that Israel or that many countries in Latin America have experienced. For in these small countries, particularly in Latin America, the currency becomes only hand-to-hand cash; all investments move to the U.S. and the dollar. The United States would not be so fortunate.

America, in sum, must choose, and the choice is a vital one. In three years, perhaps sooner if necessary, another Gold Commission should be established to make more recommendations to the Congress. At that time, the choice will be perfectly clear to all, even to those now opposed to gold. Either we must move to the gold standard and monetary freedom, with long-run stability of prices and business, rapid economic growth and prosperity, and the maintenance of a sound currency for every American; or we will continue with irredeemable paper, with accelerating core rates of inflation and unemployment, the punishment of thrift, and eventually the horror of runaway inflation and the total destruction of the dollar. The failure of irredeemable money nostrums is becoming increasingly evident to everyone—even to the economists and politicians. Congress must have the courage to move forward to a modern gold standard.

APPENDIX

The Purchasing Power of Gold and the Dollar, 1792–1981

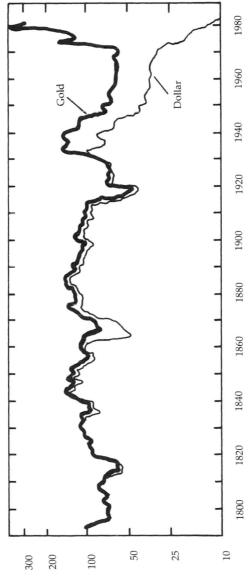

Source: **American Institute for Economic Research**

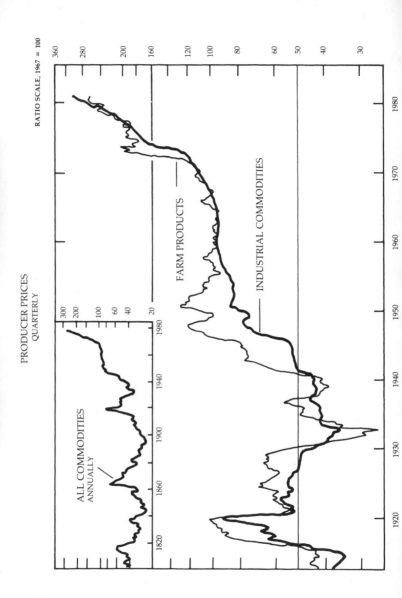

PRODUCER PRICES
QUARTERLY

RATIO SCALE, 1967 = 100

FARM PRODUCTS

INDUSTRIAL COMMODITIES

ALL COMMODITIES
ANNUALLY

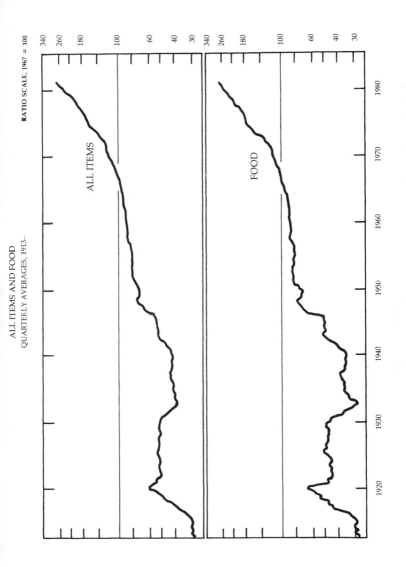

ALL ITEMS AND FOOD
QUARTERLY AVERAGES, 1913–

RATIO SCALE, 1967 = 100

ALL ITEMS

FOOD

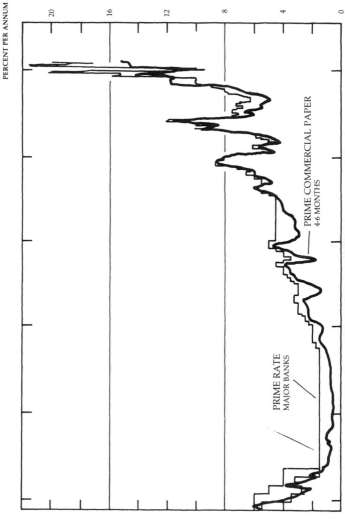

SHORT-TERM INTEREST RATES
BUSINESS BORROWING
PRIME RATE, EFFECTIVE DATE OF CHANGE: PRIME PAPER, QUARTERLY AVERAGES

PERCENT PER ANNUM

PRIME COMMERCIAL PAPER
4-6 MONTHS

PRIME RATE
MAJOR BANKS

MONEY MARKET
DISCOUNT RATE, EFFECTIVE DATE OF CHANGE; ALL OTHERS, QUARTERLY AVERAGES

PERCENT PER ANNUM

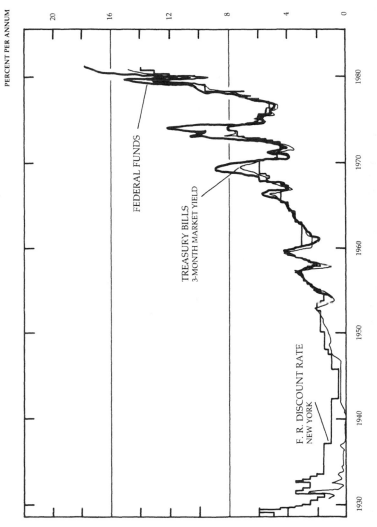

FEDERAL FUNDS

TREASURY BILLS
3-MONTH MARKET YIELD

F. R. DISCOUNT RATE
NEW YORK

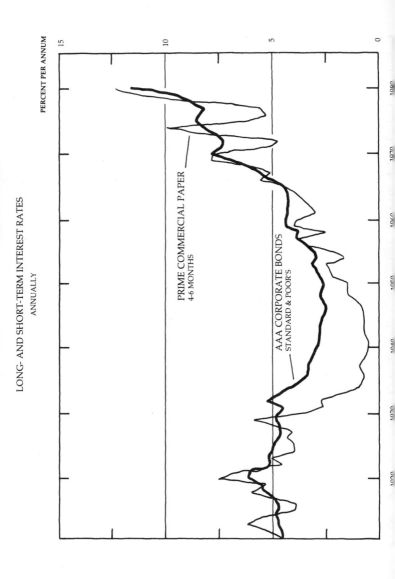

LONG- AND SHORT-TERM INTEREST RATES
ANNUALLY

PERCENT PER ANNUM

PRIME COMMERCIAL PAPER
4-6 MONTHS

AAA CORPORATE BONDS
STANDARD & POOR'S

COMMODITY RESEARCH BUREAU FUTURES PRICE INDEX

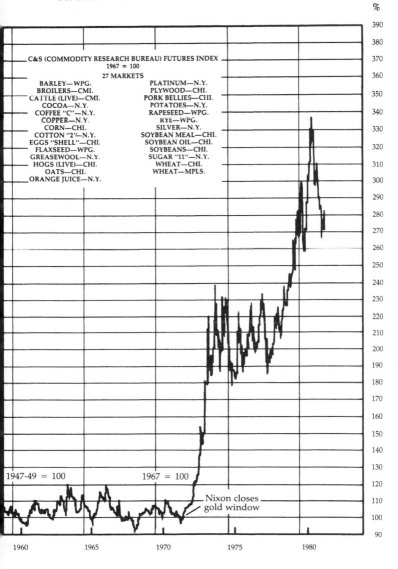

C&S (COMMODITY RESEARCH BUREAU) FUTURES INDEX
1967 = 100
27 MARKETS

BARLEY—WPG.
BROILERS—CMI.
CATTLE (LIVE)—CMI.
COCOA—N.Y.
COFFEE "C"—N.Y.
COPPER—N.Y.
CORN—CHI.
COTTON "2"—N.Y.
EGGS "SHELL"—CHI.
FLAXSEED—WPG.
GREASEWOOL—N.Y.
HOGS (LIVE)—CHI.
OATS—CHI.
ORANGE JUICE—N.Y.

PLATINUM—N.Y.
PLYWOOD—CHI.
PORK BELLIES—CIII.
POTATOES—N.Y.
RAPESEED—WPG.
RYE—WPG.
SILVER—N.Y.
SOYBEAN MEAL—CHI.
SOYBEAN OIL—CHI.
SOYBEANS—CHI.
SUGAR "11"—N.Y.
WHEAT—CHI.
WHEAT—MPLS.

1947-49 = 100

1967 = 100

Nixon closes gold window

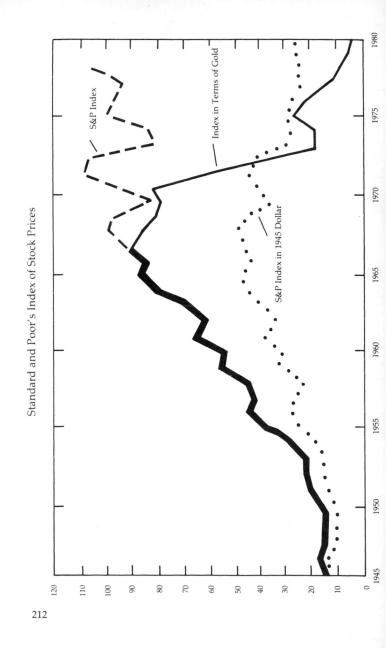

Standard and Poor's Index of Stock Prices

S&P Index

Index in Terms of Gold

S&P Index in 1945 Dollar

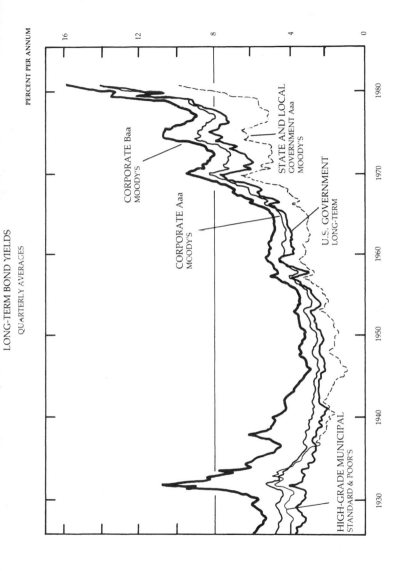

LONG-TERM BOND YIELDS
QUARTERLY AVERAGES

PERCENT PER ANNUM

CORPORATE Baa
MOODY'S

CORPORATE Aaa
MOODY'S

STATE AND LOCAL
GOVERNMENT Aaa
MOODY'S

U.S. GOVERNMENT
LONG-TERM

HIGH-GRADE MUNICIPAL
STANDARD & POOR'S

16

12

8

4

0

1930   1940   1950   1960   1970   1980

213

Standard and Poor's Index of Bond Prices

Sources: Standard and Poor's Corporation, U.S. Department of Labor, Bureau of Labor Statistics, U.S. Department of Interior, and Bureau of Mines

(S&P Index)

(Gold)

(Constant 1945 dollars)

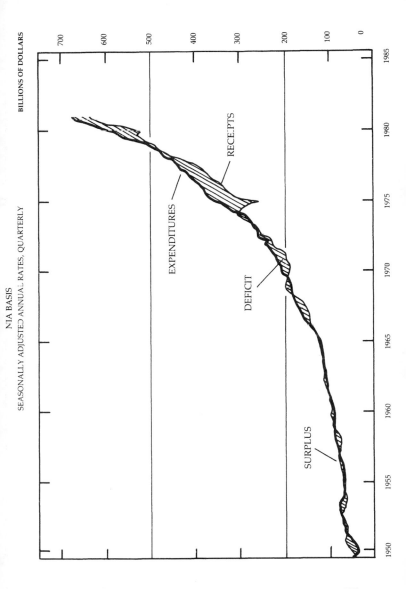

NIA BASIS

SEASONALLY ADJUSTED ANNUAL RATES, QUARTERLY

BILLIONS OF DOLLARS

EXPENDITURES

RECEIPTS

DEFICIT

SURPLUS

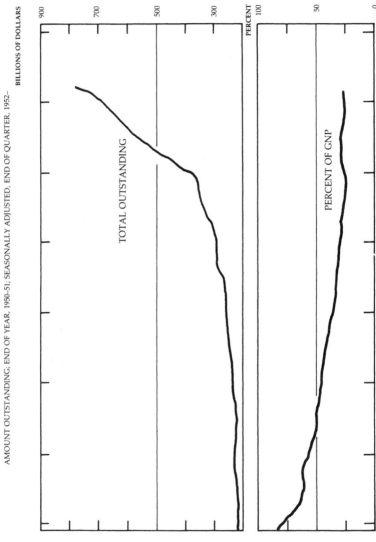

NET FEDERAL DEBT

AMOUNT OUTSTANDING; END OF YEAR, 1950–51; SEASONALLY ADJUSTED, END OF QUARTER, 1952–

BILLIONS OF DOLLARS

900
700
500
300

TOTAL OUTSTANDING

PERCENT

100
50
0

PERCENT OF GNP

216

Gold Value of Major Currencies
United States and Britain
January 1968 to February 1982

Index
(January 1968 = 100)

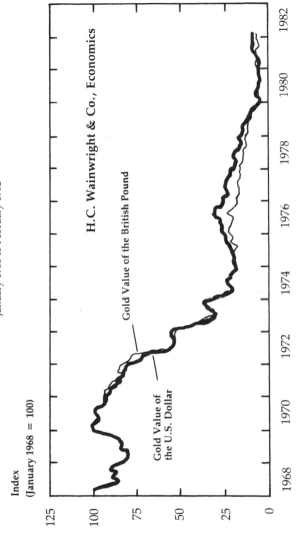

H.C. Wainwright & Co., Economics

Gold Value of the British Pound

Gold Value of
the U.S. Dollar

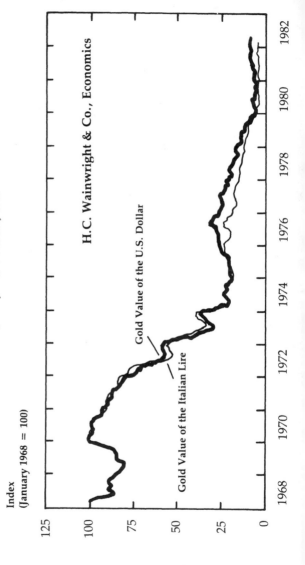

Gold Value of Major Currencies
United States and Italy
January 1968 to February 1982

Index
(January 1968 = 100)

H.C. Wainwright & Co., Economics

Gold Value of the U.S. Dollar

Gold Value of the Italian Lire

Gold Value of Major Currencies
United States and Japan
January 1968 to February 1982

Index
(January 1968 = 100)

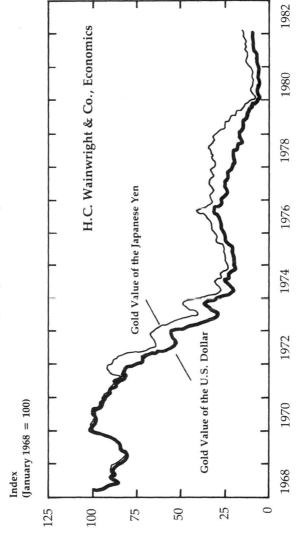

H.C. Wainwright & Co., Economics

Gold Value of the Japanese Yen

Gold Value of the U.S. Dollar

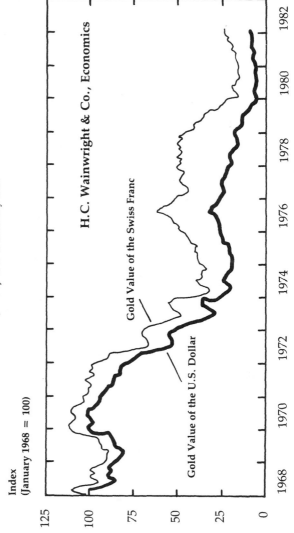

Gold Value of Major Currencies
United States and Switzerland
January 1968 to February 1982

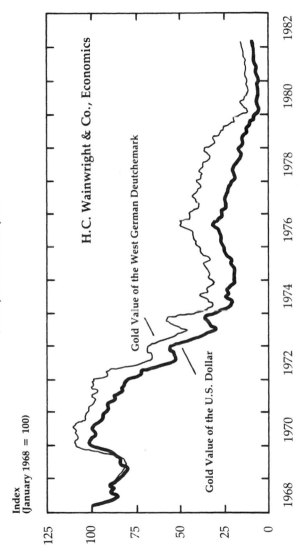

Gold Value of Major Currencies
United States and West Germany
January 1968 to February 1982

Index
(January 1968 = 100)

H.C. Wainwright & Co., Economics

Gold Value of the West German Deutchemark

Gold Value of the U.S. Dollar

INDEX